Helena Normanton and the Opening of the Bar to Women

Judith Bourne

With a Foreword by Mary Jane Mossman

WATERSIDE PRESS

Helena Normanton and the Opening of the Bar to Women
Judith Bourne

ISBN 978-1-909976-32-0 (Paperback)
ISBN 978-1-910979-16-7 (Epub ebook)
ISBN 978-1-910979-17-4 (Adobe ebook)

Cover design © 2017 Waterside Press.

Main UK distributor Gardners Books, 1 Whittle Drive, Eastbourne, East Sussex, BN23 6QH. Tel: +44 (0)1323 521777; sales@gardners.com; www.gardners.com

North American distribution Ingram Book Company, One Ingram Blvd, La Vergne, TN 37086, USA. Tel: (+1) 615 793 5000; inquiry@ingramcontent.com

Cataloguing-In-Publication Data A catalogue record for this book can be obtained from the British Library.

Printed by Lightning Source.

e-book *Helena Normanton and the Opening of the Bar to Women* is available as an ebook and also to subscribers of Myilibrary, Dawsonera, ebrary, and Ebscohost.

Published 2016 by
Waterside Press
Sherfield Gables
Sherfield-on-Loddon
Hook, Hampshire
United Kingdom RG27 0JG

Telephone +44(0)1256 882250
E-mail enquiries@watersidepress.co.uk
Online catalogue WatersidePress.co.uk

Table of Contents

About the author

Judith Bourne is an academic at St Mary's University, Twickenham and Co-Director of the Centre for Law and Culture. She founded and chairs the First Women Lawyers in Great Britain and the Empire Symposia. With a doctorate from King's College, London, Judith formerly practised as a barrister. Her research focuses on Feminist Perspectives on Law, Land Law and Equity and Trusts Law. She is an advocate of taking higher education into prisons.

Acknowledgments

With special thanks to Pat Thane for all her help, guidance and patience. Much gratitude is owed to the librarians at the British Library, the Inns of Court, in particular Lesley Whitelaw at Middle Temple, and the Women's Library for their assistance and kindness. Many thanks are owed to Judith Hodson, archivist at Varndean, for her generosity. I am indebted to Frances Burton for her unfailing kindness during the preparation of this book and in particular for our monthly 'reading' meetings in the British Library (and for all the tea and cake). Gratitude is also owed to Lady Brenda Hale for reading and commenting on an early draft of the book, and to Caroline Derry and Avis Whyte for their constant encouragement and help. Mary Jane Mossman answered an unsolicited email from me and returned it with an abundance of information and warm encouragement then agreed to write a Foreword for which I am extremely grateful. Patrick Polden also met with me and provided invaluable help. Thank you to the researchers who have found me: Rose Pipes and Elizabeth Cruickshank and for sharing their knowledge. Thanks are also due to Mari Takayanagi for sharing her work on the Sex Disqualification (Removal) Act 1919. I am grateful to Robert Walker and Christopher Forsythe who have been invaluable in providing information about the Bar. I am sincerely grateful to Bryan and Alex Gibson at Waterside Press for all their help in the publication of this book. Bryan in particular has understood and shared my desire to tell Helena's story; I was very lucky to have been put in touch with him. I am also grateful to my whole extended 'family' (that includes friends) for their support and love. Many thanks are owed to Sister Francoise for all her confidence in me. And finally, apologies to my children who have suffered an often absent mother, and to a husband without whom this would never have been written.

Judith Bourne
June 2016

List of Abbreviations

AWB	Association of Women Barristers
Bebb	*Bebb v Law Society* [1914] 1 Ch. 286
CLE	Council of Legal Education
CMW	Council of Married Women
DLRU	Divorce Law Reform Union
LNSWS	London and National Society for Women's Service
MPITRC	Married Person's Income Tax Reform Council
MT	Middle Temple
MWA	Married Women's Association
NFWT	National Federation of Women Teachers
NCEC	National Council for Equal Citizenship
NCW	National Council of Women
NUSEC	National Union of Societies for Equal Citizenship
NUWSS	National Union of Women's Suffrage Societies
NWCA	National Women Citizen's Association
TNA	The National Archives
UWV	Union of Women Voters
WL	Women's Library
WFL	Women's Freedom League
WSPU	Women's Social and Political Union

For my parents

Foreword: (Re)Discovering Helena Normanton

Judith Bourne's account of Helena Normanton is timely and important. It is timely because the centenary of the Sex Disqualification (Removal) Act 1919 is approaching, and the story of Normanton's experiences as one of the first women barristers in the United Kingdom needs to become more widely known and appreciated. And it is an important one because she was among the earliest cohort of pioneer women lawyers in Britain, women who necessarily challenged male exclusivity to enter the legal professions initially, and then all too often continued to experience problems as *members* of the Bar and the solicitors' profession. At the same time, however, Normanton's background and experiences often differed from other early women lawyers in ways that demonstrate her personal tenacity in the face of formidable barriers.

As the book reveals, Helena Normanton's experiences reflect what Carol Sanger described as women lawyers' 'piecemeal progress and circumscribed success'[1] as members of legal professions. Normanton's early life, including financial insecurity after her father's death when she was very young and then her mother's death while she was just a teenager, meant that her first career as a highly-regarded school teacher resulted because she was determined to achieve financial independence, a goal she achieved through hard work and scholarship support. Her progressive values and commitments to social justice and equality resulted in lifelong support for women's rights, including suffrage; as Judith Bourne notes, Normanton encouraged others by suggesting that 'it takes no moral courage whatever to walk in a procession.' Yet, these same values resulted in her decision to cease teaching history when her views about British imperialism in India (and the need for Indian independence) clashed with prevailing views in history texts and school curricula. Moreover, unlike a number of the earliest women lawyers in the United Kingdom, Normanton did not attend Oxford; a 'rarity' in this cohort, she obtained her BA degree as an external student at the University of London in 1912 while she was teaching full-time. Nonetheless, when the British Parliament finally enacted legislation permitting women to become barristers and solicitors, Normanton was the first woman to join one of the Inns of Court, the beginning of her ambition to become a barrister and 'as good as any man.'

Helena Normanton was called to the Bar in November 1922 (at the age of 40), and although she had married the previous year, she was determined to be called as 'Helena Normanton' rather than in her husband's name. As the book recounts, her background meant that she had few personal or family connections to assist her at the Bar, and her notoriety as a *female* practising barrister (as well as her interests in women's rights) meant that she often appeared in press reports—reports that sometimes resulted in disciplinary proceedings in relation to the issue of 'self-advertising.' It seems that she also encountered difficulties in obtaining clients, although she represented some in 'dock briefs,' but she continued to encounter negative decisions, being rejected as a member of the Western Circuit, and passed over for appointments to the Bar Council and the judiciary. Nonetheless, she provided excellent leadership at the Old Bailey during and after World War II, and in 1949, she was appointed King's Counsel along with Rose Heilbron; Helena Normanton was then 67-years-old. Overall, however, like so many other early women lawyers, she succeeded in gaining access to the legal professions, but then faced challenges of male exclusivity *within* the Bar.

This account provides a rich history of Normanton's life in the context of women's roles in 'gendering' the legal professions in the first half of the twentieth century. Although many of her experiences were similar to those encountered by women in other jurisdictions in the late-nineteenth and early-twentieth centuries, the challenges women faced in the United Kingdom were not exactly the same as those faced by women elsewhere. And we need to understand her personal responses to these ongoing challenges, just as we need to assess other women lawyers' responses to difficulties and discrimination—not only because historical contexts are different but because women lawyers' ambitions and temperaments are not all the same. Judith Bourne's detailed examination of press reports, archival sources, interviews, and academic literature enliven the day-to-day realities faced by Normanton and by a number of other women who were among the first to seek access to the legal professions in the United Kingdom, creating at once a contextual and personal account of the reception of early women lawyers at the Bar and in the solicitors' profession. As Joan Wallach Scott asked in a slightly different context, 'How do the new arrivals understand their relationship to the place they have entered?'[2]

Moreover, it is evident that Helena Normanton was highly regarded by women lawyers in the USA and Canada, as well as in a number of European jurisdictions, particularly because of her active involvement in various international organizations. Perhaps more importantly, the book illuminates how Normanton remained steadfast to the end in relation to her values and her commitments, often in the face of significant and continuing barriers and setbacks. Yet, although it is clear that the author admires Normanton, she is attentive to her foibles and flaws as well as her ambitions and perseverance. As Paula Backscheider argued:

> 'The great questions of biography are the essential questions about human experience in the world…They are the stuff of humankind's puzzling out its relationship to the world, how individual desire and ambition are confounded or aided by social, historical forces and other human beings.'[3]

Judith Bourne has succeeded both in rendering Helena Normanton as a human being, a woman with grit and aspiration, whose experiences were as often disappointing as they were celebratory in the context of her time and place — and by showing how her initial efforts paved the way for women who later entered the legal professions with greater personal success. This is a fine achievement: and Helena Normanton would be very pleased!

Mary Jane Mossman, November 2016

The author of the Foreword

Professor Mary Jane Mossman has taught at Osgoode Hall Law School, York University, in Ontario since 1977 and was Director of the Institute for Feminist Legal Studies 2002–2010. She was also a faculty member at the University of New South Wales and a Visiting Professor at numerous other university law schools. Her research focuses on property law, family law, access to justice and issues of gender and the legal profession. Among her recent books is *The First Women Lawyers: A Comparative Study of Gender, Law and the Legal Professions* (Oxford: Hart Publishing, 2006).

Introduction

Helena Normanton was the first woman to be admitted to an Inn of Court, immediately after the passing of the Sex Disqualification (Removal) Act 1919. She took her exams and was called to the Bar in 1922. Until then the Bar was closed to women whatever their abilities, skills or qualifications. Though not the first woman to become a barrister (that accolade goes to Ivy Williams) nor to hold a brief, she was the first to be briefed in the High Court of Justice and Old Bailey, and one of the two first female King's Counsel (nowadays Queen's Counsel) in England and Wales.

A single goal in life

Her ambition stemmed from a childhood vow forged after witnessing her single parent mother being patronised by a man during a visit to a solicitor's office. Helena declared that her one goal in life was 'to open the legal profession to women' and this book looks at the role she played in this. It examines her early life, subsequent legal career and fight for substantive equality—to be a barrister on an equal footing with men. Her career was a constant struggle due to misogyny, prejudice and continuing discrimination. A negative narrative grew up about her because of her pioneering status.

Helena's was not a solitary agent, rather her personal battle was part of the wider feminist campaign for equality during this great era in the history of women's rights. That struggle is still ongoing but its origins, particularly in the legal field, owe much to her determination and tenacity.

A hidden story

So what is known of Helena Normanton and why has she remained largely hidden from public view, unlike other early-feminists or women activists? Maybe she has been 'forgotten' by traditional history that is often related in a linear fashion: women 'earned' the rights to vote and enter the professions because of their 1914–1918 war work. But this explanation fails to examine and recognise women's organized campaigns and efforts to demand formal equality.

Despite the fact that Helena's personal records and surviving archives are sketchy, much of her journey *can* be charted, especially when placed in the context of the wider women's movement. History tends to choose for itself who to remember and who not, who to credit with progress and achievements and who to relegate to a 'walk-on part.' Surprisingly, little has been written or publicly proclaimed about the first women barristers. Yet pioneers need documenting and their contribution to history needs to be acknowledged.[1] I think it is especially important to place on record Helena's story and achievements because, '[W]e must bring women "back" into history' and 'study the material forces that have shaped their lives and experiences.'[2] We need to understand her role in order to comprehend how a glass ceiling was breached and prejudice resisted, and most importantly draw lessons from the past. Female lawyers, especially, need to know about and be able to contextualise their rich heritage.

Women and the law

The book examines male misogyny, the idea that the legal profession was dominated by men resistant to women's admission. When women were finally admitted in 1919 they were expected and had to adapt to a male approach. It seeks to further our understanding of why feminist scholarship has led us to a different approach in biography,[3] and why Helena may not have had the 'success' or 'celebrity' that male barristers may have had during her time. It also looks at the various allegations of self-advertising that were brought against her and that seem to have had their roots in misogyny.

Women now total half of all law undergraduates and increasingly occupy roles in the legal system, including senior positions. Helena Normanton's entry to an Inn marks the beginning of these developments and successes. It can be argued that women have still not achieved substantive equality, so that measuring her success is artificial or unnecessary. My view is that her story is not just interesting and informative in itself but provides valuable insights into women's position at the Bar and in the legal profession today.

Arrangement of chapters

The book follows Helena's progress in chronological order and considers those themes that affected her life, legal practice, writing and involvement with the women's movement.

Chapter 1 looks at her early years, background, education, teacher training, embryonic writings, and tries to understand why she set out for a career at the Bar in the first place.

Chapter 2 examines and 'situates' her feminism in context, enabling us to understand the difficulties that she faced in realising her ambition. It also locates her within the women's movement and describes her marriage.

Chapter 3 focuses on her high profile campaign to be admitted to an Inn. It examines Middle Temple's initial rejection of her application and the Parliamentary developments towards women's emancipation. The period after her eventual admission to that Inn is considered in *Chapter 4*: the exams, her pupillage, call to the Bar and first disciplinary inquiry by Middle Temple in relation the claims of self-advertising.

Chapter 5 explores the development of Helena's emerging legal practice from 1922–1924 and deals with items such has her decision to use her maiden name professionally, but style herself Mrs Helena Normanton, whilst her lecture tour of America which started in December 1924 is described in *Chapter 6*.

Chapter 7 looks at her post-America and inter-war years in practice, including some of the cases that she was involved in, and her continuing struggle for substantive equality. It also looks at her attempts to become a judge.

Chapter 8 recounts her later legal work and reflects on her attitudes towards practice as well as her achievement in becoming one of he first two women King's Counsel.

Chapter 9 considers other campaigns in which she was involved alongside her concern for social justice; and *Chapter 10* records her death and bequests including that to the University of Sussex 'if it comes into existence' (as it did in 1961).

Helena Normanton's legacy

Helena enjoyed her legal work. This was probably bound up with her own view of herself as a pioneer who not only opened the profession to women but continued in practice despite the difficulties. She sometimes lamented that she was seen as the poor relation of Rose Heilbron, and yet without her there would perhaps have been no Rose Heilbron, or indeed Helena Kennedy or Cherie Booth.

So far as I am aware, this is the first in-depth examination of her life and legacy.

CHAPTER 1

Helena Normanton's Early Years

'I have a most vivid recollection of accompanying my own mother, at the ripe age of 12, to her solicitor and most eagerly drinking in all his remarks ... My mother evidently failed to understand their purport, and the kindly old man said, "I am sure that your little girl understands what I have told you, from the look on her face". And turning to me: "Do you?" he asked. And he then and there made me repeat his observations. After I had shyly survived the ordeal, he then remarked, "Quite the little lawyer!"…"Well", I thought to myself, "so I will be when I grow up". I did not like to see my mother nonplussed in that way, and I still do not like to see women getting the worst end of any deal for lack of a little elementary legal knowledge which is the most common form amongst men.'

Helena Normanton, 1932[1]

Helena Normanton held an ambition to become a barrister following this experience in a solicitor's office when she was 12-years-old. The event, at such an early age, exposed her to the idea of gender inequality. Her mother was unable to understand the solicitor's advice because she lacked, as Helena put it, elementary legal knowledge, which she felt, was common amongst men. For Helena this was an example of sex discrimination, though, in reality, many men at this time would have lacked such education. This provides us with an insight into why she wanted to become a barrister, when the legal profession was closed to her at that time. All women faced this discrimination.[2] The Bar was only open to men and was suffused with practices associated with men such as dining and going on circuit. There were no female role models for her to follow. Her initial desire was to help other women gain access to the law. The only way for her to achieve this was to become a lawyer.

How did she come to sit in that solicitor's office formulating a near-impossible ambition? Answers are suggested by the details of her family and childhood. They also provide a clue as to why her practice was not as 'successful' as it could have been. The word 'successful' is used cautiously here, as, by practising law for much of her adult life and achieving the rank of King's Counsel (KC), she certainly was successful. However, she never became a judge, something she desired, and she failed to earn enough to live entirely on her earnings at the Bar.

It is clear from the extract above that she saw her future legal role as both opening up the Bar to women and as a way of helping women (and men), which is not the everyday ambition of a lawyer or an obvious route to conventional success at the Bar.[3] Conventionally, a barrister is expected to act like a taxi-driver, 'picking-up' the next client in the queue (the cab rank principle), dealing with their individual case and then moving onto the next 'fare.'[4] It is not normally a job of social service (although it always has been for some).[5]

Even though the above extract from Helena's *Everyday Law for Women* explains the trigger for her ambition it tells us nothing about her personal background. An analysis of this private history is essential to produce a comprehensive account of her life and career. Who was she? What was her life like before she entered the Bar?

Who was Helena Normanton?

Helena Florence Normanton was born on 14 December 1882[6] to Jane and William Alexander Normanton,[7] in Stratford, East London. Her obituary[8] describes her as being born in Kensington, but the records show this is a mistake.[9] William was a pianoforte-maker.[10] His first wife died in 1881. Jane, his new wife and Helena's mother, was born on 5 December 1850.[11] Before her marriage to William in 1881, she was employed as a milliner. Helena had a sister, Ethel, born in 1884.

In 1866 when Helena was just four-years-old her father died.[12] He was found, mysteriously, with a broken neck on the Metropolitan Railway, between Praed Street junction and Bishop's Road, West London. Evidence was given at the Coroner's Court that the carriage door was open on arrival at Edgware Road, and his 'untouched' bag was found in the carriage.[13] He was just 34. A verdict of accidental death was recorded, indicating that there were no suspicious circumstances and it is possible that he committed suicide.

According to Helena's niece, Elsie Cannon, Helena's parents were separated at the time, but planning a fresh start together.[14] There is no evidence as to why they separated, but this was a drastic step for any married woman to take at that time. Great social stigma attached to it,[15] and Jane's legal rights as a separated married woman and single mother were extremely limited[16] as we shall see in *Chapter 2*. For a short time after her husband's death, Jane seems to have let rooms in Woolwich to the wives of officers, and then returned to her pre-marital home town of Brighton where her sisters lived.[17] However, the 1891 census records that Jane and Helena were living in Ramsgate. Jane is described as a 'retired publican' and Helena a 'scholar.' So they perhaps went to Ramsgate from Woolwich, then settled in Brighton,[18] where Helena attended school.

Wherever they were living after William's death, Jane's economic position would not have been much improved from that of a separated woman, though as a widow she had more legal rights, including custody of her children.[19] She was 36, with two small daughters to care for and support.[20] Ethel was not listed in the 1891 census because she was at boarding school. Jane was well-informed and clearly had high aspirations for her daughters. This is suggested by the fact that she found a boarding school for fatherless children in Wanstead, for which she had to pay no fees.[21] Initially she intended to send Helena there.[22] However, as Elsie Cannon explained,[23] the length of time it took to secure references and votes of confidence from trustees in order to gain a place meant that Helena passed the age of admission before this formality was complete. Ethel took the place instead and the sisters spent a great deal of their childhood apart, because the boarding school had few and short holidays.[24] We can only speculate as to her mother's ambition for her daughters. Her main motivation may have been their financial security. She perhaps wanted to educate them to be independent in view of her own experiences. Schools at this time sometimes failed to train women to earn a living and she would have had to choose carefully for her daughters with that in mind.[25]

On her return to Brighton, Jane ran a grocery store and later a boarding house.[26] We can see that Helena's early life was full of change and upheaval, due not only to the separation of her parents and death of her father but to the changes of location. She had a taste of female independence at a very young age and this may have influenced her views. The two-parent nuclear family was regarded as the norm at the time, though a high proportion of marriages were interrupted by death. Her mother's situation would have given Helena a different experience of Victorian family life.[27] Her feminism, and indeed her life, involved a rejection of the idea of a benevolent male as 'protector'[28] of women.

The popular myth of male protectiveness can be seen in many legal judgments at this time.[29] This protection was seen as one of the 'glories of our civilisation …' and as a 'privilege' of the female sex.[30] Until the First World War, and long afterwards, many women's experiences were strongly determined by marriage and childbirth.[31] Marriage gave women social status and, in some cases, financial security. Unmarried women were often considered not to have succeeded in life.[32] Most women married, but a certain number did not due to the unbalanced sex ratio. In the late-nineteenth century, 88 per cent of women who had reached age 40 had married and this figure remained above that percentage through to 1921.[33] Marriage came with dangers, for example until the 1839 Child Custody Act women were denied custody of their children on separation[34] and until 1882 they were denied control of their own property and money even whilst married.[35] But Helena's mother strove to give both her daughters an education that would ensure that they would always be financially independent.

Education

In about 1894, Helena made her visit to the solicitor's office with her mother and decided more or less there and then to become a lawyer. Her mother Jane's aspirations for her daughters were not uncommon;[36] many middle-class parents educated their daughters because they knew they might not marry because of the female surplus in the population.[37] Jane might have been aware of this, conscious of her own failed marriage and financial situation, and determined to avoid this fate for her daughters. This may have influenced Helena's decision as a child to become a lawyer and maybe also her later behaviour. She was prepared to be autonomous and self-supporting, not supported by a man. Her decision also demonstrates a strong sense of justice: she believed that men had access to basic legal education and she did not like to see her mother (and therefore other women) so disadvantaged.

A year after the incident in the solicitors' office (in 1895), Helena joined York Place School (now Varndean) in Brighton having won a scholarship.[38] There is no evidence concerning where she was educated before this date, except that she was at school somewhere in Ramsgate. She was by now 13-years-old. York Place was a state school which opened in 1884,[39] originally a Board school.[40] It was subsequently chosen to become a Higher Grade School,[41] which meant that it could offer education beyond the elementary stage, sometimes including science classes.[42] The Upper School followed a four year course laid down by the Board of Education in preparation for the Cambridge Local Junior and Senior Certificates, the best route to the London Matriculation Certificate. When Helena joined, the Science Department included 54 girls rising to 100 by 1898.[43] Students were expected to study science for at least six hours per week. This course allowed women from the lower middle-classes (such as Helena) to seek training for paid work. The rationale behind this expansion of the curriculum was twofold: to enable women to become better wives and mothers because they were educated; and also to enable unmarried women to work and support themselves and other family members if necessary. It made it so that qualified women could seek positions as teachers in these expanding schools while also encouraging them to think beyond teaching as a career. For those who were fortunate enough not to need to work it provided an opportunity to engage in the public sphere, for example as a teacher.[44] It would have been clear to Jane that her daughters needed both an education and, potentially, a career. Somewhat better educational and career opportunities were opening up for girls at this time, including for working class girls following the 1870 and 1880 Education Acts.[45]

Pupil teacher

In July 1900 Helena officially left the school, then returned in the autumn to become a pupil teacher[46] at its secondary school.[47] She was 17-years-old. She remained in this position until 1903.[48] This was effectively an apprenticeship. Her CV records that she held three scholarships during this period.[49] The system of pupil teachers, in which she was employed, sustained poorer pupils in secondary school and put them on the career path to teaching.[50] Introduced in 1846 by Her Majesty's Inspectorate (HMI), children over 13 could be apprenticed to a qualified teacher for five years, enabling them both to study and earn. They could later take national examinations to enter normal schools or training colleges to gain teaching qualifications. The schools employing them benefited from an extra grant. HMI inspected pupil teachers each year. Students could compete for a Queen's Scholarship which would enable them to attend training college. By 1859 there were 15,224 pupil teachers, mostly female. By 1899, two years before Helena qualified, there were 62,085 certified teachers and 30,783 uncertified teachers in England and Wales (pupil teachers who did not complete their apprenticeships).[51]

Helena probably followed this route. Surviving records do not provide a clear indication of the detail. If so, this offered her a limited career ladder, which many young women at this time were climbing.[52] By the time she became a student teacher, Sir Robert Morant,[53] a Government education reformer and civil servant at the Board of Education,[54] had begun to reform the pupil teacher scheme. By 1900, to take part in the scheme, students had to be aged 15, approved by an HMI, passed as fit by a medical officer and had to pass a Board of Education exam in reading and recitation, English, history, geography, arithmetic, algebra, Euclid (boys) or needlework (girls), and teaching.[55] As a pupil teacher Helena was only allowed to teach for a maximum of five hours a day or 20 hours per week. She would have been examined each year by HMI. According to her CV,[56] she matriculated with a first-class grading and was the 'twentieth King's scholar[57] of 12,000 in the country' (the first 19 were bracketed equal).[58] No corroborative evidence of this achievement can be found.[59] When a pupil-teacher's term of service was completed they could sit the 'Queen's' (until 1901, 'King's') Scholarship exam.[60] A first or second class pass qualified the pupil-teacher to enter training college, though it did not guarantee entry as there were too many students for each teacher-training place, in 1900 barely 44.5 per cent of eligible pupil-teachers gained a college place. A reference from the former Headmistress of York Place, Miss A M Syson,[61] notes that Helena had 'exceptional ability,' and was a kind teacher with an excellent character.[62] The principal of the Education Committee for the County Borough of Brighton commented in another reference for her that she was top of her very large class and she had 'read much more than girls ordinarily do …'[63]

Also in 1900, Helena's sister Ethel returned home from boarding school.[64] It is unclear why she did so. She would have been about 16 and it is possible that she had completed her studies in Wanstead. She may also have returned because of their mother's poor health: Jane died that year and their 'Aunt Lizzie' moved to Brighton from Liverpool to run the boarding house and look after her nieces. The sisters were recorded in the 1901 census as living with their maternal aunt, Eliza Whitehead (a widow), in Brighton. Aunt Eliza was classed as a 'Lodging House Keeper.' Despite being in mourning for her mother and having partial responsibility for her sister, Helena was clearly happy at York Place. In July 1947 she gave a talk at the Special Reunion to celebrate the school's twenty-first birthday.[65] She stated that 'a school is not a building, a place or a staff, but the whole living, breathing texture that moves on through generations.' She urged that enterprise should be encouraged, begging all old girls with influence over the careers of the young, not to stand in their light, but prepare them to take what life offered and to follow their chosen path with tenacity.[66] In 1951 she donated a copy of the *Complete Works of Shakespeare* to Varndean as a prize. In her will she left a substantial donation for the establishment of Sussex University in thanks for her education.

Teacher training

In 1903 Helena entered Edge Hill College, Liverpool, for further teacher training. She presumably wished to gain the maximum qualifications available to her to enhance her career opportunities. Edge Hill was an all-female college where she was in residence until 1905.[67] It was the first non-denominational college in England and Wales, established due to a concern that there were no non-denominational teacher training colleges in England and Wales.[68] The idea for the college was formed in 1882 and it formally opened in 1885,[69] taking 160 students a year.[70] Helena's archives contain no evidence of her holding a religious faith, which may explain her attending a non-denominational college so far from Brighton.[71] Edge Hill College also had a strong suffragette movement.[72] Given that the college recruited mainly from the North West,[73] its non-denominational status and suffragette link are the most likely reasons why she studied there.

Students were required to sit an entrance exam in order to attend. Also, good health was regarded as a paramount qualification for teaching, since it was seen as extremely onerous.[74] Students had to provide character testimonials and demonstrate both ability to draw and a knowledge of science. It was desirable for a student to speak French, German and have a knowledge of Latin[75] and to be good at needlework, music and domestic economy.[76] Helena would have had no problem in meeting these criteria. However the uniform would have caused considerable expense, consisting of a waterproof cloak, two pairs of stout walking boots, galoshes or rubbers, two pairs of shoes, a dressing gown, flannel underwear, a white or cream dress, navy blue serge dress for school or classroom, and aprons. Also two toilet covers and two bags for linen were required. Helena also needed a PE kit: one cream and one crimson shirt blouse in 'Delaine' fabric, made with yoke, turn down collar and full sleeves with loosely fitting cuffs.[77] A sailor hat with college band and badge was compulsory for weekday wear.[78] Students were expected to be neat and properly attired at all times and their teeth had to be in good order.[79] Fees were £10 for former pupil teachers who had passed the entrance exam with a first-class, as Helena is likely to have done. Although there is no evidence, except her CV reference,[80] to being a 'King's Scholar,' she probably secured a scholarship after her period as a pupil teacher.

Study at Edge Hill was intense. The college day began at 6:15 am and ended at 10 pm with lights out.[81] Class work began before breakfast and every hour of the day was accounted for, with each meal lasting about half an hour.[82] The syllabus included practical teaching, reading and recitation, arithmetic, music, grammar, literature, geography, history, maths for teaching boys only (which may have made Helena angry), needlework (for girls),[83] school management,[84] science or a language, hygiene, singing, theory of music, physical training and domestic economy.[85]

Following establishment of Day Training Colleges by the government, Edge Hill developed its syllabus further from 1890–1906.[86] The college could now offer university level study provided by Manchester University, allowing students a third year of study. Later the degree would be offered by Liverpool University but taught by Edge Hill lecturers.[87] Helena did not take up this opportunity perhaps for financial reasons.

The ethos of Edge Hill was one of 'order and control.'[88] Helena would not have been allowed out after 5 pm on a weekday. She was allowed to leave the premises on a Saturday afternoon, with permission, but had to return by 7 pm.[89] Sundays were free. It appears students could go anywhere throughout the day. She slept in a cubicle within a dormitory,[90] consisting of a wooden panelled partition, about four to five feet from the ceiling, with a small chest of drawers, wash stand, single bed, desk and one or two bookshelves.[91] For an avid reader like Helena, the fact that the only light allowed was from the corridor must have been painful. There was no hot running water, only a jug of water carried down the corridor.[92] She was forbidden to wash in her cubicle between 9 am and 9 pm and baths were taken according to a roster, for a maximum of 15 minutes.[93]

Helena's advocacy skills were honed at Edge Hill. The food, according to Mary Sheppard, a fellow student, was 'shocking.'[94] Wednesdays and Fridays were known as 'Psalm, Fish and Mystery' because they sang psalms instead of hymns at morning prayer and at dinner had a 'Mersey Whale' (a whole fish swimming in a sea of greasy water) and 'mystery', a sloppy mixture of flour, bread crumbs, dried fruit and huge lumps of suet. On Wednesdays, one girl on a table of eleven was allowed to buy cake for tea. However Helena, as head girl, was instructed by the principal, Sarah Hale, on one occasion to ask students to forego their cake and donate it to the benevolent fund. The girls asked Helena to tell Miss Hale that they would rather give up their dinner and give the cost of that to the fund. Helena did so and an annoyed Miss Hale replied that she did not understand why no one had complained before! The food improved.[95]

A reference from Edge Hill written by Sarah Hale[96] described Helena as 'possessed of ability much above average' and '… she is a fearless but temperate critic, and brings to bear on any question under discussion a lucidity and a sanity of judgment too infrequently found in those of her sex.' Although Miss Hale disapproved of feminism, she recognised that Edge Hill students demonstrated 'a healthy interest in feminism.'[97] They held frequent debates and, as early as 1894, the college debating society decided by 64 votes to 15 that the suffrage should be extended to women.[98] As stated before, this feminism may have been a reason for Helena's choice of Edge Hill. It may have increased her commitment to gender equality. Even after she left, Helena encouraged the students in militancy. In 1908 she wrote in the *Edge Hill Magazine*: 'To all Edge Hill suffragists I give this advice — it takes no moral courage whatever to walk in procession!'[99]

Teaching career and further education

From 1905–1907 Helena held a teaching position as an assistant mistress at Anfield Road Higher Grade School, Liverpool, where she taught a special class for Oxford Preliminary and Junior Examinations.[100] She rented a small house that she shared with Lilian Fuller[101] another former student from Edge Hill, a lifelong friend who nursed Helena until she entered the nursing home in which she died.[102] The headmistress described Helena as a 'good organizer' who had an 'excellent' influence on the younger teachers.[103] Ethel moved from Brighton to live with her sister. She kept house and began training as a nurse.[104] On 14 February 1907, Helena received her Board of Education Teacher's Certificate[105] and in August of the same year also received a *Diplome Francais* from the University of Dijon.[106] She spent a few months at Dijon University in 1907.[107]

From 1907–1913 she worked as an assistant mistress in Central Schools, Acton, London The principal of this school, Ernest Rayns, commented, 'I feel that the high intellectual standard, the wide outlook and the great ability of Miss Normanton, make her eminently fitted for a much higher educational post than she now holds.' Clearly she was good at her job and was destined for higher teaching roles, presumably such as a head teacher.

On 18 December 1912, Helena graduated from the University of London with an external BA honours degree in History, first class.[108] Her degree was a considerable achievement since she was working full time and studying in her spare time. Ernest Rayns, noted that '… the more advanced the work, the more enthusiastically she throws herself into it …'[109] Also in 1912 she sat for the London external LLB Examination at Honours (Intermediate) level which she uncharacteristically failed. She gave the reason for her failure in her CV:[110] 'Had to leave examination room at final LLB because of violent coughing paroxysm and so failed that paper. Had no time to sit for the final LLB subsequently, but had covered all the ground for Final.'[111] Maybe she was taking on too much (she did however complete and pass this degree in 1930).

Her CV records further considerable academic successes, but which are undated:[112] Board of Education Diploma, Double first class, Associateship of College of Preceptors, First Class Advance Certificates (South Kensington) in Hygiene, Physiology and Freehand Drawing, Ling Physical Training Diploma, and Diploma for Secondary teaching (Scotch Board of Education). Was this collecting of qualifications a sign of insecurity or of a need to be accepted?

Helena took her next post at Glasgow High School for Girls in 1913, where she stayed until 1915, as senior mistress for History. This promotion was probably the reason for her leaving Acton. The Glasgow school had almost 1,000 pupils and her position involved preparing students for their Lower and Higher Leaving Certificate examinations. In April 1914 the Glasgow Provincial Committee for the Training of Teachers[113] recognised her as a Specially Qualified Teacher of History.[114] This enabled her to teach post-graduate teachers. It is possible that she met her future husband during this job, as he was from Scotland.

At some point in or about 1915 Helena became tutor[115] to the sons of Baron de Forest, a Liberal MP who was also one of her referees.[116] It is unknown for how long she did this. This was a controversial and bold choice of employment. De Forest was a twice married man of Austrian origins. The sons to whom she was tutor were from his failed second marriage (1904–1910) to the Hon. Ethel Gerard. His first attempt to become an MP ended in failure because of a vitriolic Conservative campaign against him which concentrated on his Austrian background.[117] He was MP for West Ham North, 1911–1918. *The Times* reported that his election address included his commitment to many controversial policies including Home Rule for Ireland, equality of religion (he was a convert from Judaism to Catholicism and believed in the disestablishment of the Church of England) and female suffrage.[118] He was rich, influential, a good friend of Churchill, and committed to equality. His life was similar to Helena's in that he was an upright member of society but not quite accepted, as a divorced Austrian Jew/Catholic, just as her gender and class excluded her from full acceptance at the Bar. We can only assume that she met him through the suffrage movement.

By 1914, Helena was a member of the Women's Freedom League (WFL). The league was formed in 1907 by Teresa Billington-Greig and Charlotte Despard in a break from Women's Social and Political Union (WSPU).[119] The WFL was a democratic, militant organization, calling for suffrage. Its methods included direct action such as passive resistance to taxation and non-cooperation with the census, rather than attacks on people and property. The WFL was responsible for the 'grille incident' in the Ladies Gallery in the House of Commons in 1908.[120] In June 1915 after 13 months preparation, the WFL celebrated the 700th anniversary of the *Magna Carta*.[121] A pageant, procession and pilgrimage to Runnymede had been planned but then cancelled because if the outbreak of the War. Celebrations instead took place in Caxton Hall with Helena as the guest speaker.[122] This would suggest that she was extremely influential within the movement. She had previously published an essay 'Magna Carta and Women'[123] and her talk followed this. She argued that *Magna Carta* was the source and legal basis of the English woman's national rights. Antoinette Burton argues that this was 'shrewd' advocacy,[124] because Helena successfully linked female emancipation with the emblem of British nationalism at a time of war-time crisis. Helena drew out that equality was historically and culturally British and that the country had a commitment to political equality. We can see from this that she was very involved in the call for the vote and was part of a network of women, maximizing their social influence and developing a sense of community.

Also in 1915, Helena produced a pamphlet, *Sex Differentiation in Salary* for the National Federation of Women Teachers, in which she espoused equal pay for work of equal worth.[125] This suggests that she was an equality feminist; whatever her category of feminism she was radical, assertive and forceful in her ideas. By 1916 she was definitely living in London, centrally located for the cause.[126] On 24 February 1916 she became a University Extension Lecturer[127] of the University of London,[128] lecturing on: Modern Methods of Teaching History, The History of Europe 1814–1914; The History of France—Tenth Century to the Present Day; Modern Reformers and the Reforms Associated with Them; Western European Womanhood in Literature; and History, Economics and Politics, with special reference to the British Isles. Her name appears in the index of lecturers, along with Dr. Marie Stopes among many others, which suggests she was mixing with other intellectual and actively feminist women. She appears to have worked in this capacity until 1920.[129]

Helena was clearly a good teacher, her references describing her as having great potential,[130] enthusiastic,[131] a 'good disciplinarian and an earnest and successful teacher.'[132] She cared about teaching and had strong views on education throughout her life. On her CV she commented that she had always been in the best of health. She wrote, 'In ten years only one continuous absence (a fortnight) from duty—tonsillitis, contracted from a pupil. And a very few odd days for colds.'[133] This adds to the picture of a woman who was not only healthy but also extremely driven, hardworking and committed. Why then she did give up schoolteaching and move to London? The answer lies in her work for the weekly publication called *India*.

This came at a particular moment in the struggle for Indian independence. The First World War, which saw Indian soldiers fighting for Britain, triggered important debates on the Indian independence movement and its future direction. While the younger faction led by Mahatma Gandhi would ultimately come to the forefront of the Indian National Congress, others actively involved included the British feminist, socialist and later theosophist Annie Besant (President of the Indian Nationals

Congress in 1917).[134] Helena was therefore very much part of a political movement which was engaging the passions of contemporaries on two continents, including prominent women. Campaigns by Gandhi during the First World War and the outrage caused by the Amritsar Massacre on 13 April 1919 had helped to prompt the Government of India Act 1919 (Royal Assent 23 December 1919, the same day as the Sex Disqualification Removal Act) which expanded participation of Indian citizens in the government of their own country. However it was inadequate on its own to assuage Indian nationalist feeling.[135] In India, the Indian National Congress was expanding enormously, widening its appeal with its campaigns of civil disobedience.

It is perhaps unsurprising that Helena, with her concern for social justice, was swept up in the movement. In her collection of the most influential articles she explained that she gave up teaching because she could not toe the official line with regard to the teaching of history:

'My own conception of India's case came to me entirely from laboriously historical delving when studying for an Honours degree of London university; and from the study of India's connection with Great Britain, I emerged permanently saddened by the amount of duplicity from intellectuals which Governments can apparently almost invariably command. The acquisition of India is written about by nearly all historians as something glorious, wonderful and beautiful on the part of England and as something beneficent and helpful of India...This point of view entirely permeates our popular text-books and school courses. I suppose a teacher who taught to the contrary in a British State School would soon be dismissed. The tragic thing is that very few would ever want, simply because the Indian side of the case is not available to them, to realise what they are doing. Personally I am not anti-imperialist in the sense of hating the British Empire as such. I see no harm whatever in the colonisation of all but empty areas like Canada and Australia...But the imperialism based on force and fraud is not distinguished from legitimate expansion in imperialism disseminated though and by the School, the Press, the Pulpit and the Historian. That is the Quadruple Alliance of India's enemies.'[136]

She continued that, as a teacher, she was under the control of the 'Quadruple Alliance', 'of cobweb softness but of the strength of steel.' She felt that she was only nominally in control in the classroom, so she resigned and had never regretted it. She stated that she had never found a truthful textbook account of the acquisition of India. She was, in short, a woman of strong convictions and morals.

India was a weekly publication and an organ of the Indian National Congress. It cost three pence and did not have a wide readership, so was always short of money. However, the readers it did have were influential. Helena became editor in 1918/1919 when the policy of the paper was to attack Edwin Montagu in his capacity of Secretary of State for India[137] She admitted in her volume *India in England* that she was ashamed that *India* was not edited by an Indian national, but they had 'never found anyone suitably qualified.' This comment is difficult to reconcile with her strong beliefs, as there must surely have been someone? Past editors included Sir Gordon Hewart[138] (Attorney General in 1921) and Frederick Pollock,[139] a supporter of Helena's, and legal academic and barrister. She wrote that from November 1919 she was entirely alone as editor, doing the work of three people. She regarded Gandhi's non-cooperation as 'magnificent' and felt that there was a need for India to educate Britain. She begged patience by the Indians, she knew from experience that England moved slowly, but insisted that the end result would be a victorious one. Her future father-in-law was very involved with *India*. Her husband to be came from a family with similar persuasions to hers.

As good as any man

Helena's early childhood was difficult: her parents separated and her father died while she was an infant. She was separated from her sister and moved homes and locations often. Her mother, Jane, died while she was a teenager. Jane was the probable source of a handed-down rugged individualism, hence Helena was determined to support herself and succeed. Jane seems to have had clear ambitions and aspirations for her daughters and actively encouraged them to learn and make the best of any education open to them. The experience in that solicitor's office exposed Helena to possible sex inequality. Her loyalty to her mother and empathy for other women in her mother's situation probably inspired her to depart from conventional norms and aspire to join a profession that was at the time resolutely closed to women. From her early life she seemed restless. Her mother's situation instilled in her the need to be financially independent of a man, and she became a teacher, one of the few professions open to women. Her collection of academic achievements suggests that she needed to be constantly stimulated and acknowledged by the elite as being 'as good as any man.'

CHAPTER 2

Helena in Context: The Struggles for Women's Equal Rights

'I longed to go to prison with the rest of my comrades in the fight [to vote] but I knew that this could never be because, if I had a prison sentence, I would never be able to open the profession of the law to women, which I regarded as my job in life.'

Helena Normanton, 1950[1]

Helena's life, from 1882–1957, spanned a long and important period in the struggle for women's equality rights. From the perspective of the twenty-first century, her ambitions and activities can be characterised as 'feminist': they reflect the goals of women (and men) who challenged the status quo to achieve equal rights for women in the public sphere and in their private lives. Thus, although it is often difficult to define 'feminism' precisely, both now and in earlier decades, it is appropriate to examine the context of Helena's life from the perspective of feminism.

Locating Helena's feminism

Feminism traces its origins to Mary Wollstonecraft, Fanny Burnley and Lady Mary Wortley Montagu.[2] Women's position had changed in the seventeenth century.[3] As the change in industry occurred their status was diminished as all 'valuable' production became commercial and happened outside the home. Husbands and wives were no longer considered to contribute equally to the household as the emphasis was placed on that outside commercial industry. As a result of this women grouped together and discussed issues relating to women and this became more organized in England in the early nineteenth century, with working-class women seeking better pay and working conditions[4] and middle-class women initially becoming involved in politics[5] (albeit through men). These groups concentrated on public affairs such as opposition to the Corn Law[6] and spread to more moral radicalism, such as anti-slavery.[7] This movement provided a vehicle for women to voice their views as independent, political individuals, who questioned men's authority. These groups provided an outlet for women with diverse and wide-ranging views; there was not just one united voice (just as there is not one united voice today). By the mid-1800s a co-ordinated campaign to reform property laws concerning women was formed;[8] and feminism had become a movement in its own right.[9] The movement was now one of sisterhood, moving from liberalism to exploring the sexual oppression of women and sexual double standards.[10] There were many campaigns, for example, Josephine Butler led one against the Contagious Diseases Acts, which provided a means by which middle-class women and working class women could unite. Likewise, Barbara Hutchins, in 1915 focussed on the slum conditions of women and the double standards that existed in working women's wages.[11] Millicent Fawcett[12] argued initially that the vote should only be for unmarried or widowed women, a view that differed from many other campaigners.[13] It is important to understand that the feminist voice was not one central, united voice, as many held different views.

Feminists also began to focus on marriage and the idea that it was a contract that worked to the detriment of the wife.[14] The view that marriage was the ideal for women was being questioned and it was suggested that men made their wives slaves, exposed them to venereal disease[15] and that their only use was to ensure the legitimacy of their husband's children. A younger generation of women, often termed 'new feminists' questioned whether there could be 'good' marriages. This opposed the older mid-Victorian feminists' ideas that there could be good marriages, based on love and equality between two parties.[16]

Different generations of feminists worked together in the 1890s.[17] Questions for feminists had moved away from the debate on sexual difference[18] and the model of female excellence and were now focused on marriage and sexuality.[19] The Victorian ideal of women as feminine beings was challenged by stronger images of more powerful women, such as Joan of Arc.[20] Suffrage activity increased. We shall see in later chapters that Helena was not alone in her goal of opening the Bar to women, but it was a goal that often concerned people of wealth, with good connections and an elite education, because a private income was necessary to follow such a profession:[21] it did not necessarily affect the working-classes; it was a middle-class debate, but it would have a wider effect on how women were treated and viewed by society.

Certainly Helena was concerned with working-class women's issues, such as pay (we will see later that she assisted the attendants in the Royal Courts of Justice in a pay dispute). Her life spanned the labour movement and she could not have been unaffected by working-class women's demands for change;[22] they questioned whether their identity was determined by their sex or their class. This was a time of factory expansion and women (and men) were campaigning for better terms and conditions.[23] They raised questions about child care and family responsibilities, as well as about whether women should marry, and if so whether they should have children, especially in view of new ideas such as eugenics.[24]

By the 1890s, the question of women's rights had been raised to the fore both publicly and politically. There was a new word: 'feminist' and a fresh term 'the new woman.'[25] 'Ellis Ethelmer'[26] attempted to define the term for the first time in 1898[27] but we have seen it was not a new movement. The word came about at a time when new ideas were surfacing. Not all women, such as Beatrice Webb,[28] saw it as a useful term.[29] We can see why today: definitions of 'feminist' can be artificial, and often crude, falling under headings such as 'mid-Victorian', 'New Woman', 'militant', 'socialist', 'radical' and 'post-modern.' For Normanton's generation there were many categories that women might associate with, in particular: 'old feminist'—for these women the central issue was rights for women (such as the vote); 'equality feminism'—these women focused on the similarities between men and women, with the ultimate goal of complete equality; and 'new feminist'—this movement viewed men and women as complimentary rather than one sex's superiority over another.

The influence of feminism on Helena's career

Helena's feminism is problematic as she does not appear to fit into a particular feminist definition or group. Her membership in 1921 of the Six Point Group[30] suggests that she promoted strict equality and that she was an 'old' feminist or an 'equality' feminist,[31] but her notions on female independence were very much of the 'new' feminist variety (such as Eleonor Rathbone). Her mother did everything in her power to enable her daughters to be independent, which was very much a feminist theme in the 1890s (the period of Helena's education).[32]

Helena's feminism can be seen by her desire in practice to *feminise* the law. Later, on entry to the Bar, she would comment that

> 'Women often say that they cannot get a man lawyer to understand what their real grievance is. Something has gone wrong with their marriage and they are not able to convince a man as to the cruelty of the case ...'[33]

However she was quick to add that, 'I do not mean to confine myself to women's cases.' In reality these early women barrister's careers were often restricted to crime and family work. They did not manage to move into more lucrative commercial fields of law for some time. This highlighted the dilemma at the heart of her campaign and subsequent career: while part of the argument for admitting women was that they would bring something different to the law, at the same time they were forced to defend themselves against charges that they were incapable of thinking legally and acting as disinterested professionals as men were presumed to do. She obviously did not want to pigeon-hole herself as a specialist only in family law cases as some of the first women doctors had been confined to women's health.[34] She clearly hoped she would have a choice of cases and that she could bring about real and much needed change to the legal profession. She was careful to promote herself as not challenging the establishment, one that had been coerced into accepting women.

This feminisation of the law is the subject of academic debate still today. It is unclear to what extent Helena wished to feminise it. She expressed a desire to change the way that barristers operated,[35] in particular she perceived that male barristers did not *listen* to their female clients.

Carrie Menkel-Meadows wrote about female lawyering in 1985.[36] Many of her comments relate to Helena and her actions 60 years earlier and describe the practice of law as male and our knowledge of lawyers as being based on a male norm.[37] Meadows described how present women lawyers wish to demystify the law,[38] this is something Helena would try to do in 1932 by writing a book on general legal knowledge for women. Further, Meadows illustrated how women lawyers now have a concern for the interconnection of the personal life and professional life,[39] again, something Helena would go on to try and organize in the form of an Association of Women Barristers in order to do this. Menkel-Meadows showed how today's women lawyers share information and sustenance[40] which is something Helena was part of: a feminist network of women. Finally, Meadows argued, women lawyers today personalise and contex-tualise their practice by asking broader questions and developing a fuller understanding of their client's lives which Helena illustrated by her recognition of the complexities of legal and social problems suffered by her clients (she supported her clients long after she represented them). Menkel-Meadows concluded that it is unclear about the impact of the woman lawyer yet,[41] and this is an ongoing debate and can be seen in the work of McGlynn,[42] and Bacik, Costello and Drew.[43] In the past it was debated that there was an essential woman: women being more caring and conciliatory with a morality responsibility orientation compared to men who were described as having a justice orientation.[44] This idea has now been rejected and a more pragmatic approach adopted, i.e. that women make up half of the population and therefore they must be represented within the legal personnel.[45]

Normanton's involvement with the feminist movement

We saw in *Chapter 1* that, by 1915, Helena was at the heart of the campaign for the vote. This was not her only involvement in feminist organizations. She was not a lone figure in her attempt to open the legal profession to women, but rather part of a bulging network of women. She was a member[46] of the Committee for the Admission of Women to the Legal Profession.[47] Founded in 1903 by Christabel Pankhurst in Manchester after her application to Lincoln's Inn was rejected,[48] Pankhurst acted as its secretary in 1904.[49] Only fragments of information exist about it,[50] yet it is clear that it was a well-organized group that lobbied and raised public awareness.[51] It is possible that this was an extension of the group set up in 1878 for the Promotion of Legal Education for Women. We will see in the next chapter that, from their victory celebrations, membership included prominent feminist activists such as Ray Strachey (chairperson), Gwyneth Bebb, Chrystal Macmillan[52] and Nancy Nettlefold.[53] Newspaper reports from 1903 show that women, such as Lady Strachey, were organizing dinners to raise the profile of women who attempted to enter the legal profession.[54]

After the franchise was obtained Helena was a member of the Union of Women Voters (this was after the right to vote had been secured and they demanded equality of franchise). She was also concerned about the correct use of the vote and was also part of the National Women Citizens Association,[55] she would be their first secretary. This group centred on how women could be active citizens and first met in Hampstead, near Helena's home in Willesden. She was also one of the first members of the 1921 Six Point Group.[56] This was set up by Lady Rhondda[57] to promote strict equality.[58]

Helena's feminist networks and activism were not just contained to England, but extended to Europe.[59] In 1924 she became an honorary member of the Kappa Beta Pi International Legal Sorority, promoting the highest professional standards for women,[60] later the Grand Dean for Europe.[61] Her belief in the highest professional standards for women is further demonstrated by her membership in 1936 of the British Federation of Business and Professional Women[62] and such membership supports the argument that she believed in equality—women should meet the perceived professional standards of men.

She also called for the reform of tax legislation, again equalising the law for both men and women. This is evidenced when in 1929 she became the chairman of the Married Persons Income Tax Reform Council,[63] campaigning against Rule 16 of the General Rules made under the Income Tax Act 1919. These rules purportedly supported the family by providing husbands with a married couples allowance in recognition of the fact that wives would not be in paid employment after they married.

Helena called for the separate assessment of married person's tax. The legal situation continued until long after World War Two. Helena resigned her chairmanship because of a dispute with other members over the way forward.[64] This was not the first or last time she did this.

Certainly her determination to be financially independent and non-reliant on a male figure is in line with other women's views at that time. Enid Locket (née Rosser) who practised at the Bar from 1927–1933 wrote to her step-granddaughters in the 1970s:

> 'To your grandfather and me your future is one of hopeless horror. We are only too conscious that what we thought we were helping to shape in the way of a better life for future generations has become so distorted and scorned that we can only regard as tragedy the world of today in which you are growing up. Women have virtually discarded the visions we had of what life should offer them. Instead of a status of dignity women appear to us to have reverted to becoming irresponsible, unthinking, selfish primitives in their apparently limitless desire to want to breed more and more humans.'[65]

The National Council For Equal Citizenship (NCEC)[66] counted Helena as one of their members.[67] This group was formed in 1932 out of the National Union of Societies for Equal Citizenship (NUSEC), which in turn had been formed in 1918 out of the National Union of Women's Suffrage Societies (NUWSS) which decided to revise its aims after the passing of the Representation of the People Act 1918. Helena sat on the Legal Profession and Sex Disabilities Special Committee of NUSEC until 1920, when it was disbanded. NUSEC's aims were not just to promote equality of franchise between men and women but also to extend this equality to the social and economic fields, working family allowances and the political education of women.

The inter-war years saw a change in feminist behaviour.[68] Women had achieved a major goal with the Representation of the People Act 1918. As Thane explained, there was not a revolution of gender roles but rather a change in the way women lived their lives, this is in turn allowed subsequent generations a greater range of possibilities and the capacity to control their own lives.[69] This quieter work of feminists has been forgotten after the drama of the WSPU, and we should recognise and revise their contribution. They had achievements in legislative change.

We will see in *Chapter 9* that Helena was also President of the Married Women's Association (MWA) in 1952. The MWA had been set up in 1938 after the failure of the Six Point Group to persuade the League of Nations to incorporate the Equal Rights Treaty that would have promoted equality for married women. The MWA wanted to secure the rights of housewives. She prepared and submitted evidence to the Royal Commission on Divorce (1951–56) without consulting the association. She proposed that husbands' should pay their wives an allowance and if the wife misappropriated it she should be answerable in law. She believed in individual property rights and not in the pooling of resources. These radical ideas would lead to her break from the group and her formation of a new group, the Council of Married Women (CMW).

Helena was not campaigning for change alone. She was part of organized feminist activities, part of a strong and powerful network. That feminist network would have been influenced by women's lack of legal personhood.

Lack of legal personhood

Helena's feminism and subsequent feminist activism was shaped by her lack of legal personhood which the rest of this chapter will now focus on. This can be seen by looking at significant events throughout her life. Her parents were separated and at that time her mother's custody of her daughters could potentially have been thwarted by her father, as we will see later in the chapter. She studied teaching because it was one of the few subjects that could provide her with a career and an independent lifestyle. Before she entered the Bar she had only just been granted the right to vote. When she married in 1921, elements of the doctrine of coverture still operated, affecting matters as fundamental as the basis upon which she held property. When finally a legal career became open to her, many of her cases involved the breakdown of marriage.

Jane, her mother's right to custody

As we have seen, Helena was the child of separated parents.[70] Her mother was in a potentially problematic position regarding the custody of her and Ethel. The Custody of Infants Act 1839 gave mothers, for the first time, the right to petition the courts of Chancery for custody of a child under, but not over the age of seven. Helena's mother would have been governed by the later Custody of Infants Act 1873, which allowed mothers to petition the court for custody of children under the age of 16, though it did not give them the right to custody. There was still no equality between men and women, still an assumption that men had absolute custodial rights over their children. The principle that custody should be decided in the 'best interests' of the child did not apply until 1925 and section 1 Guardianship Act 1973 was the first time a statutory declaration was made of equality between mothers and fathers as having equal, separate and exercisable rights.[71] Women had to show that they were of good character before they could be awarded custody.[72] Typically, the issue on which their claims were lost was adultery,[73] but other allegations could see a mother denied contact with her children. For example, Annie Besant,[74] a famous campaigner, birth control author and atheist, fell foul of these rules. In 1879 she lost custody of her daughter, despite a deed of separation giving her custody, on the grounds of her failure to give the child a religious education and her own assumed immorality due to having published a book on birth control.[75] Since little is known about the circumstances of Helena's parents' separation it is impossible to judge the likely outcome had her mother petitioned for custody of her daughters. She was probably aware of her situation, and her young daughters were living with her when their father died. This situation highlights the then sexual double standard, that disadvantaged women.[76]

University

Today women outnumber men at university.[77] At the turn of the last century, not only were women a small minority but some universities did not allow women to take degrees or award degrees to female students.[78] The first university college to grant degrees to women was the University of London in 1878[79] and in 1880 four women passed the external BA examination. Eliza Orme[80] attended the university from 1871 and finally took her external degree in 1888 (becoming the first woman to graduate in law in England).[81] There was often hostility towards women studying for degrees, particularly in certain subjects.[82] An example can be found in the judgment by Lord Neaves,[83] in the now infamous case of *Jex-Blake v Senatus of Edinburgh University* (1873).[84] He made it clear that the University of Edinburgh's admission of women to the study of medicine was illegal, stating that the proposal to confer on women a right of admission to study that subject was beyond the powers of the University Court. Even after the 1919 Sex Disqualification (Removal) Act it was legal for universities to exclude women. As we will see below, section 3 merely permitted universities to allow women but did not require them to do so.

These difficulties together with the cost of higher education, and social constraints upon young women, meant that attending university was not an option for many.[85] Thus Helena was atypical in achieving a degree, even if she did so through a slightly unconventional route. She did not attend university, but gained a University of London external degree in History, 1st class, through attending classes in Glasgow in 1912.[86] Also, some students at her teacher training college, Edge Hill, were examined by the University of Liverpool.[87] Due to her financial position Helena could not have afforded a full-time university education and there would have been little reason to study a subject like law that would not provide her with a career. However, we saw in *Chapter 1,* that in addition to her history degree and teaching qualifications, she obtained a law degree in 1930. This was not necessary at this time even for a would-be barrister.[88]

The vote

There is no need here to rehearse the reasons why the vote was so essential for women and why obtaining it meant that women moved towards a position of legal personality and an improvement of their social and political position.[89] In Helena's lifetime, not only Parliament but also the courts made clear their opposition to women's suffrage. In *Chorlton v Lings* (1886) LR 4 CP the plaintiff's argument centred on the principle that where an Act of Parliament was expressed in the masculine gender it should also apply to the female gender. This argument was rejected. The court said that women could be excluded not only where this was expressly stated, but also where it could be 'properly implied.' Here it was held that the word 'man' had been expressly used to describe men only. The judge, Bovill CJ,[90] went on to explain that women were denied the vote because of 'the respect and honour in which [they] are held', and that, rather than a disadvantage, it was 'a privilege of the sex' because it upheld female decorum.

As Helena became a politically-active adult, the suffrage movement was in full swing and recording successes. Other parts of the British Empire allowed women the vote: New Zealand and Australia opened the vote to women in 1893 and 1902 respectively, around the time Millicent Fawcett[91] became leader of the National Union of Women's Suffrage Societies[92] and as the WSPU was founded in England. [93] The protection that Bovill CJ spoke about in *Chorlton v Lings* was not afforded to suffragettes. Christabel Pankhurst[94] told a rally at the Savoy Theatre in 1911, 'When women are being knocked about, men do nothing. But when a £5 of plate glass is broken, it's thought to be serious.' The campaign clearly inspired Helena: she joined the WSPU.[95]

The suffrage movement has been well-documented and its story will not be repeated here. What is important to mention is the effect of World War I as in June 1914 the suffrage movement paused (although the NUWSS kept up activities).[96] During this time many women performed male work roles[97] and women's paid employment increased by 1.5 million.[98] The war brought some real changes to their working lives and education, because their wartime activities challenged the stereo-typing of women's roles.[99] Men, including Members of Parliament, had varying views on the role of women in the public sphere, for example Herbert Asquith, the Liberal Prime Minister from 1908–1916, opposed women's suffrage, yet Edwin Montagu,[100] Minister of Munitions in the wartime government, asked Parliament: 'Where is the man who now would deny to women the civil rights which she has earned by her hard work?'[101] The war influenced attitudes to extending the franchise both to men and women. The war also brought about a shift in the attitudes of many women to how they perceived their status and their participation in the public sphere, as did women's campaigns.

When women won the vote in 1918, Helena could exercise it because she was already over 30.[102] The Representation of the People Act 1918 gave the vote to women aged 30 and over who were householders, wives of householders, occupiers of property with an annual rent of £5 or graduates of British universities. At the same time, all men over 21 were granted the right to vote (provided they satisfied the residence and property qualifications[103] and had not been wartime conscientious objectors).[104] The Act was a great, but incomplete, stride forward for women. It was not until the Equal Franchise Act 1928 that women were finally given formal voting equality with men when the age limit was lowered to 21 and the property requirements dropped. From 1918 women could stand for Parliament from the age of 21, although they could not vote until age 30.[105]

Marriage

Helena Normanton married accountant Gavin Watson Clark in 1921. He was the eldest son of his family. Born in Edinburgh, a protégé of the Duke of Norfolk, schooled at Emmanuelle School, he worked in the Queensland gold mines, served in the Boer War and went lumbering in Canada.[106] There is no evidence of how they met. His father, Dr Gavin Brown Clark,[107] was MP for Caithness from 1884–1900. He was supposed to have run away to sea at the age of nine,[108] making a fortune of £100,000 before he was 23 by speculating in America. He eventually moved to South London in 1871 to set up a GP's surgery, then becoming an extremely radical MP: he opposed the Crofter Bill, supported women's suffrage and home rule for India and helped establish the Scottish Labour Party. As a doctor he delivered Queen Marie of Romania, was at one time a physician to Queen Victoria and, at the request of Mrs Gladstone, screwed Mr Gladstone into his coffin. He was such a feminist that he demanded a woman undertaker for himself on his death.

It is possible that Helena could have met her husband through her future father-in-law as both were involved with suffrage and the weekly journal *India*. However it is also possible that, as there was a Scottish connection, they met whilst she was teaching in Glasgow.

As already explained, Normanton had strong views on marriage being a legally enforceable contract between a man and woman;[109] unsurprisingly, her feminist understanding of the relationship was not consistent with the law. Having such strong views must have made married women's actual legal position extremely difficult for her.

Femmes covert and other shackles

Before Helena's birth in 1882, married women were considered *femes covert*—literally 'covered women' i.e., a married woman's legal existence was covered by that of her husband as soon as she married. This doctrine was enshrined in law by Blackstone[110] in his *Commentaries on the Laws of England*,[111] a treatise on the common law that explained the development of English law. The doctrine of coverture is contained in the volume entitled 'The Rights of Persons':[112]

> '[T]he very being or legal existence of the wife is suspended during the marriage or at least incorporated or consolidated into that of the husband under whose wing, protection and cover she performs everything.'

Blackstone claimed that this doctrine was a valuable way of protecting women, thereby improving their position:

> 'Even the disabilities which the wife lies under, are for the most part intended for her protection and benefit. So great a favourite is the female sex of the laws.'

In essence the law on coverture[113] meant that on marriage a woman's property (save her freehold property) became her husband's unless she owned property under a trust.[114] The married couple were united as one person in law and that person was the husband.[115]

Helena married late in life, but enjoyed a long and, according to her niece, happy marriage. However her views on a wife's need for financial independence was a 'new' feminist idea and not one necessarily held by other feminists, although conversely her emphasis on equality in areas such as legislative reform in relation to tax and divorce law was very much an 'old' feminist ideal. Other ideas were also being explored such as the nature of women's sexuality.[116] Some women were considering whether sexual relationships outside of marriage were desirable.[117]

The doctrine meant that if the wife's family had not created an equitable[118] 'marriage settlement' most of the wife's property on her marriage would pass to her husband and, in return, he was legally obliged to support her.[119] This doctrine only began to relax significantly with the Married Women's Property Act 1870 and a married woman's earned income became her separate property for her own use only.[120] It did not confer full property rights on married women.[121] The position changed in the year of Helena's birth, 1882, with the second Married Women's Property Act. This Act was still in force at the time she married. The situation was that her property rights took the form of a statutory settlement (trust).[122] This adopted the 'separate property' system that was used in equitable marriage settlements. The wife's capital remained her separate property by the operation of statute and was therefore not subject to common law rules.[123] Wives were benefitted by the 1882 Act because their property no longer automatically transferred to their husband on marriage. Helena became capable of owning her own property as if she were a man or a single woman in 1935, with the Law Reform (Married Women and Tortfeasors) Act of that year.

Overcoming inequalities

Feminism was not a spent force during the inter-war years. It was a well-organized, non-violent campaign group, albeit not with a single, unified voice. Feminists did not adopt the militant ways of the suffragettes, rather their liberal methods. They understood the vote was not obtained solely through the efforts of the suffragettes. The post-war emphasis was on peace. The campaigns by the NCEC on divorce highlight competing views as to how divorce should be legislated for. There was not one standard view, the issue was fundamentally different from the equal franchise. There was not one type of feminist, Helena was neither 'old feminist' nor 'new feminist.'[124] She believed in equality but also recognised that women needed improvements in the private sphere, as well as the public one. Women worked together without sharing the same views. Many knew change would be slow, as was the campaign for the vote.

Helena's (and women's) legal position was problematic and complicated for much of her life. She came of legal and professional age at a time when this position was in turmoil. She was an active agent of change, beginning with her suffragette activities at Edge Hill.

She went on to fight to become the first woman to be admitted to an Inn, and ultimately succeeded in maintaining a practice at the Bar. At first sight it is difficult to understand why any woman would strive to be a barrister when they faced such legal opposition and discrimination. Perhaps a sense of injustice drove her. Perhaps the atmosphere of radicalism and change further fired her own ambitions. Whatever the reasons, Helena lived through and largely overcame numerous inequalities with men concerning her bodily autonomy, her desire to enter the public sphere, her property and central to this book, her career.

CHAPTER 3

Closed Doors at the Inns of Court

'In the city and the legal quarter the lady clerk had barely set foot … So life flowed confidently on … The summer [of 1914] was still unclouded but in little more than a month the Long Vacation opened to the bulges of war.'

Francis Cowper, 1951[1]

The Great War was a period of change for the whole nation. It also signified a complete change in Helena's life. She had left teaching (although she continued with her extension lecturing at the University of London[2]). Her political activity increased with her call for the vote,[3] Indian independence, her role as first secretary for the NWCA[4] and campaign for women's admittance to the legal profession. She worked as the editor of the weekly journal *India*[5] and established permanent roots in London when she leased 22 Mecklenburg Square, on the edge of Bloomsbury, London WC1, for 12 years.[6]

This chapter considers her personal struggle to open the profession to women as was already the case in other countries. In Canada for example, although admission varied by state, Clara Brett Martin was the first woman to be admitted to the Ontario Bar in 1897. Likewise in Australia, Grata Flos Greig was admitted to the Bar in Victoria in 1905. In New Zealand Ethel Benjamin became the first woman to practise in 1897 after legislation was enacted. Cornelia Sorabji had been appearing in court in Poona, India, since 1894 (at the judge's discretion). Much of Europe had also opened up the profession to women: Sweden in 1897, Finland in 1895, Romania in 1891, Norway in 1904, France 1900, and Russia in 1917. In America (where women's right to practise law also varied by state) Arabella Babb Mansfield had been accepted to an American Bar in Iowa in 1869. England and Wales was far behind.[7]

The 1919 legislation

Helena was finally allowed to join an Inn on Christmas Eve 1919, after the passing of the Sex Disqualification (Removal) Act. Her lead, experiences, ambitions and actions have not only influenced the legal profession but also the wider legal and social development of women but only after a well-organised, women-led campaign. This network of women was confident, for example Ivy Williams proclaimed:

> 'The legal profession will have to admit us in their own defence…a band of lady university lawyers will say to the Benchers and the Law Society "Admit us or we shall form a third branch of the profession and practise as outside lawyers."'[8]

The idea was not a new one, it had been suggested at least as early as 1904 by Bertha Cave after her failed attempt to join Gray's Inn.[9] However, this third branch was not required as the 1919 Sex Disqualification (Removal) Act came into force. Helena and other women could finally be admitted to an Inn and the legal profession. The Act received its Royal Assent on 23 December 1919. According to Section 1:

> 'A person shall not be disqualified by sex or marriage from the exercise of any public function, or from being appointed to or holding any civil or judicial post, or from entering or assuming or carrying on any civil profession or vocation.'[10]

In essence this provision enabled more women to access the public sphere, allowing them to enter most professions. It did not outlaw discrimination[11] and it was not an ideal piece of legislation. For example section 1(a) allowed women to be excluded by regulation from any branch or posts within the civil service or foreign service, and permitted restrictions on the mode of admission of women in the civil service (this allowed the marriage bar — the automatic refusal or dismissal of women on marriage — to continue). Section 2 permitted women to be admitted as solicitors after serving three years articles if they possessed a university degree, or had fulfilled all the requirements of a degree at a university which did not, at the time, award degrees to women. These were the same requirements as for men. Section 3 stated that, 'Nothing shall be deemed to preclude the authorities of such university from making such provision as they shall see fit for the admission of women to membership thereof, or to any degree' (in other words, the Act allowed but did not require universities to admit women). It further allowed women to be appointed as jurors and magistrates[12] for the first time. The year 1919 was described by Virginia Woolf as the 'sacred year'[13] because she believed that it allowed women the right to earn a living (though many had done so in various ways before). Enid Rosser wrote of the Act:

> 'It cannot be overstressed what a revolution it was at the time; it is almost impossible for anyone of today's generation to realise what it signified, for that Act … theoretically established women's right to a proper place in the life and work of the country …'[14]

However some historians have seen the Act in a more negative light, as 'a broken reed'[15] or 'a dead letter'[16] because it did not remove the marriage bar or bring an end to sex discrimination.[17] Helena herself angrily lamented that 'The Sex Disqualification Act is all done away with, except for the admission of women to the legal profession and justiceship of the peace … I return to the Government election pledge … And this is how HM Government carries it out!'[18]

The 1919 legislation did more than finally enable Helena to enter the Bar, it also marked the beginning of feminist campaigns during the interwar years. The high profile and well documented suffrage campaign has sometimes been considered the last united woman's movement. But this was not so.[19] This legislation is a good example of the start of those later campaigns. It was a stepping stone to other reforms.

How did this legislation come into being? What were the events that led to its passing? The Sex Disqualification (Removal) Bill was not the only Bill to be presented to Parliament proposing women's admission to the legal profession. There had been a long line of Bills presented to Parliament over the years proposing this. However, it was one of three presented to Parliament in the mid-to-late 1910s. The other two were the Barristers' and Solicitors' (Qualification of Women) Bill[20] introduced by Lord Buckmaster on 26 February 1919, followed by the Women's Emancipation Bill, on 21 March 1919.[21] The ultimately successful Sex Disqualification (Removal) Bill was introduced in July 1919 by the Government.[22] This was a period of unrest in Britain; the Great War had just ended and there was ongoing discussion of the peace settlement, there was trouble in Ireland and the further problem of returning soldiers. Women had only just achieved a limited franchise after a long and difficult struggle but were now potential voters and MPs.

Attorneys, infants and serfs[23]

To become a barrister, a man was required to become a student member of one of the four Inns. Refusals of applications to join were rare — if you were a man. They had to eat 36 dinners in their Inn before becoming eligible to be called to the Bar, as well as sitting and passing the Bar exams. We will see below that the law supported those who refused such membership to women, including Helena. She was not the first woman to be refused admission.[24] We saw earlier, in *Chapter 2,* that women had long been campaigning to enter the legal profession. But, let us look at this in more detail in order to fully understand the context of Normanton's application to join Middle Temple.

Women had been attempting to enter the legal profession from the 1870s. In 1873 Maria Grey[25] organized a petition, signed by 92 women, to attend lectures arranged by the Council of Legal Education (CLE)[26] at Lincoln's Inn.[27] This was an organized campaign of a network of those women signatories. Grey was an education reformer and a founding member of the Women's Education Union.[28] The petition was a political gesture and was, predictably, unsuccessful.[29] The Lincoln's Inn Black Book[30] records that at a council meeting on 18 February 1873:

> '[T]he Petition of Maria G. Grey and others be referred to the Four Inns of Court…Ordered: that the Resolution of the Council of Legal Education be confirmed and that the petition signed by 92 Ladies referred to therein be taken into consideration at the next Adjourned Council…'

Accordingly, at the next meeting on 11 March 1873, it was resolved:

'…that in the opinion of this Bench it is not expedient[31] that women should be admitted to the lectures of the professors appointed by the Council of Legal Education.'

Clearly women were not welcome at the Inns of Court.

Quasi-lawyers and legal challenges

Although the Bar was resolutely closed to women, one woman, Eliza Orme, circumvented the need to be professionally qualified and managed to practise law. Despite having no formal legal qualifications, she opened a law office with a colleague on Chancery Lane in London (close to the Inns) in 1875,[32] called Orme and Richardson.[33] There were probably many women working in non-qualified positions in law offices, but Orme's office was 'bold'[34] because there were women legal assistants at this time but 'few, if any' had set up an office as Orme and Richardson did.[35] Although she managed to gain an LLB in 1888, when she was 40-years-old, Orme was never qualified to practise the law. She was in practice for 25 years[36] working as a quasi-lawyer or legal assistant to qualified lawyers, by providing opinions and drafting pleadings and documents.[37] Mary Jane Mossman commented that 'Orme's decision to engage in legal work reveals a different strategy; rather than confronting the authority and legal culture of the legal professions directly, Orme chose to do legal work at the boundaries of professional jurisdictions, mainly as a conveyance and patent agent.'[38]

Miss Day also sought an indirect method of practising law in 1891. However, unlike Orme, she attempted to become a licensed conveyancer 'under the Bar.' This was a means of becoming a 'special pleader,'[39] which required a certificate from one of the Inns. It was a way of becoming a barrister through the back door.[40] However, Lincoln's Inn prevented her from becoming a licensed conveyancer (she presumably felt this was possible because she was competent and professional at her legal work). She was also a feminist campaigner.

For many women, this 'quasi-lawyering' was not enough and the battle for formal equality continued. Just before Miss Day's disappointment, in 1878, another group was established which specifically aimed to open the legal profession to women called the Promotion of Legal Education for Women.[41] This lobbied MPs and canvassed for change. By the turn of the twentieth century, women were beginning to complete law degrees.[42] This created an anomaly: women were technically exempt from certain parts of the professional exams by virtue of their law degree, yet could still not enter the legal profession.

On 5 March 1903 Bertha Cave[43] applied to join Gray's Inn. Very little is known about Cave, save she was born in 1881 in Sevenoaks, Kent, and was the daughter of a 'butler/servant.' How did this servant's daughter end up challenging the establishment, not just by her sex, but by her class? On her application she wrote:

'I am desirous of being admitted as a student of the Honourable Society of Gray's Inn for the purposes of being called to the Bar. I am aware that my application is most unusual and no doubt without precedent, but trust that the Masters of the bench will give it their serious consideration and I should, in the event of a favourable reply, be pleased to conform to any special rules they may think fit to impose.'[44]

No order was made on this application and, because she had two supporters and two dissenters, it was sent to another committee for consideration. However, eight days later the master's sitting on that committee refused her application.[45] The masters of Gray's Inn referred her application to a report of a committee, which sat in April,[46] where it considered whether they had the power to admit her. They held that not all the power the society had concerning admission was delegated from the judges. Judges alone, they held, decided on details of dress and exercise. These regulations, according to their ordinary and natural sense, indicated that males, and males alone were admissible as students, and, when the regulations were read in the light of the uniform and uninterrupted usage which had so long followed upon them, they appeared to be conclusive against the power of their society to admit women for the purpose of being called to the Bar. They referred to various legal cases, none of them on point.[47]

Cave appealed and this was heard in the Moses Room of the House of Lords on 2 December 1903 before a formidable group of judges (not sitting in a judicial capacity).[48] She was a litigant in person. She began

> 'May it please you[r] Lordships: As you already know: the committee of Gray's Inn have decided upon making no order on my application for admission as a student and I appeal to your Lordships, knowing the court has at present power to admit students. I would urge in support of my case that although there are no rules for the admission of students, there appears to be none against …'

She argued that they had the power to admit her as there were women lawyers in other countries. She finished by saying, 'Will that be sufficient?' The Lord Chancellor, Lord Halsbury replied, 'We are prepared to listen to any argument which you address to us by which you can show you are entitled to become a member of the Inn.' Boldly she replied, 'Does your Lordship know of any reason why I should not be admitted?' He countered, 'I am afraid the objection is that no lady has ever yet been admitted to the Inn; and that, dealing with legal institutions, is a very powerful argument against it. I am afraid that I cannot conduct the proceedings in dialogue. I must ask you to argue it.'

Clearly no legal precedent prevented him from finding in her favour. Bravely she asked, 'Have your Lordships anything to argue against it?' Halsbury replied, 'It is not for me to argue against it. It is for you to convince us that you have a right. I am afraid I cannot enter into an argument with you. It is for you to argue before us.'

She persisted, 'Might I argue on this principle, that there are no rules forbidding the admission of women?' Halsbury conceded: 'I think you may take it that is true. That is open to this observation, that nobody ever dreamt that a lady would ask to be admitted to the Inn, or there might have been rules on the subject. I cannot argue with you. We must hear arguments, whatever you have to urge, and then we shall decide.' She simply said, 'There is nothing else I can think of to urge, but that.' He dismissed her with, 'Very good, You may resume your seat.' Clearly the men felt challenged. Halsbury's remarks to her are belittling, a powerful man, in grand surroundings trying to make a young woman feel small. He then gave his decision:

> 'I think we are all of opinion that the appeal must be dismissed. There is no actual rule upon the subject, but long continued practice is a very powerful observation in reference to anything that is suggested as a new right, and this would be a new right which I think certainly does not exist and of which there is no trace whatever. There is no precedent for it, and therefore, I think we are all of the opinion we cannot make a precedent or suggest to the Inns of Court that they should alter the course of practice which has now lasted for some centuries. That is quite enough to justify the Inn in the course they have pursued, and we do not think it necessary to give other reasons than that there is no precedent for such a proceeding.'

He gave no legal precedent to support his decision, because there was no legal authority on which to base it. Cave made one final plea, 'Is there no possible chance of your Lordships altering your decision?' He showed no remorse saying, 'I think not the least.' She replied quite simply and with understatement: 'I am very disappointed.' This transcript was filed in Helena's application file in Middle Temple[49] and formed part of the precedent that was relied on by that Inn to deny her membership. In 1903, Christabel Pankhurst[50] also had her application to join Lincoln's Inn refused on the basis that women were not permitted to practise law.[51] Like the Bills to Parliament on this issue numerous women were constantly applying to the Inns seeking admission but being refused.

Cave was used to deny Normanton entry to the legal profession, as was the 1914 decision in the case of *Bebb v Law Society*.[52] In this case, four women took the Law Society to court in an attempt to force them to allow women the right to sit the Law Society's preliminary examination in 1914 in order to qualify as solicitors. There were four separate actions by each litigant. The women argued that the Interpretation Act 1889, section 1, laid down that, where the masculine term was used in a piece of legislation, it was taken to include the feminine. They argued that the

Attorneys and Solicitors Act 1729 should apply to women as well as men, enabling them to qualify. The court rejected this argument. They and the Law Society relied upon a mediaeval treatise, *The Mirror of Justices*,[53] which stated that 'the law will not suffer women to be attorneys, nor infants nor serfs.'[54] The court concluded that, since women could not qualify as lawyers, they would not be allowed to take the exams. When the case went to appeal, the Master of the Rolls commented that, 'There has been that long uniform and interrupted usage which is the foundation of the greater part of the common law of this country, and which we ought, beyond all doubt, to be loath to depart from.'[55]

The decision in *Bebb* was one in a string of cases known as 'persons' cases. This meant that women were not considered 'persons' in legislation, and were not to be included in the masculine pronoun despite general legislation that said otherwise.[56] The decision was also based on the idea that women needed 'protection.'[57] Whilst some judges thought upper-class and middle-class women should spend their time in the home and in voluntary work, it was clear from the legal regulation of factories and mines that the law (and some in society) had a quite different idea of how working-class women should spend their time. Although women were excluded from working in mines[58] and from night work in factories,[59] very many[60] working-class women (who were a large and diverse group) did not have much chance to study domestic skills or command their homes, but spent long hours in domestic service or, where factories and workshops existed, in appalling conditions.[61]

Membership and clientele

'The status of a profession is affected by two principal factors: membership and clientele.'[62]

Living in London placed Helena in a good geographical position to lobby for women's entry to the legal profession, since London was the central location for law at the time.[63] The Bar Council was based there, as were the four Inns.[64] Although there were provincial sets, most chambers were in London and these sets, until very recently, were required to have their chambers within the precincts of the Inns.[65] Barristers were (and still are) distinguished from other lawyers by their 'call'[66] to the Bar, which takes place during 'call night' at one of the four Inns where each barrister must have membership. Once called, the man could describe himself as a barrister. This gave him a monopoly on the rights of audience in the higher courts and he could only be briefed by a member of the 'junior legal profession,' solicitors. Therefore, the starting place for any would-be barrister was membership of an Inn.[67] The Inns had control of their own membership. Helena applied to Middle Temple in early February 1918 and was rejected on the basis of *Bebb*.[68]

The purpose of membership of an Inn of Court.

Apart from a gap from the seventeenth century to 1846 [69] the Inns were responsible for training barristers.[70] In 1852 the four Inns established the Council of Legal Education (CLE) which provided lectures,[71] and in 1872 introduced a compulsory Bar examination.[72] Helena needed to sit these exams in order to practise law. Bar students were not required to be graduates, but the Inns encouraged this by offering exemptions from parts of the Bar examinations for law graduates [73] and reduced the requisite number of terms of dining for other graduates.[74] Dining was a further reason why Helena required admission: she needed to 'keep terms' and eat three dinners in hall in each of the four terms for three years.[75] Without doing so, a barrister could not ordinarily be called to the Bar.[76]

Enid Rosser described in detail the dining practice at her Inn, Lincoln's Inn in 1927 which gives the reader a flavour of the atmosphere:

'Masters of the Bench sat at the High Table on a dais at one end of the Hall, immediately below them but with parallel tables sat the barristers of the Inn and then at cross tables running the length of the Hall sat the students of the Inn. The laying of the student tables was so arranged that we sat in messes of 4, the messes being divided up by carafes of water and when choice had been made by vote of each mess, the chosen bottle of wine and port. Each mess had its quota, choosing with burgundy or claret; the port arrived automatically. Everybody wore black gowns and no student could sit down until the senior bencher had said grace. If you had not already fixed

your companions from your friends to form your mess, it was chancy whom
you would find yourself as companions.'[77]

This was, then, a very male environment, similar to eating in an
Oxbridge college.

A legal oligarchy

'An oligarchy of older barristers who selected their successors.'[78]

Admission was controlled by the benchers[79] of each Inn. As already indicated, women apart, refusals were few.[80] Applicants had to be male, to
state their age, residence, condition in life and to supply two references
from other barristers or one reference from a bencher.[81] They were not
permitted to practise a trade. The Inns, in essence barristers and judges
(who had themselves been barristers themselves), exercised total control
over who could be admitted as students.[82] Not only the legal authorities
opposed women joining the legal profession, so did many barristers.
Evidence is the motion in favour of admitting women moved by Holford
Knight,[83] a barrister and supporter of Helena,[84] at the annual meeting of
the Bar in 1913, which was rejected by a majority.[85] Again, in January 1917
he proposed a similar motion to the Bar Council which was defeated
by a majority of 178 to just 22.[86] Knight believed that women could no
longer be denied entry to the Bar because of their contribution to the
war effort during the Great War.[87] He was not alone, Lord Buckmaster
could not understand the Bar's refusal of women and had hoped that
they would voluntarily open their doors to them. He reflected:

'I thought it possible that the Inns might take what I regarded as the courageous course of saying that in exercise of their unlimited and undoubted
discretion they would admit women to the Inns without further delay.'[88]

Despite the overwhelming majority of barristers seemingly opposed
to female barristers there were clearly some strong and influential male
sympathisers such as Holford Knight.

Helena's application to join Middle Temple

On 6 February 1918 women obtained the right to vote with the passing of the Representation of the People Act. Against this backdrop, Helena applied to Middle Temple. It is unclear exactly why such press interest followed her in particular, especially as she was not the first to apply. We will see that she made use of the press to publicise her campaign; she understood the value of publicity. There was also a sense that, because the vote had been granted, the campaign to open up the legal profession had a chance of success.[89]

An example of the press interest is the *Observer*, 10 February 1919,[90] which (among others) reported that Helena had applied for admission to Middle Temple. Many of the reports were sympathetic, such as the *Daily Graphic* (16 February 1918) which argued, '[I]f women cannot stand in court, they will get no clients!,' and that women did not want special treatment or privileges in court.[91] This was a direct answer to an argument put forward at that time that women would detract from the workings of the courts because of their sex or 'sex attraction'. The paper dismissed this argument, saying that this hardly deserved serious attention because it was a reflection on the male judiciary and jury, and not on women: 'We would need to remove women from all public offices and place a grille across the public gallery of the House of Commons so that men do not get distracted!'[92] Helena reassured the reader that she did not wish to enter the Bar as a feminist but as a human being desirous of serving the community. This is another indication that she saw the Bar as a means of helping people. She argued that the law courts were not a proper arena for sex grievances; rather they existed for the administration of justice 'pure and undefiled by political prejudices or personal feelings'. She is portrayed as non-confrontational, rational and non-threatening. This is an early example of her using the press as a means of promoting the cause, as well as the press having an interest in her.

The press certainly did have a fascination with the first women barristers that is difficult to understand today. They followed her campaign avidly. Enid Rosser, a barrister called in 1927, wrote an account of the press attention afforded to her during the trial that year into the murder of PC Gutteridge, who had been shot in the face. She was purely in court to assist her pupil master and yet she wrote '… the consequences were overwhelming to me personally for it was more than the Press could resist."[93] Fleet Street had placards saying, 'Woman appears for the crown.' Photographers were waiting for her at chambers. She said the press attention was a 'ghastly fate and burden,' which was only 'lightened' by her chambers colleagues sweepstake to see who would collect the most press references. But they also helped Rosser find a way out of the basement so that the press could not take pictures of her. However the press would knock on the front door at 11 pm. She concluded:

> '[I]t was more annoying as it did me and woman barristers generally a lot of harm as it is a very strict rule of the profession that publicity must be avoided …I never, hard though I tried, succeeded in suppressing this Press interest in my doings. It was extremely silly, apart from its high nuisance value, or lack of value … there was little I could do about it and had to put up with constant photographs in the Press taken of me as I walked to the Old bailey or Police courts …To you all this fuss must seem very odd as you take in your stride women cabinet ministers and women holding every kind of job in all walks of life. But in those days we were still battling along and it was not difficult to be the first woman to do anything … they [the press] caused me much misery.'

The press were clearly sympathetic to Normanton's cause, something that Bertha Cave discovered in 1903 (one could argue the visibility of her Gray's Inn application tested the waters in terms of the press response). Also, as mentioned above, some men were also sympathetic. She had supporters who wrote references in aid of her application.[94] Holford Knight wrote to Middle Temple asking them to give sympathetic consideration to it, saying that he supported her, she had high credentials, her public work was full of distinction and her personal character would keep the traditions of the profession secure. Finally, he stated that he was satisfied that the admission of women would enhance the profession and its service to the State.

John Wells Thatcher prayed his recommendation for Helena be put before the benchers. He wrote that he had known her for three years, she was well qualified and well read. Women, he said, would enhance the profession. David Murray LLD also wrote a reference, stating that he saw a great deal of her in Glasgow, she had a brilliant university career and was widely read with a quick apprehension. Sarah Hale supported Helena with a reference stating that all her lecturers at Edge Hill were impressed by her intellectual ability, power of concentration and clarity of judgment. These references had no power of persuasion.

First rejection

On 21 February 1918, Middle Temple held a parliament[95] to consider her application and refused to admit her as a student.[96] The outcome was predictable and widely anticipated. *The Vote* for example reported that the 'Londoner' in the *Evening Standard* had indicated the benchers would not admit women unless Parliament forced them.[97] Helena received official confirmation of this on 23 February in the form of a letter from the under treasurer at Middle Temple, but not the actual judgment.[98] The letter informed her that her application had been considered and 'unanimously refused.' She must have known that this was the most likely response, but had hoped that, following women's enfranchisement, the Bar would concede that women's public position had changed. Such was the misogyny at the Bar that they would not change unless forced to do so by law.

Her plight was commented on by the *Standard* and other publications. A crudely cut newspaper article from another newspaper was sent to Helena anonymously (dated 25 February 1918), with in ink at the top: 'WITH LOVE FROM A BENCHER.'[99] The cutting stated that she was refused admission and reported her comments that she felt that this was just the first stage in the contest and that it would 'not be a long one.'[100] The article further quoted her saying that she had six million enfranchised women behind her who would not tolerate 'this absurdity from the Benchers.' The 'With Love' suggests that it was sent maliciously. Whatever the motive behind the correspondence it must have been unsettling for her.

The stated reasons for Helena's rejection

The minutes of the Middle Temple parliament record the grounds for her rejection. These were agreed unanimously and the parliament ordered that no reasons should be given to Helena. At some point, she must have been supplied with a transcript, as there is a copy of it in her archives.[101] The decision consists of a lengthy statement from the treasurer, which stated, in summary, that they followed the *Bebb* decision and the ruling in Bertha Cave's application to Gray's Inn (it should be noted that this was a tribunal appeal against an institution, not a legal precedent). Further, they held that, under the Solicitors Act 1843, and the common law, women were under a disability by reason of their sex.[102] Therefore they had decided that they were bound by precedent. If they were indeed bound by *Bebb* it would have been correct that they were restrained by legal precedent. Parliament had not given them the tool with which to admit a woman: legislation. But was this legally correct? The *Bebb* judgment concerned solicitors and attorneys, not barristers. Therefore it could have been treated as irrelevant. Alternatively, they could have been brave and held that it was absurd to deny women entry to the legal profession when they had been granted the vote and performed roles in the public sphere during the war. This behaviour was, as Rosemary Auchmuty commented concerning Gwyneth Bebb, one of 'the defensive strategies employed by those whose privileges are under threat.[103] The decision of Middle Temple to refuse Helena entry to the Bar is difficult to understand, except in terms of conservatism, prejudice, misogyny and discrimination. *Bebb* is a poor decision. The judge had no authority to distinguish the Interpretation Act on the basis of a medieval treatise.[104] It is clear that he had no intention of allowing women to become solicitors and used any means necessary to achieve that result. He used a 'protection' argument and rummaged around for some kind of legal authority. It is hard to understand why Middle Temple felt obliged to follow the ruling. The judge held that 'The law will not suffer women to be attorneys...' i.e. solicitors. Before 1873, when law and equity cases were heard in different courts, solicitors practised in the Chancery Court, attorneys in the Common Law Courts and proctors in the Ecclesiastical Courts. After the Judicature Act 1873, attorneys became solicitors of the Supreme

Court. As a consequence of this, section 89(6) of the Solicitors Act 1860 provided that any reference to attorneys was to be read as a reference to solicitors and so did not apply to barristers. Nonetheless, the effect of Middle Temple's decision was that Helena was frustrated in her legal ambitions. This would change only in 1919, with the passing of the Sex Disqualification (Removal) Act.

Helena's character is demonstrated by her reaction to the rejection: she lodged an appeal. Again, she was not acting on her own. She had tremendous support from women's organizations and prominent male establishment figures. Holford Knight wrote regularly in the press. His sentiments can be seen in an article written in 1913.[105] Where he wrote that he failed to understand why England was not progressive and had not accepted women legal professionals when 'other modern states' had done so; he believed that it was only a matter of time. He countered arguments that women were physically incapable of being lawyers with the fact that women already, under the stress of economic need, undertook a wide range of employment. He dismissed arguments that women suffered from 'defect of temperament and mind' that 'would lower the standard of professional conduct,' stating that he was not sure whether this was true and that many men suffered from this disability. He concluded by saying that 'only exceptional women will be admitted.' Was it true that only 'exceptional' men were practicing as barristers at the time?

Even some of the judiciary indirectly backed Helena's application. Charles Swinfen-Eady,[106] Lord Justice of Appeal[107] (and later Master of the Rolls)[108] was reported as saying,[109] whilst presenting prizes at a girl's school in Pimlico, that he had 'no doubt' that women would be admitted to the Bar. At its meeting[110] in the Middle Temple Common Room, the Hardwicke Society,[111] moved 'That there is no reasonable ground why admission to the Bar should not be granted to women on the same terms as men.'[112] Frederic Mackarness J[113] wrote to *The Times*[114] publicly endorsing women barristers. He stated that he did not believe that there were any judges or barristers who thought that women would lower the high standards of the profession. He felt that the current position was not a courteous or happy reflection on the sex who were wives, mothers and sisters to men, and had during the last four years produced thousands of brave, capable, and devoted women of the highest quality. He pointed out that women already appeared in court: as witnesses and litigants in person and there were already women barristers in the Dominion of Canada.

Helena had a following among women's organizations. The *Christian Commonwealth*[115] reported that the National Union of Women Workers (which became the National Council of Women later that year), the most powerful body of organized women in the country, which included in its 153 affiliated societies no fewer than one-and-a-half million women, 'cordially' endorsed her application at its executive meeting. The Women's Freedom League wrote to her offering their support and confirming a lecture she was to give them the following week. They urged her to 'try & work up the press.'[116] Helena also had private letters of support such as this one from Inga Hawkins, of Latchgrads, Chipstead, Surrey, who wrote to Middle Temple on 26 February:

> 'I am sorry for you that it was your lot to tell the women of England that the door to the Middle Temple is closed. It is only a matter of time when the Masters of the Bench will have to swing the door wide-open to women the Masters will with humble, bent heads stand by the door saying "Come welcome, we want your help to make laws…"'[117]

With the support of so many women continuing the campaign must have been both daunting and inspiring.

Claud Schuster[118]

Helena had one other significant ally, and probable supporter, Claud Schuster. [119] Schuster became a civil servant in 1899 and moved to the Board of Education in 1903. In 1915 he was chosen by the then Lord Chancellor, Lord Haldane, to fill the office of Clerk to the Crown in Chancery and Permanent Secretary in the Lord Chancellor's Office. By the time Schuster started this job Lord Haldane was no longer Lord Chancellor, having been replaced by Lord Birkenhead.[120] We have no evidence of any prior acquaintance or introduction between Helena and Schuster.[121] There is no previous correspondence between them in her archives or in the National Archives. On 10 June 1918 she received a reply to a letter she had sent to the Lord Chancellor's office requesting advice about how to appeal against a decision of the parliament of an Inn. His letter[122] explained in detail with whom to lodge her petition and where.[123] He set out the grounds 'upon which it is desired to appeal' and attached a copy of an appeal. It is fairly simple and reads:

1. That by recent legislation your petitioner has become a parliamentary elector & she now claims a disability under the common law to exercise public functions in the state has been removed thereby (this is fairly self-explanatory, as women have been granted the right to vote and participate in the public sphere then they should be able to participate fully in that sphere by being able to enter the professions).

2. The Bar hitherto raised against the admission of women to the legal profession should be considered by your lordships & removed (again this just means that the judges should consider the law, such as *Bebb*, and remove it by admitting women).

3. That testimony as to personal character from responsible persons as is required by the Consolidated Regulations aforesaid with reference to the fitness of your petitioner has been furnished to the Masters of the Bench of the said Honourable Society of the Middle Temple and copies thereof are appended hereto (this just means that she has the appropriate references).

4. Your petitioner therefore prays that your Lordships will be pleased to grant:
   (1) That your Petitioner may have audience before your Lordships to prosecute this appeal (this is fairly self-explanatory, it is just asking for her to present her appeal in person).
   (2) That your Lordships may be pleased to set aside the aforesaid refusal of the Masters of the Bench of the Honourable Society of the Middle Temple (this just means to set aside their previous decision).
   (3) That your Lordships may be pleased to direct the said Masters of the Bench of the Honourable Society of the Middle Temple to reconsider the Petition of your Petitioner presented to them

on the date above mentioned (this just merely asks them to reconsider their decision).

(4)   Such further and other relief as to your Lordships may see fit.

Helena lodged this appeal as directed in July 1918,[124] but it was not heard until 11 February 1919.[125] The passage of time was explained in the *Daily Telegraph* as due to her appeal being deferred because of the introduction of Lord Buckmaster's Bill.[126] Elsie Lang explained that Helena had been given an official explanation to insert in *The Times* that her appeal had been fixed for March 1919, unless the Government made a statement that they would deal with the admission of women by legislation.[127] Elsie Lang referred to this as the first official statement about the intended Sex Disqualification (Removal) Act.

Seeking publicity

Helena responded actively and did try to 'work up the press'. She gave numerous public addresses, including at two meetings, at 3 pm and 7.30 pm, of the Derby Women Citizens' Association,[128] on 'Women and the Legal Profession'. She was described on the flyer as

'[T]he pioneer in the movement to open the Legal Profession to Women, and is shortly to appear before the Lord Chancellor and 26 Judges of the Country, to personally conduct her appeal.'[129]

This description as 'pioneer' is interesting.[130] Although she was only one of a number of women who had attempted to open the legal profession to women, she had become 'the pioneer' in the eyes of the press and many women's groups. This label was to become a hindrance in her later career and may help to explain why she was not as successful as could have been expected. There was also a backlash to this role.

She also spoke at the Kingston Church of Humanity, Kingston-upon-Thames, Surrey[131] on 'Women & the Legal Profession.' She took part in debates, for example at the Union of the Society of London,[132] at their annual Ladies' Night Debate, at Old Hall, Lincoln's Inn.[133] She moved '[T]hat all Branches of the Legal Profession should be open to women.'

She gave an address, 'That the exclusion of women from the English Bar is to the Public Detriment,' at the Pioneer Club, 9 Park Place, St James's, London SW1.[134] Helena was fearless in these public debates, openly arguing 'That all Branches of the Legal Profession should be open to women.'[135] This was reported widely. For example the next day the *Evening Standard* described her arguments as ranging from relying on authority ('Why when Mr Justice Eve had the other day given a judgment that opened the profession of Chartered Accountants to women, didn't he go further and open it up to his own profession?'), to entertainment ('I myself would have a horror of being heard by a women judge — if I were guilty!') to non-threatening sincerity ('I'm not arguing from a narrow feminist point of view … but because there might be among women as rich a capacity for service in the law as they had shown in medicine, nursing, and other forms of activity').[136] In this debate she was vehemently opposed by Mr I A Symmons, a metropolitan magistrate. He admitted some women might have the intelligence, industry, and accuracy of the lawyer; they could study law, even teach it, but not practise because they lacked judgment. He accepted that women might have deeper consciences than men, sympathy, and a love of right and justice, but they lacked honour — the regard for the rules of the game that was embodied in the professional sense of honour. He warned that women were not all law-abiding and that they did not respect law because it was law. He further warned that the barristers' profession was the hardest apprenticeship of any in the world and the world at large knew the successes at the Bar, but not the failures. There were failures in spite of talent and industry. Of over 100 people present, 35 voted in favour of Helena and 24 for Symmons. This result was reported as a surprise.

At another event Helena publicly promoted the Barristers and Solicitors (Qualification of Women) Bill,[137] by calling for a resolution

'That this meeting calls upon the Government to give facilities for its passage through the House of Commons to the Barristers and Solicitors (Qualification Of Women) Bill, which has already successfully passed through the House of Lords so that it may become law at the earliest possible date.'

She also spoke of the social work and support that women's participation in law could bring.[138] She described criminals not as 'a peculiar type, but rather as a slightly sub-normal person—who was the product of under-nourishment and under-development.' She saw the criminal as a brother or sister who had gone wrong, needed help and should be helped. Women's function for her was the 'humanising of the law.' She strongly believed that the general interests of the community were not served by the continuation of the existing system. As enfranchised persons, women should accept their due responsibility; to neglect it would be a dereliction of duty; to attend it would make the country more humane and moral. Clearly she hoped to 'feminise' the profession.

Appeal outcome

Obviously fed up with waiting, Helena wrote again to Claud Schuster[139] on the 15 January 1919,[140] venturing 'to bring to his notice that [her] Petition of 23rd July is still unheard' and could he 'please' fix a date for the hearing of it? He replied two days later,[141] informing her that the benchers of the Middle Temple had not yet lodged their reply. He said he would write to them and call their attention to this fact. He asked whether she had actually served the petition upon the benchers and to which judges it had been addressed (accusation is the best defence).

Unknown to Helena her appeal was heard at Middle Temple on the 30 January 1919.[142] The judgment stated:

Case for the Benchers of the Honourable Society of the Middle Temple on the Petition of Helena Florence Normanton:

IN THE MATTER OF

THE PETITION TO THE JUDGES OF HELENA FLORENCE NORMANTON on Appeal from the refusal of the Benchers of the Middle Temple to admit her as a Student.

Case for the Benchers of the Middle Temple

1. The Benchers do not dispute any of the facts stated in the petition which relate to the Appellant and her qualifications, personal character, and attainments.

2. The Benchers considered the application of the Appellant for admission as a student, and decided that by the Common Law there is a disability on the part of a woman to be admitted as a student of an Inn of Court with a view to being called to the Bar, which disability has not been removed by statute.

3. The Benchers further considered that they were bound by the statements of the law contained in the judgments by the Court of Appeal in *Bebb v. Law Society* (1914) 1 Chancery 286, and by the decision of the Judges on the Appeal of Bertha Cave against the refusal of the Benchers of Gray's Inn to admit her as a student. That appeal was heard on the 2nd of December, 1903, and in dismissing the Appeal the Lord Chancellor (the Earl of Halsbury) said as follows:

   'I think we are all of the opinion that the appeal must be dismissed. There is no actual rule upon the subject, but long continued practice is a very powerful observation in reference to anything that is suggested as a new right, and this would be a new right which I think certainly does not exist, and of which there is no trace of whatever. There is no precedent for it, and therefore I think we are all of the opinion that we cannot make a precedent, or suggest to the Inns of Court that they alter the course of practice which has now lasted for some centuries. That is quite enough to justify the Inn in the course they have pursued, and we do not think it necessary to give any other reasons than there is no precedent for such a proceeding.'

4. Assuming that their Lordships consider that, as Visitors of the Inns of Court, they have jurisdiction to entertain an appeal to them by a person who is not a member of an Inn of Court, appoint on which

reference may be made to *R. v. Benchers of Lincoln's Inn* 4 B. & C. 855, the Benchers submit that it was their duty to refuse the present Appellant's application for the reasons above stated.

It is unclear when Helena had news of this outcome, whether at a meeting with Claud Schuster in February or at some other date. The outcome would not have been unexpected given her original rejection, though it must have been extremely disappointing. It also had the effect of passing the responsibility for women's admission to the legal profession onto Government. It was certainly a missed opportunity by the Bar. It might have been hoped, as Lord Buckmaster said when reflecting on the failure of his Bill,[143] that the Inns might have taken the 'courageous course of saying that in the exercise of their unlimited and undoubted discretion they would admit women to the Inns without delay.'[144] The decision to open the Bar up to women was not going to be achieved without the Inns being forced into it.

February 1919

On 11 February, Helena received an intriguing letter from Claud Schuster.[145] She clearly had not been informed of the appeal outcome at this date, as he told her that Middle Temple had lodged their answer to her petition. He did not tell her what the outcome was, but asked, 'Before the next step is taken will you arrange a conversation with me [and . . .] conveniently come here?' She was asked to fix an appointment with his private secretary Colin Smith. There are no formal records of this meeting in the National Archives or in Helena's files. In a much later letter to the BBC, in 1952,[146] Helena wrote that the purpose of the meeting was to prevent her bringing litigation. The Government requested that she withdraw her appeal since they were introducing the Sex Disqualification (Removal) Bill. In the letter to the BBC she said that she had evidence of the negotiations in writing and had kept a copy, though none survives in her archives and this would certainly seem contrary to her declaration of betrayal by the Government in 1921.

Helena had written to the BBC in response to a programme they were broadcasting on the opening of the legal profession to women, in which they attributed the success of the movement to Ray Strachey. In this letter she stated that the clause on opening the profession to women in the Sex Disqualification (Removal) Bill was drafted in her presence during this meeting with Schuster. There is no evidence to support this assertion but this meeting would explain her failure to take legal action between February and December 1919.

It has always been difficult to understand why Helena (and indeed other would-be women barristers) did not test in court the Inns' refusal to allow women students. The idea that the lawfulness of the exercise of power might be tested in court was several centuries old. In particular they could have brought an action to obtain a declaration that their admission would be lawful by relying on *Dyson* v *Attorney General*.[147] Why did Helena and the other women not do this? Perhaps, in Helena's case,because she 'struck a deal' with Schuster or because it would have been expensive and time consuming, therefore a more liberal approach was considered more expedient? As an aspiring lawyer she could have brought an action herself. Bertha Cave appeared in the House of Lords in person. Perhaps Helena felt such a case was unlikely to succeed because Bebb had not, or she believed that, without legislation, the judiciary (and therefore lawmakers and benchers of the Inns) were extremely unlikely to find in women's favour, especially as such men had already refused them admission to an Inn.

Lord Buckmaster's Bill

In February 1919 Helena had indirect support from Lord Buckmaster as he introduced into the House of Lords his Bill to admit women to the legal profession, the Barristers' and Solicitors' Bill.[148] This managed to pass through the Lords with virtually no opposition less than a month before the other two Bills. Lord Buckmaster had appeared as a KC for Gwyneth Bebb in the *Bebb* case. He had been a successful barrister, indeed a KC, a bencher of Lincoln's Inn, Standing Counsel to Oxford University, and Liberal MP for Keighley.[149] His Bill was considered unnecessary by the Government because of the passage of the Sex Disqualification (Removal) Bill, and did not reach debate in the Commons. Lord Buckmaster stated in the debate, 'Nobody thinks that the passage of this Bill is going to flood the legal profession with women. It will enable a few women, who are peculiarly qualified, to earn an honourable living.'[150]

Buckmaster summarised his Bill and the rationale behind it in the radical *Pall Mall Gazette*.[151] He argued that a woman who was intellectually capable of qualifying for the profession should be allowed to try to succeed in it. He dismissed the idea that women could be excluded from the profession due to assumptions about their physiology, as this was not based upon 'sound premises.' He denied the suggestion that all women were subject to 'emotional cataclysms.' Women, he stated, differed from one another as men differed. He argued that his Bill was permissive: it merely provided that women should not be excluded from the profession because they were women. It did not compel women to become solicitors, nor compel anyone to employ them. His final point was that rules that secured a monopoly for men were unfair, given the effort of women during the war. His Bill initially only covered the solicitors' profession as he believed that the Bar had no legal precedent that prevented women from being admitted.[152] He was under the impression that an Inn could change its rules without recourse to legislation or case law. This was because the *Bebb* case centred on 'attorneys', meaning 'solicitors'—not to mention the Bar's long history of emphasising its separation from the solicitors' profession, a factor which made Middle Temple's reliance on *Bebb* the more surprising.

Support

Buckmaster's Bill was widely supported by women's organizations such as the National Council of Women. At their annual general meeting they passed a resolution: 'That this meeting of the Representative Council of Women of Great Britain and Ireland calls upon the Government to redeem its election pledge to the women of Great Britain, by granting the House of Commons full facilities for the Barristers and Solicitors (Qualification) Bill, which has already passed through its stages in the House of Lords, so the provisions of this Bill become the law of this land at the earliest possible moment.'[153]

Much lobbying preceded his Bill, by Millicent Fawcett and Mrs Humphrey Ward, among others. They wrote a letter to all MPs asking them to support it.[154] Helena campaigned too, not only in public speeches, but also by courting press attention and the support of other people. She was a prolific letter writer. On 4 December 1918 [155] she wrote to the Prime Minister, David Lloyd George, urging him to pledge to open the legal profession to women. His secretary[156] replied, acknowledging receipt of her letter and referring her to a previous speech. There is also a letter[157] from the Labour MP and party secretary, Arthur Henderson,[158] pledging that the Labour Party was entirely in favour of both branches of the legal profession being opened to women and that they stood for absolute equality in matters between the sexes. This pledge was proven by the Labour Party's Women's Emancipation Bill, which was introduced in March 1919. In June 1919 she spoke at a National Council of Women (NCW) conference on 'Women as Magistrates, and to Serve on Juries' at De Montfort Hall, Leicester, and to the Women Teachers' Quarterly General Meeting, Essex Hall, Essex Street, The Strand on 'The Power of Women's Political Influence.'[159]

Carrying the burden

This period of Helena's life must have been difficult, yet she continued campaigning. She appears to have had a strong sense of public duty, a desire to fight an injustice that prevented women from entering the profession. She also had her childhood ambition and a sense of moral duty towards women like Millicent Blewell Stone, who wrote a very personal letter of support to her, though they were strangers.[160] She urged Helena to 'persevere' with her aim to become a barrister, and stated that she wanted Helena to be successful. She wrote: 'The women of England are not catered for in the laws man made at all or become the victims of unprincipled or amoral men.' She then told her own story of domestic violence, implied marital rape and her husband's refusal to provide her with money to feed her children and herself. She had been advised by a solicitor that there was no redress except to go to the High Court (which was too expensive) or to divorce him (she would not give him that freedom and that too would be too expensive). With no allowance from her husband, in desperation, she moved out of the matrimonial home with the children and relied on his food handouts and her own ingenuity to feed and clothe them all. She was in her thirties. She ended the letter by urging Helena to continue her fight and stop this kind of 'living torture' and 'slow murder.' How could Helena possibly stop her struggle in the face of this need from other women? She bore not just a personal ambition but also a tremendous burden on behalf of others.

The second Bill: Women's Emancipation Bill[161]

This was a private member's Bill, introduced by Labour MP Benjamin Spoor on 21 March 1919 and was promoted by the Labour Party. In her papers, Helena describes it as a 'radical' bill.[162] It was extremely wide-ranging, proposing the enfranchisement of all women aged 21–30, that women be allowed to sit and to vote in the House of Lords, that all professional and judicial posts be opened to women and, finally, that women MPs be allowed to hold ministerial positions. It successfully passed all stages in the House of Commons, but was defeated by the introduction of the Sex Disqualification (Removal) Bill by the Government. Both Bills had their second readings[163] within days of each other.[164] However, the clauses on civil and judicial appointments in the Women's Emancipation Bill became incorporated into the Sex Disqualification (Removal) Act and became law.

Lord Buckmaster's Bill empowering women to become barristers and solicitors had successfully passed its second reading in the House of Lords by March 1919,[165] but this Women's Emancipation Bill was demonstration of the Labour Party's commitment to Helena and to women by introducing their own Private Member's Bill.[166] It had the support of some feminist groups (they opposed the Sex Disqualification (Removal) Bill).[167] The National Union of Societies for Equal Citizenship actively promoted the Emancipation Bill with deputations, processions and public meetings.[168]

The Women's Emancipation Bill had its second reading on 4 April 1919. As Mari Takayanagi comments, the tone of the debate on the second reading was sympathetic.[169] Seven MPs spoke in opposition and their main concern was the equal franchise; some felt this was too soon after the initial extension of the franchise. Twenty-seven MPs spoke over 67 columns of debate which centred on women deserving the legislation because of their role in the war effort. They felt that women would bring additional qualities to the professions and to public life; that 'a woman matures much more quickly than a man' so they were more suited to these activities than men in some ways. Almost nothing was said in opposition to women becoming solicitors, barristers and justices of the peace; this was the least controversial part of the bill, at second reading and at all later stages in both the Commons and the Lords. The Women's Emancipation Bill passed the second reading by 119 votes to 32.[170] Why did male MPs support it? Ray Strachey commented that MPs 'hardly dared to vote against it, not knowing what their female constituents might have to say.'[171] Legal opinions seemed to be changing too. The Law Society passed a resolution: '[I]n view of the present economic and political position of women, it is the opinion of this meeting expedient that the obstacles to their entry into the legal profession should be removed'.[172] This was passed by 50 votes to 33. However, in the same month, the benchers of the Middle Temple voted against opening the profession to women.[173] This was a clear sign that they were not prepared to open their doors without being forced to do so by Parliament. The Bill then went before a standing committee on 14 May 1919 and was passed. Although there are no records of what was debated at that standing committee we know from the third reading of the Bill on 4 July[174] that no member of Government attended that committee and an amendment suggested by Sir Kingsley Wood, the Parliamentary Private Secretary to the Ministry of Health, deleting the clause on franchise extension was rejected.

At the third reading it was argued by the Government that the Bill had been badly drafted, but this was vehemently dismissed.[175] However, Major Astor, Parliamentary Secretary to the Ministry of Health, moved to delay the Bill because the government was about to introduce the Sex Disqualification (Removal) Bill in the House of Lords.[176] He made clear that the franchise clause would not be included. The Women's Emancipation Bill then moved to the House of Lords under the name of Lord Kimberley. However, by this time, the government had introduced its own Bill as Major Astor had foretold. On the second reading of the Sex Disqualification (Removal) Bill, the Lord Chancellor verbally destroyed the Women's Emancipation Bill. It had its second reading in the Lords on 24 July, but the Lord Chancellor[177] again destroyed it and the peers understood that the only way forward was to go ahead with the Sex Disqualification (Removal) Bill.

Sex Disqualification (Removal) Bill

On 16 July 1919 Helena signed the lease on her Mecklenburgh Square house for £265.[178] She intended to let out the considerable amount of rooms in this former foundling hospital to fund her career at the Bar, but it was a monetary failure as she struggled to tenant, staff and maintain it, especially as the roof leaked so much. It is unclear how she could afford this. She obviously intended to put down permanent roots in London. A few days later Lord Birkenhead, the Lord Chancellor, on behalf of the government, introduced the Sex Disqualification (Removal) Bill.[179] He used his speech again to systematically destroy the Emancipation Bill.[180] The government strongly opposed the Emancipation Bill because of fears about women working after marriage and competing in open exams for entry to the civil service. They felt that women should not enter on the same terms as men and that such work was incompatible with married life. It was also suggested that women became less efficient with age.[181]

The Bill had two clauses, the first stating that a person would not be disqualified by their sex from exercising any public function, being appointed to any civil profession or vocation (the civil service was excluded from this section), or serving on juries; the first clause contained a proviso that a judge could use his discretion and exempt a woman from a jury by reason of the nature of evidence or issues contained in a specific case.[182] The second clause was to allow women who inherited peerages the right to sit in the House of Lords in their own right. The Bill basically allowed women to join the professions, public offices and jury service.[183] The franchise clause of the Women's Emancipation Bill was absent. The Bill was later amended to include admission to incorporated societies.[184]

July 1919

This Bill demonstrated that the Government had no plans at this stage to extend the franchise or remove the marriage bar (although this was included in the legislation which passed). The Labour Party's

Emancipation Bill was defeated on 24 July at its second reading in the House of Lords. Ray Strachey commented that the non-elected Lords did not have constituents.[185] The Emancipation Bill had been the Bill of choice for women's organizations. Their support can be seen from a letter of thanks sent by the London Society for Women's Service (LSWS) to MPs who voted for it.[186] There was much regret for its failure because it was so comprehensive. However, for some, like Millicent Fawcett, the Sex Disqualification (Removal) Bill was welcome, as it was better than nothing:[187] 'being half a loaf was better than no bread.'[188] Strachey saw the Emancipation Bill as a chance to sweep away women's remaining disabilities.[189] She warned women that the Sex Disqualification Bill was a 'trap'[190] but all her attempts to have it amended were unsuccessful.[191]

On 11 August a deputation of women was received by the Lord Chancellor. This had been arranged by Pippa Strachey[192] on behalf of the London Society for Womens's Suffrage[193] and other societies in order to discuss amendments to the Sex Disqualification (Removal) Bill.[194] It was attended by Lady Emmott (for the NCW), Emily Penrose (Principal of Somerville College, Oxford, for the Federation of University Women), Edith Major (Headmistress of King Edward VI High School for Girls, Birmingham, for the Headmistresses' Association), Ray Strachey and Olive King. The Lord Chancellor left before three other women had the opportunity to speak,[195] which could not have been done without his approval. The NCW urged the Government to make good its manifesto commitment to remove inequalities.[196] The Sex Disqualification (Removal) Bill completed its progress through the House of Lords on 4 August 1919. From there it went to the House of Commons where it had its second reading on 14 August. There was no debate. Its move to committee stage was delayed deliberately, probably a delaying tactic.[197] There were fears that it would be shelved. It finally went to committee stage on 27 October 1919.[198] Some amendments were passed, such as the clauses allowing women to become solicitors in three years if they had a degree (as men were) and giving universities the power to admit women to membership or degrees if these doors were not already open to women. The marriage bar in the civil service remained in what would become section 1(a), but, concerning other professions the words of Clause 1 were amended to read:

> 'A person shall not be disqualified by sex or marriage from the exercise of any public function, or from being appointed to or holding any civil or judicial post, or from entering or assuming or carrying on any civil profession or vocation.'

This removed the marriage bar from the legal profession and other professions outside the civil service.

By November 1919 it was clear that the Sex Disqualification (Removal) Bill would become law, so Helena rang the under treasurer at Middle Temple (12 November) and asked to be admitted as a student. She received a letter later that day from him informing her that, as the treasurer was absent, he had spoken to the ex-treasurer who ordained that her admission 'must stand over until the Act actually become law.'[199] Middle Temple were clearly not going to accept women until they absolutely had too. Again, this is another example of misogyny. Three days later the press announced that she would be admitted before Christmas (she was described as having a 'considerable' reputation as a speaker and an authority on constitutional law).[200] Middle Temple wrote to her on 19 December explaining that they had received a reference from Lord Robert Cecil which they had attached to her application which confirmed that her papers were in order. They informed her that the office would be closed from 24 December to 31 December.[201]

Victory

Finally, on 23 December 1919, all the effort by Helena and other women came to fruition with the passing of the Sex Disqualification (Removal) Act 1919. Although Ray Strachey had suffered disappointment about the Emancipation Bill, she was positive about this victory in the battle to enter the legal profession: 'one of the objects of the feminist societies for many years.'[202] On the day the Bill passed into law Helena received a letter from Middle Temple. The under treasurer, Major Henry Beresford Peirse DSO, had obviously relented and wrote:

'[W]e are waiting in this office until five minutes past four today in case you should call. I was told the Royal Assent was to be given at 3 pm today. In the event of you not calling I am giving you my private telephone number and address.'[203]

He continued that he was sorry to trouble her, but wished (ironically) to cause as little delay as possible over this matter, as he appreciated that she would wish to have her application for admission to the Inn completed at the first possible moment. She must have gone to Middle Temple the next day, or, as Elsie Lang described it, 'with characteristic promptitude'[204] as her receipt was dated 24 December (the first day of the Inns' Christmas holiday). Attached to this letter in her archives is a Middle Temple library card with the 'Mr' scrubbed out in ink and 'Miss' written in. There is also a receipt for £40. 7s. 6d from Middle Temple (dated December 24 1919, presumably her membership fee) and a note to the chief porter, asking him to allow 'Miss H Normanton' into the commons, signed T F Hewlett, also dated 24 December 1919.[205] Middle Temple probably contacted her because her original application form was allowed to stand,[206] or perhaps because they had been forced to admit women and so wanted to make history. Predictably, she was also well-known to the Treasury Office. This enabled her to become the first woman to join an Inn. She had achieved the first stage of her ambition, admission to an Inn of Court, the only body that could call her to the Bar.

CHAPTER 4

After Joining an Inn

'A woman on the Woolsack is another contingency the medievally-minded must brace themselves to face, for since the passing of the Sex Discrimination (Removal) Bill our first woman barrister-to-be has become a reality in the person of Miss Helena Normanton, who jokingly remarked that she goes to the House of Lords "to study the correct deportment for the Woolsack" but added that she does not think she can "hope to emulate the present occupant."[1] But there is, it seems, no reason why women should emulate the manner of men in politics or law. Provided they are "in order," let us hope that women will introduce something new and invigorating into both these ancient professions.'

The Gentlewoman, 27 December 1919[2]

Triumph

The Gentlewoman's comments reveal that the New Year of 1920 brought much hope and optimism to many women. There are no records of where Helena spent Christmas 1919, or with whom, but it may have been the most exciting and hopeful time of her life. She was possibly full of trepidation too: joining an Inn was just the beginning of her journey to becoming a barrister. She would now have to complete the Bar exams, dine at Middle Temple, find chambers and procure work in the form of briefs (which entailed forming relationships with solicitors and also the clerk of her chambers). She would have understood that the prejudice she experienced on trying to enter an Inn had not instantly evaporated. Would the Bar live up to her childhood dream and expectations?

The press reports

Three days after Christmas, Helena is reported to have given an interview to the *Evening News*[3] where she described how she had longed to be a barrister since she was 19-years-old[4] and had considered becoming naturalised as a French citizen so that she could practise there. This may not have been an idle comment as she spoke good French for the purposes of teaching and had spent time in Dijon studying for a diploma. Women in France had been able to enter the legal profession from December 1900.[5] She was expressing the sentiment that England was slow to admit women and that she was determined to become a barrister. She commented, 'I do not mean to confine myself to women's cases.'[6] This highlighted the dilemma at the heart of her campaign and subsequent career: while part of the argument for admitting women was that they would bring something different to the law, at the same time they were forced to defend themselves against charges that they were incapable of thinking legally and acting as disinterested professionals as men were presumed to do. We saw in *Chapter 2* that she did not want to pigeon-hole herself as a specialist only in family law cases. She hoped she would have a choice of cases and that she could bring about real and much needed change to the legal profession.

Although there were many newspaper reports expressing hope and optimism, some were more cautious, such as another in the *Evening News*.[7] They reported that Helena had taken her first step to becoming a barrister and predicted that she would achieve this,[8] but poignantly asked, 'What success will come to these ladies?' and questioned whether they would get work. Would clients want them? These questions became the critical issues for women barristers until the 1960s and are particularly relevant to Helena's legal life. There was some confusion in the Press as to who exactly was the first woman to be admitted to an Inn. The *Daily Chronicle*[9] reported, wrongly, that it was Mrs Gwyneth Thomson (née Bebb).[10] This mistake by the 'London papers' was keenly corrected by the *Manchester Guardian*.[11] It stated that the 'honour goes' to Helena Normanton 'who has fought the battle against the entrenched powers of the legal profession so resourcefully and steadily for years and has so much to do with the final victory ... There is no doubt as to her historical position as the first woman law student'. They commented that she was noted for her 'militant feminist campaign.' It is interesting that they characterise it in this way because, although her politics were indeed militant, her tactics were not: she used the formal procedures of the Inn, liaised with government officials, and lectured at public meetings. This was the start of the negative narrative that grew up around her. Perhaps this was a reference to her views rather than her methods, or to the aim of her campaign.

Despite the Sex Disqualification (Removal) Act 1919, and Helena's admission, the press still found it necessary to justify women's new found status. The *Evening News*[12] cited two examples of women acting as litigants in person. Firstly Miss Lind[13] (an anti-vivisectionist) brought an action for libel.[14] The newspaper reported that she made an opening statement lasting nine-and-a-half hours and a closing speech of three-and-a-half. Although she lost her case, the judge (Lord Bucknell) said she cross-examined as well as any other counsel, her final speech was a fine one, and she was a woman of 'marvellous power.' Likewise, they mention Miss Emily Mary Howe, who, they report, argued her case in 1907 and won £25 damages, making a two-and-a-half hour opening speech. Why they focused on the length of the speech is mystifying. Length does not necessarily equal quality. Similarly, the *Daily Chronicle*[15] found it necessary to argue that, if women could vote, there was no justification for denying them the right to plead in court. They stated that a certain number of women barristers was highly desirable, just as a certain number of women doctors were needed, and remarked that 'exclusion is unthinkable.' However, from the tone of the article, they appear to have believed that women were only good for certain types of case, such as those concerning divorce and the family.

Helena clearly enjoyed the attention (we shall see in *Chapter 5* that this would not last). She took newspaper space, prominently on the front page of the *Observer* on 4 January 1920,[16] to thank her supporters.[17] The same paper reported a recent meeting in East London where Helena had spoken. On being heckled by a male member of the audience, she demanded he stay and have his say because, 'he never gets a chance at home, his wife never lets him.' Not surprisingly, the man left.

Congratulations

Letters of congratulation abounded. Her archives contain a telegram from the National Federation of Women Teachers (NFWT) congratulating her on her entry as a law student;[18] they also mischievously sent one to the benchers of Middle Temple and Lincoln's Inn.[19] Congratulation letters also came from the NFWT (as well as the telegram), the Voters' Council, the British Patriotic League, the National Union of Societies for Equal Citizenship, from male barristers and French lawyers, the LCC Women Teachers' Union, the Women's Freedom League, her past school students, the house captain from Tollington High School, and from friends.[20] Strangers wrote from the UK and the USA not just to congratulate her but also to thank her.[21] Her archives also contain affectionate congratulation letters from her future father-in-law to be.[22] This was a time of high celebration.

Helena's first dinner at Middle Temple

The reality of her success was evident on 11 January 1920 when Helena was formally admitted to eat her first dinner at Middle Temple.[23] She had three guests, her supporter Wells Thatcher her pupil master (a specialist in divorce and criminal law), Holford Knight (her friend and advocate of women barristers) and Hubert Sweeney (a barrister and proponent of women barristers and women's rights).[24] On a handwritten dining card her menu is listed as pea soup, followed by roast mutton, vegetable curry, plum pudding, then cheese. On the back of her menu is written a poem of hope by Wells Thatcher:

> This is the night within this regal place
> When first hath beamed an able woman's face;
> First since the spacious far off Tudor days
> When England's Queen attended Jonson's plays.
> Today the woman student breathes our air
> With highest hopes that winds may set for fair.[25]

The *Daily Express* reported on this dinner the following day[26] stating that, for the first time since Queen Elizabeth I, a woman had been allowed to dine at Middle Temple. They related how a female representative of the newspaper was mistaken for Helena and given a seat near a blazing fire in the male robing room. The reporter was eyed with 'curiosity and interest' by the men changing into their gowns. She was then given a gown, but when she attempted to enter the dining hall, was stopped for not having a valid card.

The *Daily Express* report also featured an interview with Helena in which she gave an account of the evening. How much of this report was based on her actual words is questionable. As we shall see in later chapters, Helena complained that the press concocted stories about her. She was reported to have said that she enjoyed the dinner as much as a 'debutante enjoys a first ball,' and that Elizabeth I did not behave as well as she did (it is not clear in what respect). Helena, the *Daily Express* wrote, was most impressed by the wonderful grace when dinner began and the procession of benchers. Her meal was not without incident, as she was almost fined a bottle of wine for speaking to someone in the next mess. She evaded the penalty on account of the 'leniency afforded to my sex.' Barristers sat in groups of four (a 'mess') and each mess was forbidden from speaking to another. However, this did not spoil the enjoyment of her evening as many in the dining hall congratulated her. Helena is likely to have been moved by the sense of occasion and its significance. The historical implication of her dinner would not have been lost on her.

A separate table whilst dining?

Helena had been adamant that she did not want a separate Inn for women. However, there is an indication in her archives that she was keen for women to have a separate table when dining. This is indicated by a letter to Helena from fellow Bar student, Monica Geikie Cobb,[27] politely stating that she understood that Helena wished to have a separate table for women when dining at Middle Temple. Cobb explained that she had dined with six other female students and they were unanimous that they did not want any such action. She wrote that they all felt grateful for the consideration shown to women students and wished to fall in with the arrangements that were made 'for us.' Nothing in Helena's archives supports this 'understanding' that she wanted a separate table. She had perhaps mentioned it as a possibility. If so, why? Did she feel uncomfortable or unwelcome? Patrick Polden[28] refers to various incidents where women were made to feel uncomfortable when dining: 'Hannah Cross found Lincoln's chilly' and she learned not to sit on 'smart tables', as it was complained about. He also mentioned how, in Middle Temple, some members found it 'amusing' to take their snuff in a way that would make 'Dorothy Lever sneeze.' He recounts how Gray's Inn was supposed to have welcomed women, yet their treasurer denounced women members after taking too much wine.[29]

The number of women entrants to an Inn of Court

The *Manchester Guardian* reported at the end of January 1920[30] that almost a score of women students had joined an Inn. The newspaper insisted that more than half of these had been influenced by the 'pioneer', Miss Helena Normanton. What was their evidence? We do know that, in 1920, Middle Temple admitted the largest number of women: 33.[31] The other three Inns only admitted 13 women altogether. The percentage of women entrants was 5.6. The percentage then remained between 2.9 and 4.8 until the Second World War. Total numbers of entrants each year never exceeded 27 (in 1924) and fell to as low as 16 (in 1933). Between 1920 and 1939 only 428 women were admitted,[32] amounting to just four per cent of all admissions.[33] As we saw at the beginning of *Chapter 3*, England and Wales[34] was significantly behind several other countries in permitting women to practise. This fact was not lost on the press, the *Daily News*[35] reported that 36 American law schools had admitted women and there were at least 20,000 women attorneys in the USA. Australia had two women barristers. There were 30 women advocates in France, 48 in Holland, 11 in Norway.[36]

The acceptable face of the female Bar student

In February 1920 we have a description of Helena in a newspaper.[37] She was interviewed by the *Christian Science Monitor*,[38] which stated that the reporter felt trepidation about interviewing her, because he feared that she would be 'unapproachable and terribly intellectual.' Apparently these fears disappeared as soon as the reporter met her and found her 'no dry scholar but a woman tolerant and kindly, an avowed optimist, who looks at the world with a friendly eye and not above confessing to a fondness for detective novels.' Helena apparently told him that she came from a very old legal family, since she was a direct descendant from Alice de Montacute who in the Middle-Ages presented a case concerning the right of women to enter the Privy Council and won. This may have been true though she appears to have been both appealing to the American taste for antiquity and creating a women-centred legal history. This article offers some interesting insights: Helena is described as posing no threat to the status quo. She is characterised as slightly eccentric, perhaps implying that only eccentric women wanted to be barristers, hence there was no danger of an influx of women Bar students.

Celebration dinners

There were dinners outside the Inns to celebrate the women's victory. On 19 January 1920 there was one at the New Minerva Club[39] 28 Brunswick Square, London, WC1, where the WFL celebrated women's admission to the Bar and, in particular, that of Helena.[40] Fifty people sat down to dinner and were waited on by fellow members and friends. Toasts were proposed to Helena by Mrs Schofield Coates,[41] Mrs Mustard[42] and Holford Knight,[43] and Helena responded, together with Wells Thatcher[44] and Janet Gibson.[45] Helena's speech referred to the roll of great women who had fought for women's freedom in the past and the great deeds which had been accomplished, alongside which their present-day efforts seemed very small. She was reported to have spoken of the 'real humility and sense of responsibility' with which she and other women in the Inns were facing their new careers. This was probably more than a rhetorical device: she is likely to have felt victorious but also burdened with the expectations of others. Her friends remained supportive throughout her career, but they had high expectations. A letter (addressed to 'Hellie') from Wells Thatcher in 1921[46] stated that he thought she would make a good living at the Bar and success was assured for her, but that once she was called, she would have to forsake everything else for to practise law. Sadly for Helena, along with the majority of women barristers, as we will see, this success was never the case, largely due to discrimination.

The House of Commons was the venue for the formal dinner[47] to celebrate the passing of the Sex Disqualification (Removal) Act 1919 on 8 March 1920.[48] Guests enjoyed oysters, trout, mutton with peas and croquette potatoes, chicken casserole, salad, *poires belle Helene*, and dessert.[49] The dinner was organized by the Committee to Obtain the Opening of the Legal Profession to Women, by Mrs Ray Strachey as hostess and Mr Jack Hills MP as chair.[50] Amongst the guests were the Lord Chief Justice, Lord Reading; the Solicitor General, Sir Ernest Pollock;[51] the Attorney General, Sir Gordon Hewart;[52] Viscount Haldane;[53] Lady Rhondda;[54] Mrs Fawcett;[55] Crystal Macmillan;[56] the President of the Law Society, Thomas Liddle; the President of the Divorce Court, Sir Henry Duke;[57] Cecil Chapman, representing the London magistrates (a supporter of women's suffrage,[58] described as 'a magistrate of impeccable feminist credentials');[59] Mr Withers of Withers, Benson, Birkett and Davies, the solicitors who had briefed Miss Bebb's barristers; Nancy Nettlefold, Gwyneth Thompson (née Miss Bebb); Karin Costelloe; Maud Ingram;[60] and Helena (as well as others).

The guest of honour was the Lord Chancellor, Lord Birkenhead. He congratulated Mrs Fawcett upon the success of her life's work and said that she 'was entitled to regard herself as driving in a victorious chariot over her victims.' He spoke of the great ability that he had seen in the female clerks in the Law Courts and how he had tried to persuade his daughter that the law was the career for her, but she wanted to be a movie star.[61] This is very different man from the one who left early from the meeting with the deputation led by Pippa Strachey (although he may have had a genuine reason for leaving that meeting). His sentiments were echoed by Lord Reading[62] who spoke of his anticipation of the time when women would plead in his court. Crystal Macmillan is reported by Lang[63] to have proposed the toast of the Scottish Bar as the Lord Advocate was 'unavoidably absent.' Mrs Thomson proposed the toast to the Bar of England and Wales;[64] the Attorney General, Lord Birkenhead, responded, stating that he had always supported women entering the professions. Ray Strachey gave the closing speech in which she recalled the history of the movement to open up the legal profession to women. A fund was proposed by Jack Hills for women to read for the Bar and £150 was subscribed on the spot.[65]

The newspapers reported that the 'leading lights of the law' were in attendance, welcoming the 'fledgling Portias'.[66] The *Evening Mail* took the opportunity to reflect on women's new opportunities. It argued that many women would never have a chance to fulfil their role as wives and mothers, and it was necessary on purely economic grounds to open new avenues of employment to them. The article stated that the chief argument put forward against admitting women to the law was that they were not fitted by nature to succeed at it, but that remained to be seen, since they were now given the opportunity to compete with men on equal terms. The *Evening Mail* also addressed the fear that the Bar would be swamped by women, pointing out that this had been disproved in France:

> '[T]he fact is that in the present state of the world, at any rate, it is only the exceptional woman who wishes to be a doctor or a lawyer, and it has been recognised that to keep these ladies standing on the doorstep was neither polite or complimentary to the men who might be supposed to fear their competition … After due experiment each sex will settle down to the work for which it finds itself best fitted, while the brilliant exceptions of both will have a fair chance.'[67]

There was no mention of the prejudice that women would have to overcome to succeed.

Women Bar students

The celebrations over, women Bar students needed to focus on their Bar Finals in order to be called to the Bar and practise law. Helena studied for these exams in 1920. We saw in *Chapter 3* that these exams were organized by the Council of Legal Education (CLE). The CLE teaching staff consisted of six readers, four assistant readers, and two lecturers.[68] It was only since 1872 that Bar students were required to take compulsory examinations.[69] The Inns did not co-operate with universities in the training of lawyers and there was a distinction between the way law was studied as an academic subject in university and as a practical subject at the CLE. The Bar examinations consisted of two parts:[70] Part I had four sections: (I) Roman Law, (II) Constitutional Law and Legal History, (III) Contract and Tort, and (IV) Real Property or Hindu and Mohammaden Law or Roman-Dutch Law. From 1891, law graduates who had passed Roman Law at university were exempt from this subject at the CLE and from 1910 law graduates only needed to sit for the criminal law, real property law and a separate part II exam.[71] Part II was in six sections: (I) Criminal law, (II) Common Law (specialist subjects), (III) Equity, (IV) Company Law and either Conveyancing or Special subjects in Hindu Law, or Mohammaden Law or Roman-Dutch Law, (V) Evidence and General Procedure and (VI) General Paper. All sections were compulsory for non-law graduates. All sections had to be sat at once, after the students had kept six terms (i.e. dined in hall the requisite number of times).[72] Few English students attended the lectures offered by the CLE, most opting instead for private crammers, correspondence courses, etc. (the most popular was Gibson and Weldon).[73] It was said that a law graduate could pass at a reasonable standard on six weeks' work, though a non-law graduate was likely to need more time.[74]

There appears to be only one primary source describing everyday life for a woman Bar student in 1921. This was written by Robina Stevens, in the form of a diary.[75] Robina was just 17 when she joined Gray's Inn in 1920, straight from school. It highlights the hard work and focus that the Bar student needed. Robina did not refer to the lectures delivered by the CLE, but refers to studying in the Inn. Her teaching seems to have come mainly from an institution called 'Law Notes' which was both a library and a teaching establishment.[76] Robina scored a first class in all her Part I exams and certificate of honours in the Finals. She had to wait until she was 21 to be called, in 1924. She married in 1927 and gave up her career to be a wife and mother.[77]

Robina's diary described the constant hard work of completing practice papers for the exams. Her life revolved around studying. In the published extract she referred to three other students, firstly, a man called Fielding, who is 'down on women barristers'. Next, a Mrs Jones (probably Mary Selina Share Jones, the first woman to join Gray's Inn on 27 January 1920[78]) with whom she lunched, but she disparaged Jones's lack of work.

Lastly she refers to an unnamed woman aged 23 who had just joined the Inn: 'I am so glad that some other ladies are young'.[79] For Robina, Helena at 38 must have seemed very old.

Helena noted on her own CV[80] that in her Part I exams she achieved a first class in Constitutional Law, second class in Roman Law, and a second class in Criminal Law and procedure. She commented that 'Most people take the three parts in three terms, but I did it all at once.'[81] All sections of the Bar Finals were compulsory, but could be sat at different times, and at any time after admission. Not only did she take the exams in one session but she had had only six weeks to prepare. She remarked that she did not buy her books until 1 November and the exam was on 13 December. This was because until 30 September she was editing *India*. She was not entitled to any exemptions in Part I as, although she had sat for the LLB law degree in 1912, she did not pass.

Had Helena been successful with the LLB, she would have been entitled to exemptions and might have 'beaten' Ivy Williams to the position of first woman called to the Bar of England and Wales in May 1922 at Inner Temple,[82] having been exempted from some of the Bar exams by virtue of passing the Bar finals with a first-class in the Michaelmas term (although Ivy Williams was not the first to pass the Bar Finals, this was achieved by Olive Catherine Clapham, another forgotten woman[83]). This excused her two terms of dining,[84] and so she 'overtook' the other women Bar students. However, Williams never practised law, instead she became a tutor and lecturer in law to the Society of Oxford Home Students, later St Anne's College, Oxford. Frances Kyle from Ulster was called to the Irish Bar six months earlier.[85]

Disciplinary inquiry at Middle Temple

Helena's Part I exam success was widely reported. The *Evening Standard* called her a 'wonderful woman'[86] as she had only studied for six weeks and it marvelled at her 'great ability'. The paper featured an interview with her, stating (incorrectly) that she had achieved three first-class passes.

However, Helena's excitement was short-lived. In an undated statement[87] she recounted the reaction of Middle Temple to this newspaper report. Some days after it was published, she received a letter from the under treasurer asking her to call at the Treasury at a given time (this would not be the last time that she would be accused of self-advertising).[88] She wrote[89] later that she 'expected some formality but to her intense surprise was ushered into the presence of the treasurer, Master C C Scott KC, and Sir John Edge.[90] They put her through an enquiry. She complained in her statement later that she was not forewarned or prepared. Middle Temple were asking her to account for the newspaper report and suggested that she may have been self-advertising, a disciplinary offence. Within ten minutes, whether she showed it or not, she was:

> '[I]nwardly thoroughly, but icily, angry, and it was all I could do to control myself sufficiently not to leave these gentlemen, walk out of the room and leave them to draw any conclusions they chose. It will be realised that in the mood I was in it was not very likely that I should do myself justice; and I should suppose I did not. Seems probable to me now that these gentlemen must have been a sub-committee of the Benchers appointed to deal with the press accounts of my poor little results.'[91]

She was furious she had not been warned that the meeting was really an inquiry as to her conduct. She wrote that, if she had been warned, she would not have thought it unfair and would have taken press cuttings with her, presumably to enable her to examine the material in detail, show them the inconsistencies and explain the circumstances, rather than just discuss the reports in general. She felt aggrieved at the time by the press articles and indignant that the CLE should put the results in *The Times* without permission[92] (they were always published in this way).

In her later statement[93] she explained how the 'interview' with the *Evening Standard* occurred, prefacing it by saying that she did not think there was anything special about her exam results. She explained that just as she was leaving home, a man called to congratulate her. She was surprised and flattered that he was so impressed. He asked how she had done the work while she was editing a newspaper. She replied that the examinations were not very remarkable and she had resigned as editor of *India* on 30 September. She explained, 'I just meant that I didn't deserve credit.' She protested that she had never said that she had received three firsts in her exams. At some point the man informed her that he was a representative of the press. She stated that it was a very short conversation, and referred to the fact that she 'was full of private trouble' (it is unknown what this might be). She felt that the interview was both 'ridiculous' and 'imaginative.' It is difficult to understand why she felt this when it was full of praise—but undeserved in part, and therefore damaging to her. Perhaps also she realised that notoriety would be of little help in being taken seriously in her career/getting pupillage.

Helena decided, on reflection,[94] that the meeting at Middle Temple had a three point agenda: whether it was true that she had studied so rapidly? Secondly, they assumed she was boasting and, lastly, they believed she had wrongly claimed an Oxford degree. She was pained that they thought that the press man was a personal friend. At the end of the meeting, Master Scott stated that she should not give any more of these interviews. She replied, 'I wouldn't as I had no desire ever to give any.' She also explained that she was a novice student and had only the haziest idea of Bar etiquette. That was understandable as such rules were not written down until 1953. From that year all barristers received a copy of *Boulton's Conduct and Etiquette at the Bar.*[95] Before then, Bar etiquette relied on an oral tradition of rules, one of which was that a professional man would refrain from advertising.[96] Helena argued that Middle Temple had erred by segregating men and women, which had deprived women from learning etiquette and tradition. She could only be referring to some form of segregation during dining and this calls into question the suggestion that she favoured it.

Nothing came of this meeting. She received no warning. She wrote that if she had received a warning she would have demanded a full hearing. She left the meeting feeling that she had been believed and that she parted with Master Scott in a friendly way (but maybe not with Sir John Edge?) She wrote that she did not feel any disgrace and she later consulted Master Scott over another press matter. His advice conflicted with that of her solicitor but she abided by it. She declared that thereafter she refused interviews. This incident marks the end of her 'honeymoon' at the Bar.

Understanding the inquiry

The Bar had a strict etiquette and it was part of the unwritten code of conduct that barristers would not advertise their services.[97] Such behaviour was viewed by the Inns and Bar Council as intolerable,[98] warranting discipline and possible exclusion from the profession. Helena must have been aware of this, as she was well-informed on the practices of the Bar. She should not have given interviews, as this put her membership at risk. Of course, she was not practising at that time and it is not certain that she was informed about Bar etiquette.

However, she may have had an ambivalent attitude towards the press.[99] On the one hand she had used and courted it in order to promote her goal of opening up the legal profession to women in the 1910s, but now she needed to distance herself from them. The battle for women's inclusion at the Bar was not over by 1921. Women were now formally able to enter the legal profession, but next they had to deal with the more difficult, subtle form of indirect discrimination. She may have seen the press's interest in her as an advantage in maintaining interest in the movement for women's inclusion in the legal profession. Any publicity would keep up the momentum of change. Certainly, in some quarters, the fight for admission was over, for example Helena received a letter from the National Union of Societies for Equal Citizenship, informing her that the Legal Profession Committee no longer existed and thanking her for sitting on it.[100] As the *Daily Express* understood (after the publication of Helena's Bar results), 'one might be excused at thinking that women's emancipation was complete, but the excitement over [Helena's] success shows that there is still much prejudice to be overcome' and 'why should we cry 'wonderful'? Only when [Helena] does things without us being astonished will emancipation be a fact'.[101]

To a certain extent, Helena could not control the press interest in her. Women barristers were novel and she was noted as a 'first' for her membership of an Inn. There was a great deal of interest in her. The press certainly quoted her a great deal after her exam success and Middle Temple may have been excused for believing that she was self-advertising. Of course, the press are not always reliable. Certainly a number of stories at this time were published in daily papers featuring 'interviews' with her. For example, *The Daily Chronicle*[102] reported that her exam success had 'caused a ripple of excitement throughout legal circles.' Also that Helena was not 'the least concerned,' taking her exams in 'one gulp rather than in three sips,' and that her success set a precedent. She was said to have referred to studying Hindu Law next as it was important that some women realised the legal conditions under which Asiatic (Asian) women lived: 'We white women might be pressing for the kind of world which would be beautiful for us, but which would not suit brown and yellow women at all.' She continued that she had no firm ideas of what kind of practice she would develop as it would be determined by the law of supply and demand. She said that she would be guided by what women wanted her to do for them, although she did not want to represent women exclusively. This sounds like an authentic interview, expressing views that Helena is known to have held.

The *Daily Sketch*[103] featured an interview in which she described herself as feeling like Oliver Twist, because she would have been happier with three firsts! She explained that she was taking Hindu Law next since no white woman knew exactly how Hindu laws affected women, which caused difficulty at international conferences. The affairs of Asian women were often discussed in the dark. The affairs of Asia and in particular, India, were important to her, having edited *India*, the London-based paper of the Indian National Congress party, at the time when Gandhi's non-violent civil resistance movement was becoming active.

The *Daily Telegraph*[104] also marvelled that she had only studied for six weeks since few men would take it in one go. They mentioned that she was editing *India* at a time when Indian affairs were causing a tremendous amount of work and interest, hence she often sat up until 3 am. Her determination to succeed is illustrated by her comment that she had proved that a poor woman by working hard could qualify for entry to the Bar, as many men had done. She is reported to have said, passionately, that a woman who has suffered knocks and had to fight her way would be more successful than one who had led a sheltered life. She said she was proud that she attempted the exam without coaching. Everyone had told her that she would 'come a cropper.' She praised the excellent lectures at the CLE which made employing an expensive coach unnecessary.

Second allegation of self-advertising

About two weeks later, an anonymous letter was sent to Middle Temple (stamped as received 27 January 1921) containing one sentence: 'A case for enquiry?' It enclosed three articles concerning a talk Helena gave to the WFL at the Minerva Club. It appears that Helena was unaware this complaint had been received by Middle Temple, as there is no evidence that they wrote to her either in her archives or Middle Temple's. This was the second time her behaviour (concerning self-advertising) was questioned. Nothing came of it, there was no inquiry, but it demonstrates that she was being scrutinised and that clearly many people were not happy with her admission.

The first newspaper report the letter contained was by the *Evening Standard*, 25 January 1921, entitled 'When Women Dare, Absence of Genius Due to too much Morality?' which reported Helena as saying: 'When women really let themselves go and are themselves, possibly we shall have an outpouring of genius such as the world has never known.' She apparently said women's achievements were less massive compared to those of men. No woman, she is said to have argued, was as good as Francis Bacon, Shakespeare or Plato. She believed this was because women dared to be themselves:

'I honestly tell you that there is a sort of woman I like best, the woman who likes all that is bad in life. Many of great geniuses have been people who have given enormous vent to themselves in love, rage and passion. Some of the great ladies lived scandalous lives. Probably they wanted to. They have great value for us because they dared to be themselves. I appreciate range and massiveness, and I wonder when women are going to get hold of it. I am inclined to think that there is too much morality about women; too much accepting of the fictions of the day as to how women ought to behave. So long as women accept so much modern morality, custom and fiction, we shall not see what they are capable of. Until they are really themselves there will be all kinds of mental differences which I do not think are real.'

The second article appeared in the *Sketch*, 25 January 1921, 'Too Much Morality' and the third in the *Daily Express* of the same date. They covered the same ground. Helena wrote a furious letter to the *Daily Express* the next day,[105] complaining that her talk had been taken out of context, and arguing it had been a psychological study: 'we may have our soft corners for Nell Gwynnes and Catherine the Seconds, but our instincts teach us that the highest ends of humanity will be best served by an equally high standard of morality in conduct of both sexes.' Although she doesn't seem aware of it, she must have anticipated that it might cause complaint as she sent a telegram (reply paid) to Middle Temple explaining: 'Correcting gross misreporting of speech last night if against etiquette please wire.'[106] She was obviously aware that she now had to be careful how she behaved.

Helena's peers: Other women Bar students

Helena was one of 12 women successful in the Part I examinations.[107] There is little available data on these other women. We know already that Middle Temple admitted 33 women in 1920, but that should be put in the context that they also took that year an unusual 330 men. Patrick Polden found that 428 women were admitted to an Inn between 1919 and 1939.[108] He estimated in his study of women at the Bar between 1919–1939, that approximately eight per cent of the women were married.[109] Social class is difficult to establish. As described in *Chapter 1*, Helena's father is sometimes described as a pianoforte manufacturer and sometimes a piano tuner. Having separated from her husband, Helena's mother had to earn an income, which she did by running various businesses including a boarding house and a pub. Helena herself had been schooled to gain a profession that would set her up as an independent woman. She was by no means from a wealthy or well-connected family. She was not a typical Bar student. Abel demonstrated that the sons of gentlemen were falling in number among barristers and new occupations were rising, but the sons of the working-classes were unusual.[110] Polden has shown that of the 428 women admitted to an Inn between 1919–1939 only three-quarters of their paternal occupations is known.[111] Sixteen had a father who was a gentleman or from the landed gentry. Seventy-one had fathers who were in the law and one-hundred-and-three had fathers who were professionals. Ninety-one had fathers in commerce or industry and fourteen in public service. Fourteen women had fathers who were clerical or manual workers or from journalism or similar occupations.

Polden[112] comments that most women admitted to study law between the wars (1919–1939) were university educated. Almost 60 per cent of home female students[113] joined an Inn having a degree, were enrolled on a degree or had attended university.[114] Of the 199 women admitted to an Inn 40 per cent were Oxbridge graduates, 30 per cent from London, and 28 per cent from other universities.[115] Polden points out that older universities did not confer degrees on women until 1921 (Oxford) and 1948 (Cambridge) therefore it is not 'surprising' that the proportion of women with degrees was lower than men.[116] Only after the Second World War did the majority of all students enter with a law degree.[117] Regardless of subject, Helena had a degree, but was not university educated (it was obtained through external examinations by way of an extension course). So her relatively humble background would have set her apart from most of her fellow students. She would have been a rarity. She was definitely not part of a family or social network that promoted its members. Her contacts were probably limited and not made from childhood, family or university. This also possibly contributed to much of the gossip that, as we will see later, surrounded her career at the Bar.

Photographs

In May 1921 Middle Temple requested that Helena use her influence to keep her photographs out of the papers.[118] They urged her to buy up blocks of photos owned by newspapers that had been taken of her before she was admitted to Middle Temple. On 2 June 1921 she wrote a rather desperate letter to Master Scott describing how she had tried to buy some blocks of photos, but there were so many others, which she could do little or nothing about. She stated that she had refused requests for interviews and was holding back a book and did not know what else she could do to show how genuinely she wanted to keep within the etiquette of the profession. She concluded that she was bewildered and did not want to bother him with every etiquette issue. This scrutiny was to become intense and bullying.

Bar finals

On 26 October 1921 Helena passed her Bar Finals with a third-class.[119] This must have been disappointing for a woman who had achieved a first-class in her BA History degree and a double-first in the English Board of Education Teaching Certificate. Passing the Bar Finals alone was a triumph, but the grade is very poor, especially compared to Robina Stevens and Ivy Williams[120] who both achieved firsts. This result may explain her determination to complete the LLB after she qualified.[121]

Pupillage

Once Helena had passed the Bar Finals she was in a position to begin her pupillage. Pupillage was not essential in order to be able to practise[122] (it became so only in 1958) and some barristers proceeded to practise without it, although they had to have been called to the Bar before setting-up an actual practice was possible. Finding a pupillage and setting up in chambers was not difficult for men between the wars. It was for women.[123] This was recognised by the Inns and they recommended to barristers that there should be no discrimination against women.[124] Recommending, of course, is toothless. There were no anti-discrimination laws prohibiting chambers from refusing women just because they were women.

As described in *Chapter 3*, Helena's menu card for her first dinner at Middle Temple contained a hand-written note stating that one of her guests, Wells Thatcher, was her pupil master. He had chambers in 2 Essex Court[125] and specialised in divorce and criminal law, the two main areas in which Helena would practise. However the address that she wrote from when releasing her statement to *The Times* in 1921 regarding the use of her maiden name was 5 Stone Buildings, Lincoln's Inn.[126] This does not tally with having Wells Thatcher for a pupil master. Perhaps she had chambers there initially and then took up pupillage? It is impossible to be certain. There are no Bar Council records on where she did pupillage let alone for how long and whether she completed it.[127] Pupillages were worse than unpaid, since the pupil barrister had to pay for the privilege and also maintain himself or herself.[128] It was recommended that the pupil spend one year with a conveyance or an equity draughtsman, six months with a special pleader or common law barrister, six months with a solicitor and then, after call, a further six months with a barrister.[129] In 1950 it was recorded that only one-fifth of barristers followed the recommended training.[130] Enid Rosser completed her pupillage and described it as a happy experience as her chambers were friendly, and she was grateful for the welcome she was given, and the kindness they gave her, remarking: "They hid cleverly any misgivings they may have had about the prospect of a female invasion of their happy male community and appeared to regard it as something of a joke."[131]

Helena must have saved money from her teaching career in order to fund herself. Some scholarships from the Inns were available[132] and, according to Polden, were granted to two women: Sara Moshkowitz (1922, called 1925) and Muriel Walker from Lincoln's Inn.[133]

There is further confusing evidence that she applied for a pupillage at other chambers. In June 1922 she received a letter from a Mr Skinner (from the Common Room, Lincoln's Inn). Apparently Wells Thatcher had put them in touch. Mr Skinner said that he could not discuss pupillage with her as his 'Head of Chambers would not approve' because he had 'old fashioned principles' and a lady in chambers would be too 'upsetting for him.'[134] This, apparently, was not unusual. According to Patrick Polden, the usual excuse chambers made to women applying for pupillage was that there were no female lavatories. He cited Hannah Cross as having to undertake to use the public lavatories in Lincoln's Inn Fields.[135] It was not just chambers lavatories that women struggled with. There was also a shortage of court facilities. Enid Rosser explained:

'One of the difficulties, purely practical, which I discovered was the question of lavatories. There was no lavatory suitable for women counsel. There were lavatories for female prisoners and for female witnesses but clearly women counsel could not share with prisoners, and it would be highly improper for them to use any cloakroom accommodation provided for witnesses. It is an unbreakable rule, for obvious reasons, that counsel in a case must never speak to witnesses. They might "suggest evidence" or some such. Lavender Hill [South London Police Court] was much concerned with this problem for my comfort. When next I went there they had solved it and a kindly female attendant led me to a room completely empty except for a table with jug and basin, a small mirror on the mantelpiece, and an old fashioned commode. I was deeply touched by this kindly attention for it is a long day from ten in the morning until four thirty in the afternoon with a short lunch break in some primitive café for restaurants did not abound in those outskirts in those days.'[136]

26 October 1921

On the same date as her CLE certificate was issued, 26 October 1921, Helena married Gavin Watson Clark. Polden estimated that from 1919–1938 only 23 per cent of women were married when starting at the Bar.[137] Robina Stevens left the Bar on her marriage. It would seem that Helena waited until she had fulfilled her ambition before marriage and had no intention of giving up her career. She was 39-years-old. She probably believed she was too old to have children. Childbearing would have required a career break and had its dangers for older mothers (as it did fatally for Gwyneth Bebb). Interestingly, Polden points out that all the women who were successful at the Bar were married.[138] Helena's niece remarked that 'they had no children, and it was a marriage in which sparks could fly, for both had quick tempers, but I think it was basically a happy one.'[139]

They were married in St Pancras Registry Office.[140] She wore a fur coat and was accompanied by her friend Florence Daplyn (she was a witness to the marriage as was Helena's new father-in-law). The event must have been fraught, as the registrar leaked the news to the press. Helena had attempted to keep it a secret (she only let three or four relatives know at the last moment) but it took place in front of reporters (to her disgust). They followed her to the railway station and took her photo without her consent.

Her professional name

Before Helena actually practised law she made a decision as to the name she would use. She chose to retain her maiden name, but took the title 'Mrs.' 'Ms' is commonly used for women today who do not wish to be known as either 'Miss' or 'Mrs' but this was unknown in 1922. Helena said that she used 'Mrs' to put her divorce clients at ease and that she preferred to be addressed in that way:

> 'I like the prefix of "Mrs" Because it is more dignified. If people do not wish to address me as 'Mrs.' they can call me Helena Normanton, which I like very much. I think it is quite a good name for professional purposes, too. I have never given up my maiden name, and shall always use it with the "Mrs" before it.'[141]

She went on to say that a woman who has made her name professionally or commercially was justified in using it.[142] Further, she said that, if a title was to be used, 'let it be Mrs as Mr is used by men, single and in bondage, and Miss is prudish and silly.'[143] As we shall see later from her campaign on divorce, what she really resented was women's loss of identity on marriage.

Before her call, in late October 1922, she wrote to the treasurer of Middle Temple stating that she had married on 26 October and asked if she could retain her maiden name. They replied on the 3 November stating that they saw no reason for calling attention to the fact that Helena Normanton was not her name [144] and asked her to present a formal petition to the benchers, which was then considered by the four Inns. She had to assure them that she would permanently adhere to that name, not change it later, or use any other name but 'Helena Normanton'.[145] She was allowed to be called in her maiden name.

This retention of her maiden name was extremely unusual in 1922. We have seen in *Chapter 2* that, although coverture had supposedly been removed by the Married Women's Property Acts, women were still socially and economically bound to their husbands. It was extremely unusual for them not to take their husband's name on marriage. It was a radical move, but an understandable one. She wrote: 'No one who ever knew my wishes ... would ever call me Mrs Clark.'[146] She had achieved so much as an independent woman. Why should she change her name on marriage? Her name was her own. It conjured up a whole identity and to an extent a movement to open the law up to women. Her name would also have been useful for future practise and was known by both clients and solicitors. She probably hoped that it would bring in work.

Her public explanation for wishing to keep her maiden name involved her new mother-in-law.[147] She said that Mrs Gavin Clark was her mother-in-law's name and her mother-in-law 'was naturally offended' by newspaper reports publishing accounts of both Helena's private and professional life. Letters began to arrive addressed with her mother-in-law's name but intended for Helena. Both Helena and her mother-in-law found this unpleasant. Whether her mother-in-law was really offended is unknown, but probably unlikely as it was the norm for a wife to take her husband's name.

There was a movement in America at this time, called the 'Lucy Stone League.' Their motto was 'My name is the symbol for my identity and must not be lost.'[148] Ruth Hale (1887–1934) was president of the league and demanded that the US State Department issue her a passport in her own name, despite being married.[149] The lawyer who represented the league, Rose Falls Bres, was to become the president of the National Association of Women Lawyers, who would later invite Helena on a lecture tour of America. The society visited London in July 1924.[150] This connection may have had something to do with Helena's radical stand.

This retention of her maiden name attracted much comment throughout her career. The *Evening Standard* remarked in their report on her call that she was called in her maiden name 'even though she is Mrs Clark.'[151] In January 1925, the *Oxford Times* reported[152] that everyone had heard of a professional name so famous that the husband's name paled into insignificance, but few had followed the example of Helena and retained their maiden name, prefixing it with 'Mrs.' They referred to the Lucy Stone League and commented that no more significant symbol of emancipation could be found than the desire of married women to retain their own name. Helena later needed to defend herself against an accusation of self-advertising[153] and commented on a correction that she drafted, inserted and paid for in *The Times* newspaper: 'Mrs Helena Normanton announces that the above is her legal and only name in public and private life and that she hereby formally denies all statements to other effect.'[154] Her intention was to stop the press discussing her name and she felt that it was successful. But only after the insertion did she discuss it with the secretary of the Bar Council. This was to have devastating consequences on her career, as we shall see in the later chapters.

Helena fiercely defended her maiden name. On being described as Mrs Clark in *Woman's Who's Who* Helena wrote and furiously complained. The editors replied confusedly that, although they apologised, they were within their rights to refer to her as Mrs Clark as she gave them her husband's details.[155] She immediately responded that she was in Rome when their letter had arrived and therefore someone in chambers must have filled it in as a practical joke. She threatened to inspect their document. She finished by saying that they had no right to refer to her as Mrs Clark 'as every person in this country has the right to choose their own surname ... it cannot be thrust on them by a third party.'

Call night 17 November 1922

'The women barristers' wigs made them look like men':[156] Helena's call night was symbolic: she had achieved her childhood ambition. She was called, as requested, by her maiden name.[157] Ten other women were called that night,[158] eight of them at Middle Temple: Monica Mary Geikie Cobb, Auvergne Doherty, Ethel Bright Ashford, Naomi Constance Wallace, Sybil Campbell, Elsie May Wheeler, Lillian Maud Dawes, Beatrice Honor Davy,[159] and one at Inner Temple Theodora Llewellyn Davies.[160] The speech was given by the treasurer,[161] Sir Forrest Fulton. He made little mention of the women called that night, but told them to persevere, as there were 'sure to be difficulties.'[162] It was a tremendous achievement and one that had been denied to a list of women before them. It must have been a remarkable night.

Helena had every intention of practising. However, like Ivy Williams, not all those called to the Bar were intending to practise law. The Bar was a frequent choice of training for men of a certain class and was often viewed as a finishing school for young men.[163] Polden commented that in 1919 at least half of all home students did not intend to practise,[164] and two-thirds of women called during the period 1919–1939 did not intend to practise.[165] Women were no less likely to drop out of their studies than men.[166] At least some of them must have entered the Inn hoping to make a career as a barrister, but Polden concluded that barely a score made even a modest success at the Bar.

Would the Bar live up to Helena's expectations? Would she live up to the hopes of her many supporters?

CHAPTER 5

Helena Normanton's Emerging Legal Career

'[W]omen at the Bar are portrayed in much too sorry a view. I am afraid that I know personally far too many women in both branches who have never been able to make even a start in practice to think it at all wise to encourage more women to come into [the law] unless they have ample private means to sustain themselves during their period of waiting. It is not in my view to achieve success at the Bar (i.e. in the ordinary acceptance of the term) when able women accept relatively trivial Civil Servant positions when one gravely doubts whether men of equal ability would be at all likely to accept such positions.'

Helena Normanton, 1933, in a letter to the
London and National Society for Women's Service[1]

By 1922 Helena was 40-years-old. She had achieved her purported main goal in life: to open the legal profession to women. However, the contest was not over. She and other women barristers now faced the struggle for substantive equality; they had to break down discrimination and prejudice in order to practise at the Bar as men did. She would also have to contend with class and education prejudices that would affect her life as a barrister, as well her high expectations of how barristers should behave.

Number of women called to the Bar in November 1922

We saw in *Chapter 4* that Helena was not the only woman called to the Bar in 1922, there were ten others. All were an unknown quantity to many solicitors, the majority of whom were men. They may have been wary about putting briefs into their hands. Their preconceived ideas about women may have led them to behave according to presumed gender stereotypes, for example by giving Helena divorce and other family type cases. The thinking may have been that, as a woman, she was fit to deal with these because women traditionally inhabited the private sphere and therefore were best suited to such cases.

The situation did not change much in the next ten years. Richard Abel has shown that in 1923 a further ten women were called to the Bar, in 1924 18 more, in 1925 only nine, and in 1926 just 15. These are typical of the figures until 1946, when his stop.[2] In 1935 *The Northern Daily Telegraph* reported (confirming these figures) that a yearly average of 14 women were called to the Bar, and at the time of that report there was a total of approximately 200 women barristers.[3] The article questioned the woman barrister's standing. Many, they said, never intended to practise, they just wanted the status and privilege of wearing a wig and gown. Many left on marriage, went overseas or used the Bar as a stepping stone to a more lucrative job. They suggested that the Bar was not a welcoming place, along with widespread prejudice from a supercilious public and even unfriendly criticism from some superior judges, although it was felt that the Bar had finally accepted the situation. The article argued that the women were still on trial. Optimistically, the reporter believed that another generation would witness the female barrister's heyday.

The age of Helena Helena's female contemporaries

As noted above, Helena was aged 40 in 1922. She already had considerable life experience and was a seasoned professional, a teacher. Polden has reported, that between the wars, the ages of 262 of the 428 women Bar students were known (60 per cent).[4] He calculated that the median age at admission to an Inn was 21.2 years. About 20 per cent were teenagers and over a quarter over 30. He found that there was a correlation between age at admission and whether a woman Bar student proceeded to be called to the Bar. Of the very young, only 60 per cent were called whereas, among the over-forties, 80 per cent went on to be called. No comparable figures existed for men. Seventy-five per cent of female Bar students were younger than Helena and the same is probably true of those called with her. It is difficult to assess to what extent her age affected her career. It may have put off solicitors more familiar with briefing younger members of the Bar for their junior work. This may explain why she suffered a shortage of briefs, so necessary to forging a successful career. However the converse may be true, solicitors might have been attracted by her age, experience and maturity. Her shortage of briefs may have been due not only to prejudice but to the length of time it took to become established.

Women in practice in 1922

It is well-known that Ivy Williams (the first woman to be called to the Bar) had no desire to practise and instead settled into academic life. The Bar Finals pass rate was high, 85 per cent in 1922.[5] In 1919, 594 men were admitted to an Inn and in 1922, only 377 were called.[6] Even if women were called to the Bar it is difficult to establish exactly how many of them practised. Barristers then did not have to take out annual practising certificates (as they do now) so it is impossible to give numbers with certainty, because no records exist. In February 1925 the *Northern Evening Dispatch* stated that there were at least 40 female barristers, 25 of them having put their names up outside chambers and been briefed at least once.[7] The *Liverpool Courier* reported in 1926 that women were doing well at the English Bar, stating that there were 80 women members.[8] The *Newcastle Journal* in 1926 suggested that there were 12 women practising, with fair practices. Strachey wrote in 1935 that 79 were practising[9] compared to Hughes' 1936 estimation of only 12 to 18.[10] Polden guessed that at no point between 1919 and 1939 were as many as 20 making a living exclusively from the Bar.[11] There was probably no year in which 40 held a brief. Similarly, there are no figures for men's practice. Polden concluded that 'while it seems to have been generally accepted that women were disproportionately unsuccessful, the extent of the gender gap is quite unknown.' What is clear is that Helena was not alone in her struggle.

Class

We should not underestimate the effect of her class on her standing at the Bar.[12] Although there is little direct evidence as to class prejudice we can see from Enid Rosser's account of Helena Normanton that it must have been present. She describes Helena as 'an old war horse,' who terrorised her male colleagues with aggressive ways (described as wanting to storm the male only club preserves of the men barristers 'that not even their wives wanted to join'). She illustrates Helena as being 'comic and without fear,' 'physically unattractive,' 'large,' 'blowsy,' 'amusing,' 'incredibly common not to say vulgar,' 'feminist and militant,' who later in life 'mellowed.' Rosser believed that Helena although a 'character,' did damage women barristers by her aggression, but 'was human and without malice.'[13] Her choice of adjectives are interesting — 'common' and 'vulgar,' which can only equate to Helena's social background. She was being penalised for her class, but in fact these traits are positive: a threat to the established order.

'[D]espite being present in the divorce court with another female barrister she still had not been briefed'[14]

Irrespective of Helena's well-known status, briefs did not just appear. On 20 November 1922, three days after her call, the *Evening Standard* and other papers reported on her 'first day in court'. She was described as having been present in the divorce court but 'still not briefed.'[15] These reports later became an issue between Helena and Middle Temple about further self-advertising, as discussed later in this chapter. She vigorously denied giving an interview to the *Standard*. Despite these issues, the reports are interesting because they describe her first day as a barrister and the expectations resting on her. She was dressed as a barrister and, although she was not professionally employed, she was observing, learning and making it visible to solicitors that she was ready to be briefed.

She was extremely unlikely to be briefed immediately.[16] To make a living at the Bar, barristers needed their own briefs, which were generally dependent on their social networks and family connections. They needed a private income when they started. They were not allowed to form partnerships but were autonomous individuals who had to build up a practice, unlike solicitor's articled clerks who could rely on their salaries. Many women called to the Bar sought other careers[17] such as becoming solicitors,[18] reporting and writing,[19] and in academia and public service.

As to the appearance of women barristers, the wig was a male wig. It would have had to go over their hair, as prescribed for men. Wigs, and the blue bags in which robes, wigs and briefs were carried, were purchased from Ede and Son and Ravenscroft on Chancery Lane.[20] Rosser wrote that one of the problems faced by women barristers was how to make the neckwear stiff enough to carry the white bands properly.[21] She explained that there was no standard style at the time, and she solved this problem '… by calling in the aid of Harvey Nichols who made me [a] sort of linen vest to which was stitched a white collar of linen similar to man's dress collar with "butterfly bows" and with the co-operation of the laundry they were laundered properly and remained stiff for several days. For the rest we were uniformly clad in black with black silk stockings and shoes.'

A lack of cases was not confined to Helena, it was true of many of her contemporaries who found it difficult to stay at the Bar. Certainly Enid Rosser complained of having few cases,[22] she devilled (stood in) for her old pupil master, Roome. Although she felt she was becoming known and accepted, she had to leave the Bar on her father's death, as she no longer had his financial support. She also found other difficulties, such as the nervous strain: the need for technical knowledge, and to keep that knowledge in detail during a trial, which took a great deal of concentration. Cases she found, left her nervously exhausted and also low from anti-climax. Then, there were the other cases that were 'boiling.' Rosser also found the travel difficult, transport was bad, trams were museum pieces that rattled and clanged their bells over Blackfriars Bridge.

The barrister's clerk was (and often still is) the key to success in the early days in practice. The clerk plays a central role in securing work for the set; he (or nowadays she) liaises with solicitors and allocates briefs to barristers and negotiates fees. In Helena's time these clerks often found women a 'bad investment.'[23] Clerks earned a percentage of their barrister's fee, therefore they needed to make a 'good investment' in high fee work.[24] Barristers could not (then or now) rely solely on their clerk to bring in work; they also needed relationships of their own with solicitors. This is where coming from a legal family could be particularly useful, but Helena did not benefit from this. The Poor Persons Procedure[25] and the dock brief were the only occasions when a barrister could by-pass a solicitor. At this time the majority of solicitors were men.

Rosser, a contemporary of Helena, gives us a contemporaneous explanation of the importance of the barristers' clerk in her account of her practice from 1927–1933:

'The staff consisted of Robert Eldridge, the Clerk, and Ernest the "boy". No barrister's clerk is ever known except by their Christian name because they always started as boys and acquired the status of Clerk when their predecessor either died or the Head of Chambers became a judge and the clerk went with him to the Bench. The Clerk is the most important person in your professional life. It is he above all others who can hold your destiny in his hands. He is the link between you and solicitors; he agrees with the instructing solicitor the fee you are to be paid; he sees that you are in the right place at the right time and that your robes and books are waiting for you. If you require throat lozenges on the bench in front of you in Court he sees they are there. It was rumoured in certain Chambers the clerk drafted all the pleadings. There is nothing your clerk doesn't know about you and your doings and very little he won't do for you if he likes you. He completely identifies himself with your life and for all this he receives from you no salary. He is paid by the client a clerk's fee on every brief and he gets all the shillings off the guineas marked on briefs. He therefore has a vested interest in the quantity of work he manages to get for you and on the size of the fee. The clerk of a successful barrister can make a very large income. I was advised by Henry Roome to start well with Robert by giving himself a handsome tip, which I duly did, and he and Ernest cherished me warmly despite my sex and the little likelihood that I would ever bring in sufficient guineas for the shillings upon them to add up to much…It was in 1927 a far from rosy outlook for women at the Bar. We were not only regarded somewhat as figures of fun all dressed up in our wigs and gowns. Solicitors regarded us with horror and it was a courageous solicitor who gave us a brief…Women were an unknown and untried quantity as advocates…'[26]

Searle v Searle

Helena had to wait nearly a month for her first brief, becoming the first woman to hold a High Court brief. Monica Geikie Cobb[27] was the first woman to hold a brief when she appeared before Birmingham Assize

Court on 1 December 1922.[28] Helena's first case, on 21 December 1922, was *Searle v Searle*.[29] She appeared at the Royal Courts of Justice in The Strand, in a divorce matter,[30] before Horridge J.[31] There is a full transcript of this case in her papers, kindly supplied to her by 'C. Damer Snell, Official shorthand writer at the Royal Courts of Justice.'[32] He kindly wrote '[As] it is your first case I felt sure that you would like a memento of what I hope will be a successful career at the Bar.' Helena was instructed by Messrs. Dehn and Lauderdale[33] to appear for the petitioner.

We saw in *Chapter 2* that divorce was a cause which concerned Helena. She campaigned tirelessly for changes in the law, at great personal expense. Her practical experience of acting for clients in such matters placed her in a good position to understand the issues and lobby for change. In 1922, divorce was governed by the Matrimonial Causes Act 1857 which allowed a man to divorce his wife if he could prove she had committed simple adultery, whereas the wife had to prove that her husband had committed aggravated adultery (adultery plus incest, bigamy, desertion for two years, cruelty, rape, sodomy or bestiality).[34] In the *Searle* case, the wife sued for divorce for desertion for five years and adultery.

Helena opened her first case with the words: 'This is a wife's petition, my Lord for dissolution of marriage on the ground of adultery and desertion for two years and upwards': the first words to be heard by a woman barrister in the High Court. After opening the case, her next task was to take the petitioner through her examination-in-chief. This was vital because the petitioner was required to mention everything that she wished to be considered, to state her case. The petitioner was Mrs Violet Rose Searle, of 28 Ravensdon Street, Kennington, London. She revealed that she had no children and supported her husband financially. When leading her witness, which was acceptable in an examination-in-chief in a case of this kind, Helena made an error in asking her to explain that her husband had a 'bookkeepers business' instead of 'bookmakers.' Horridge picked her up on this. She acknowledged her mistake and moved on, saying, 'That was my mistake, my Lord, I meant a bookmaker's business.' This business had failed and in 1913 and the marriage became unhappy due to his failure to support the home. In 1915 he was discharged from the army and found a job at an arms factory, but she said he refused to work unless Mrs Searle gave up her job or left him.

By Mrs Searle's account the marriage continued to go badly. She gave examples of how he took away her war loan and the furniture, forcing her to leave the matrimonial home and move in with her parents. They enjoyed a temporary reconciliation, but her parents' house proved an inconvenient meeting place so they met at weekends. He never said where he spent the week days. He asked to spend Easter week with her but never turned up; she waited at the station, but never saw him again. He wrote to her, making various allegations against her, which she denied. Finally, Mrs Searle had heard rumours that he was living with another woman. She confirmed the service[35] on him of the legal papers relating to her action. Helena then called her next witness, Mr Horace Rowe, who had rented his house for five years to Mr Searle with his 'wife' and their two children. Helena produced birth certificates for the two illegitimate children. The register confirmed that the children were registered only to their mother. Horridge commented: 'That doesn't help you then.' Helena replied that she had two witnesses to corroborate the adultery. Horridge responded that he did not need to hear anymore and ordered the divorce. She had won her first case.

It is difficult to know whether such a quick resolution of a divorce was usual. Certainly those who sought a divorce were normally successful. Between 1858 and 1861, 416 divorce decrees were granted and only 29 petitions denied, Cretney could see no reason to suppose that the ratio would have changed over the coming years.[36] Certainly, to be successful, the petitioner had to come to the court with 'clean hands,'[37] as Mrs Searle did. Section 22 of the Matrimonial Causes Act allowed the court to act in an inquisitorial way to establish the truth. Horridge certainly did not do this in *Searle*. There could be no connivance by the petitioner,[38] or collusion, but any condonation by the petitioner would result in the petition being rejected.[39] It was clear in *Searle* that the wife had been keen to make the marriage work, but had been unforgiving once she became aware of his 'second family.'

Searle v Searle was widely reported internationally, as can be seen from Helena's Scrapbook.[40] For example, the *Chicago Tribune*[41] reported (wrongly) that a 'woman barrister for the first time in history conducted a case in the English law courts.' They commented that Helena 'took her place in a row of members of the junior bar, wearing a wig, gown and bands not distinguishable from those of the men.' With this publicity came letters from the public. Some were extremely pleasant, such as that from Miss L Broad, Headmistress, of Tollington High School, Grand Avenue, Muswell Hill, London N10,[42] which informed Helena that they had named a school house after her and asked her to 'do a favour for the school' by taking a little interest in it, providing them with a motto and suggesting dates that would be suitable for a special day in her honour.

Other letters were less pleasant and may have placed a burden on Helena. For example, on 27 December 1922 she received one from Agnes Roberta Littlejohn of 68 Sutherland Avenue, Maida Hill, London W9 which begged for help, stating that she was 'desperate', although she did not say what the trouble was.[43] On 1 February 1923 she received a letter from a woman whose name is unknown asking to see her regarding a case concerning children, but only in 'an unprofessional capacity'.[44] On 7 April 1923 Helena received a letter addressed to her at the divorce courts from two women asking if she would take any kind of case: 'ours is a defrauding & breaking up case to rob and demoralise two innocent women of their power, living and home.'[45] She had a tremendous sense of duty towards the sections of society with no access to justice. She is likely to have found these letters expressing such personal difficulties hard since she could not help. They suggest something of the public impact of her presence at the Bar. The frequency of Helena's cases in her first years of being in practice is hard to ascertain as her case book for 1922–1930 is missing.[46] But it is certain that they were few and far between and of an extremely junior nature, such as a 'dock brief.'[47]

Gathering storm clouds: Rejected by the Western Circuit

All practising barristers needed to be a member of a circuit. England and Wales was (and is) divided into circuits, routes throughout the country that the King had originally travelled and then his judges in order to dispense justice throughout the realm. Circuits changed and became more formal as barrister numbers expanded and transport improved in the late-nineteenth century. Membership was required to practise within each circuit as higher fees were passed on to the client if barristers practised outside of their own circuit.[48] This, in practice, made it impossible for most barristers to practise on a circuit of which they were not members. The existing members of a circuit controlled who could or could not join.

Helena attempted to join the Western Circuit in November 1922.[49] At a meeting of the circuit her application was considered by its members. She was proposed by Mr S H Leonard and seconded by Mr W Blake Odgers.[50] Mr H Gregory KC responded that her conduct had already been considered by the benchers and she had been 'warned' (this must have referred to a previous inquiry by Middle Temple in 1921 that we examined in *Chapter 4*). Extracts from the *Daily Graphic* report of her call night dated 18 November 1922 were then read aloud by Mr Emanuel KC, as was her announcement in *The Times* that she was to be known professionally as 'Mrs Helena Normanton.' Members asked if a man in such circumstances would have been elected, he 'thought not'. Mr Odgers had obviously anticipated this might happen and had brought letters of support for Helena from newspaper editors and solicitors. However a Mr Broderick proposed the election be postponed for one year, seconded by Mr Duckworth. Mr Percival Clarke suggested that the circuit should deal with the matter at once, although it is unclear what he meant: reject her outright? Mr Charles KC argued that the meeting was representative of the mess and not a tribunal of conduct. Further, he said that the meeting had to decide, after hearing facts, whether to admit candidates as members of the mess. Mr Bousfiled KC then summed up, a vote was taken and the motion was lost: Mrs Helena Normanton was not elected.[51]

The issue of self-advertising, April 1923

Her rejection was a damaging setback. In response she wrote to Master Scott, master treasurer at Middle Temple[52] and requested that the Bar Council hold a searching and full enquiry into whether she advertised herself. She wrote that the Western Circuit's refusal was primarily on the grounds of her self-advertising:

'…although some additional personal calumnies of a very wicked nature had been circulated before the Election Meeting about me. With these I don't propose to trouble you, because Time and the Event are the best indicators, but I can pin down the advertising legend, because it must take two to manoeuvre an advertisement, viz. the editor as well as the notoriety hunter, and I am confident that I can secure very emphatic repudiations of such practice from the leading editors to place before the Council.'

She wrote that her sponsors were told by a 'Western Circuiter' that she had been admonished before call for advertising. This, she said, was untrue, although she did have an 'interview.' We know from *Chapter 4* that this was more than an interview, it was an inquiry and a warning about her future conduct. Her letter continued that one of her Western Circuit sponsors had been distressed and felt that the comment was meant to infer that at the time she was called she was under censure. She said that this 'shook' and 'weakened his advocacy' on her behalf. She concluded: 'However, I suppose that any weapon is fair against a woman, and I am learning day by day.' Clearly, she saw her rejection as straightforward sex discrimination. Indeed she commented that men used their family and connections in order to be briefed and yet this did not fall foul of the code.

As she understood it, the accusations centred on six pieces of publicity surrounding her marriage, her call night, the 'Eldon Junior' publicity,[53] photos supplied to the press, her first day in court, and the use of her maiden name. She produced an undated 'General Statement,'[54] written on opinion paper. It gives a flavour of how she felt about these accusations and as to how she would behave throughout her time at the Bar. This statement was in the form of a legal document. She explained that she had lived a life under the public eye, not only because of her legal work, but because she had been a female lecturer to post-graduate students in Glasgow, an extension lecturer at the University of London and the first General Secretary of the National Union of Women Citizens Association. She explained that having delivered hundreds of lectures her name had legitimately appeared often in the press. Subsequently, she was the first woman to be admitted as a law student. She was clearly furious, as she explained, that she had forfeited a handsome income by not writing for the daily press. Nothing came of her demand for an inquiry.

Rose Heilbron: Similar problems

Helena's career and life were naturally of public interest because she had been the public face of women's admission to the Bar. Due to the lack of written material on women at the Bar at this time it is difficult to assess how great a problem it was for them. Rose Heilbron certainly had similar issues in 1952 when an article was written about her, with information inadvertently supplied by her sister. This resulted in a letter from Gray's Inn's Discipline Committee. Nothing came of the inquiry,[55] but Heilbron continued to suffer from 'incessant' publicity throughout her career.[56] She later had to appear before a special committee to consider whether she had self-advertised after similar articles were written about her.[57] We should not underestimate how serious these allegations could be, potentially resulting in being disbarred. Again she was exonerated. Interestingly, Heilbron steadfastly denied requests for photographs of herself[58] which could have been a result of the controversy over Helena's photographs. In the late-1950s, Heilbron was again asked to account for her conduct in relation to numerous articles that had been written about her, but as always she was cleared of any wrongdoing.[59] This illustrates that Helena's problems were not unique to her, or necessarily anything to do with her own conduct. Both women were 'victims' of public interest and the commercial awareness of editors.

Professional jealousy

Heilbron's daughter wrote that Rose Heilbron had supportive and sympathetic colleagues at the Bar, although 'it is inconceivable that there would not have been some envy at her huge Press coverage, particularly as she was so much junior to many of her colleagues...'[60] Helena had a stark problem with one colleague who caused her great difficulties and drawbacks. In November 1924, she received an anonymous letter on Middle Temple notepaper purporting to have been written by a group of barristers, but signed by a 'well-wisher'. Anonymous letters are always sinister. They render the recipient powerless because there is no effective means to reply. It warned her that there was still more than one person opposed to women joining the Bar. This fear was justified as being due to jealousy which has always been a feature of life at the Bar. This had been aroused by Helena and the letter instructed her that the time had come for her to consider how she should limit the gossip about herself. It continued, with a back-handed compliment, that her 'partial successes' had caused the envy of other women.

In essence, the letter was a warning against a Miss Ashford, stating 'are you really unaware of the origin of comments about you?' Ethel Bright Ashford was admitted to Middle Temple in 1920 and called in 1922 with Helena.[61] She intended to practise at the Bar and joined a local government set and the South Eastern Circuit.[62] She went on to become a local councillor in Marylebone and active in social work.[63] It seems that she did not manage to practise[64] but was a prolific writer of books on local government and local history. According to the letter, there had been 'trouble at Winchester & Clerkenwell.' This can only have referred to the courts or the circuits. They continued that in 'every case they all have one feature in common-they have been friends of Miss Ashford. It is not a secret that she openly makes statements about you: your mode of life, work, marriage and professional code.' The letter insisted that the writer did not think the comments were true, but they all commented on Helena's passivity. It maintained that Miss Ashford was responsible for the complaint to Middle Temple. Interestingly they informed Helena that it had 'fallen flat.' It finished by advising Helena to stop inviting Ashford to her house or continuing to treat her as a valued friend.

This letter is intriguing, but who wrote it? Was it really from a group of well-wishers, or an attempt to divide and conquer women barristers? It purports to be assisting her, yet it is unsigned and criticises her 'passivity'. It seems designed to undermine her. It suggested that Helena was not isolated or detached, as she can sometimes seem, but was active in professional relationships and friendships in inviting other women barristers into her home and life. Her suggested passivity is in direct contrast with her earlier behaviour when attempting to enter the Bar and towards requesting a judicial post (see *Chapter 7*).

We will probably never know what the personal outcome was for Miss Ashford and Helena or whether this letter defamed Ashford. If the letter was untrue in its assertions it illustrates the level of malice directed against Helena. We will never know who sent it or whether it is accurate. Needless to say it was extremely unpleasant. It was obviously of great significance to Helena or she would not have kept it in her papers. Helena later commented in a letter that Marshall Hall[65] gave her good advice on the hostility he went through when 'he went forward.'[66] We do not know what that advice was, but it is interesting that professional jealousy/envy/malice was rife at the Bar and not confined to women.

Missing case book

As already noted in this chapter, the frequency of Helena's cases in her first years at the Bar is hard to ascertain as her case book from 1922–1930 is missing.[67] Her fee book contains scant information.[68] But it is certain that her cases were few. They were also of an extremely junior nature such as a 'dock brief.' Abel has commented that 'it is extremely difficult to make meaningful statements about barristers' income: statistics are unavailable, unreliable and incomparable; and there is great variation within the profession ...'[69] A barrister's income reflected their status, age, experience and speciality (and therefore their dependence on public funds).[70] Helena may have been older than other new barristers and had a well-known status, but she was extremely junior, inexperienced and was given work that was not well paid: crime and family as opposed to chancery or common law work. Abel provides some figures for 1928, where the highest earner made £28,000, but the median barrister only £600.[71] Rose Heilbron, Helena's only well-documented comparator, was called to Gray's Inn in 1939[72] and after six months pupillage was offered a tenancy.[73] Her biographer notes:

'There was much less work available for young barristers, whether men or women, when Rose started at the Bar than in later years. Many barristers left the Bar because of lack of opportunity. Fees were much lower than they are today and there were far fewer courts in which to practise. There was no unified state funding by way of the legal aid scheme until the 1950s ... Cases tended to be shorter than they are today and there were more pleas of guilty…The availability of privately paid work was limited. Even when a young barrister obtained work, receiving payment could take an extremely long time and would have a deleterious effect on cash flow, because of chambers' overheads and travelling expenses as well as other expenses.'[74]

Although Heilbron was called almost 20 years after Helena, this passage gives us a flavour of the difficulties of the early years of practice. Heilbron's practice started to take off after two years and was in full flow after five years.[75] Her biographer puts this down to the fact that she was a local household name, her cases being reported by the press, she was a beautiful woman, a novelty and good at her work. It would seem that Heilbron was unusual. The average earnings of barristers in 1922–23 were approximately £580-£600,[76] around £25,000, in present day terms.[77]

Helena's situation was not unusual. As Abel points out, finding a tenancy was only the start, the junior barrister still had to earn a living.[78] Barristers are independent, self-employed lawyers who work out of the structure of a set of chambers. They receive no salary, so, even today, all junior barristers must attract briefs in their own right, through their clerk, from contacts, from the contacts of other barristers working in that set or by devilling. There are no figures for 1922/23, but, by 1952 barristers starting out would lose £10 in their first year and earn a net income of £100, £280, £370 and £590 in the following years.[79]

'Stick to my choice'[80]

It would seem that many of Helena's cases were dock briefs. This was a criminal brief given directly by the prisoner in the dock to a barrister selected from a panel of barristers waiting in the courtroom. No solicitor was involved. The Poor Persons procedure and the dock brief were the only occasions on which the barrister could by-pass a solicitor. The dock brief cost the prisoner £1 3s 6d (£1 1s for the barrister and 2s 6d for the clerk[81]) and there were strict rules governing it: barristers were not allowed to make gestures such as waving a wig or giving friendly glances in order to be selected. Enid Rosser described the procedure.[82] The barrister was taken down to the basement cells at the Old Bailey via the back of the dock. Each prisoner was 'locked in a minute cheerless cell with an iron barred door and it made it look like a zoo.' The interview took place in a waiting room and a warder would be present, 'that basement was a cheerless depressing place but I learnt a lot about life there. And the wickedness, hopelessness, despair and courage of humanity. Some were just derelict, some were pathetic while others were helplessly silly and had fallen by the wayside from which nothing nor anybody really could rescue them.'

On 6 February 1924 Helena became the first woman to accept a dock brief,[83] and to run a trial in the Old Bailey, for a man accused of fraud.[84] It has been suggested that men using a dock brief opted for women barristers because they believed they would be more sympathetic, though in divorce cases male clients would not risk an untested woman barrister. Again, this case was widely reported,[85] partly because it was the first case conducted by a woman in the Old Bailey, but also because it made a good story. Eyles believed that he had selected a male barrister.[86]

The Old Bailey was (and still is) the Central Criminal Court in London. Rosser, who practised from 1927–1933, described the court make-up in detail[87] as consisting of four courtrooms. Court No.1 was where the visiting judge sat. Court No.2 she wrote was where the Recorder of the City of London sat 'in state.' This office (at that time) was held by

'[A]n astonishing character disliked by all and sundry, Sir Ernest Wild. His antics were preposterous as he was vain and rude to absurdity. He used to cause intense amusement by his pomposity to the humbler members of the junior Bar, and irritation to those with an established reputation by a superior false smile with which he would greet them. He rather revelled in embarrassing female witnesses and in sentencing the convicted he would deliver long sermons with unctuous sarcasm. He did not take kindly to female barristers and I found that he [was] always only too ready to make me look ridiculous when it was my fate to appear before him. But he frequently referred publicly and personally to the woman probation officer as "our angel of the Old Bailey" much to everybody's' scorn because it was so obviously insincere and poor Miss Green would be flushed with blushes.'

Court No.3, she went on, was presided over by the Common Sergeant, who was a 'constant joy' — Sir Henry Dickens, only surviving son of

Charles Dickens, '[O]ld deaf, toothless, wig never stayed in place, used a quill, witty and a good judge.' She said he kept order in a kindly way. Court No.4 was presided over by the 'Commissioner', 'Old Atherley-Jones … a character of the old school, sentimental (would cry tears of sadness), found it hard to keep counsel in order.' The clerk of the court was the 'kindly rubicund' Sir Herbert Austin, 'all his working life spent at the Old Bailey and his knowledge of criminal law was profound.' She explained he was kind to all young and inexperienced barristers.[88]

Helena's dock brief concerned alleged fraud by Charles Eyles, a 67-year-old car dealer, and was heard before Judge Atherley-Jones.[89] Eyles faced a charge of obtaining goods (cars) by false pretences and had two co-defendants. Helena complained to Atherley-Jones that she had not been able to see letters which were part of the evidence. She stated that they were said to have been written by her client and were therefore crucial to the charge of fraud. She maintained, that without them, she would be unable to conduct a proper cross-examination. She believed the letters were essential to her defence. Desperately, she said: 'They [the letters] go all round the court, but I don't get them to cross-examine on, and I am in a state of confusion.'[90] This must have been annoying, because she could not get justice for her client, and also humiliating. The judge replied, 'You are under a disadvantage. I quite appreciate your difficulties but they cannot be helped.' Mr Abbott, for the prosecution, said that he would help Helena all he could (clearly he had not done thus far) and would give her copies of the letters. He did this, but only typed copies, which did not help her as she wanted to disprove authorship of the letters. This placed her at a disadvantage, so, with the ferocity of a true advocate, she pleaded this to the judge and demanded the originals, as it was 'all a question of handwriting', A Sergeant Gooch was in the court and said that he knew all about the letters and would explain them to her. This sounds like kindness, but she did not need them explained, she needed to see the originals and it seemed that everyone was out to thwart her. Atherley-Jones commented that the sergeant was 'ready to help a lady in distress-if you will accept help from the enemy.' Helena retorted (graciously) that she would be glad of the assistance. Atherley-Jones adjourned the case for five minutes while the handwritten letters were finally examined. This is a good example of the kinds of prejudice and discrimination that surrounded women at the Bar.

Helena's closing speech to the jury was described as business-like 'punctuated with brilliant flashes', occupying exactly one hour.[91] She declared, 'You have heard an enormous amount of evidence in this case with a great deal of patience … I should think we have made the acquaintance of a considerable number of the car man population of London, but not one has spoken to handing a single thing to my client …'[92] One witness, she argued, 'adopted an attitude a little curious in its unctuous rectitude.' Letters by another witness suggested, she added, that 'he should be running a school for the teaching of writing business letters with a "pull" in them.' Further, she believed that 'the opulent imagination of our merchants must be a great advantage to them, and when the wireless fails to interest them they must derive great satisfaction from reading their glowing correspondence.' Not perhaps the usual language or style of the dock brief barrister.

The next day, Eyles was acquitted.[93] The jury was initially unable to agree a verdict, but, after retiring for a second time, returned a verdict of not guilty. His two co-defendants were not so fortunate, both were found guilty of obtaining goods by false pretences and sentenced to nine months imprisonment (second division[94]). Atherley-Jones congratulated Helena, saying, 'You have in difficult circumstances conducted the case with considerable skill.'[95] It remains unclear why Eyles was acquitted and the others not and to what extent it was due to Helena's advocacy.

More professional jealousy

The *Manchester Evening News* not only reported the Eyles acquittal but also the alleged reaction of Helena's contemporaries.[96] According to them she was warmly congratulated on her success by fellow members of the Bar and particularly the new 'Portias'. They comment on the glare of publicity that had surrounded her career as she was one of the first to be called to the Bar, and that male barristers displayed a great deal of jealousy when they found a woman barrister getting too much of the limelight. They disclosed that one member of the Bar's irritation had led to the extreme step of complaining to the Bar Council. They conclude that the novelty of women barristers had not worn off and newspapers gave them far more publicity than they wanted or deserved. Women barristers were seldom to blame for the publicity.

Supporting women at the Royal Courts of Justice

Although Helena's cases came slowly, she continued to try to help those with poor access to the legal profession. In March 1924 she approached Henry Snell, MP for Woolwich East, regarding the issue of the poor pay of one of the Royal Courts of Justice female attendants.[97] These women waited upon women of the jury, female witnesses and lady barristers. Snell's reply (presumably he was the MP for one of the attendants) indicates that she had written a letter for one of the attendants, Mrs Smith, to copy and send to him. Mrs Smith had been at the RCJ for 14 years, on £1 a week, and her request for a pay increase had been ignored. Mr Snell concluded that the wages were adequate. We do not know whether Helena continued this campaign but her action demonstrates that she was always available to help those she believed had a worthy cause. It was an extension of her belief in the law as a form of social work. Helena was not given a locker at the RCJ until December 1927. Whether this was a direct result of her interference or whether it was because lockers were in short supply is not known.[98]

CHAPTER 6

America

> 'America achieved. Statue of Liberty, admirably lit up…entrance to the harbour is incredibly beautiful, and skyscrapers prove to be just as impressive as their reputation and just as decorative.'
>
> E. M. Delafield[1]

Helena spent December 1924 to May 1925 in the USA. By 1924, she had been in practice at the Bar for almost two years. The profession was notorious for the length of time it took to build up a practice[2] and we will see in later chapters that her earnings would remain low.[3] She must have been prepared for this. Perhaps given the controversy over allegations of self-advertising she, not surprisingly, took a career break and decided to embark on a lecture tour of the USA. This may have been a reaction to her slow progress at the Bar, perhaps she needed the money or felt that being away for six months would not affect her career, or wanted to gain some distance between the professional jealousy and gossip that had been circulating around and about her. Perhaps she also saw her visit to the USA as an exciting opportunity.

The American connection

In July 1924, a delegation of American women lawyers visited London. Enid Rosser, before practising as a barrister, worked for Claud Schuster at the Lord Chancellor's Department (LCD).[4] She was instrumental in arranging this visit. Rosser wrote that the LCD was in 'a state' about the visit, especially as the Americans were 'seeing it as a pilgrimage to the shrine of their legal ancestors.' Rosser doubted the English Bar 'took it so seriously'. The Canadians were joint hosts and Mr Bennett, the Canadian Attorney General, asked if England's Attorney General would accept £1,000 to 'squander' on more lavish entertainment than was being proposed. The money was refused by Claud Schuster. He then changed his mind and asked Rosser to call upon Bennett at his hotel and retract this refusal, which she did. Bennett shook hands and asked 'And what do you want' and she said '£1,000 please.' They had a 'cheerful talk' and she returned to Schuster with a cheque. Three thousand American and Canadian lawyers, and their wives, visited London. There were parties at the Inns of Court and the Law Society, the King and Queen even gave a garden party, as well as an official welcome in Westminster Hall.

Helena was involved in this visit. A photograph appeared in many newspapers of her leading a tour around the Inns.[5] Her existing American connections included American lawyers. Also, by this time, she had been the subject of much newspaper reporting and, to an extent, had become a celebrity: the face of women's entry to the legal profession in Britain. This made her a marketable commodity in America, where a lecture circuit had grown since the Civil War.[6]

US Publishers struggled to meet the demand for authors, so turned to the European market to satisfy the demand. Literary celebrities such as Charles Dickens and Oscar Wilde had appeared on the circuit, which could be extremely lucrative. In June 1924, Helena began to look for an agent, indicated by a letter to William Feakins asking him act as such, as she proposed 'to make a lecture tour of the United States.'[7] By September 1924, negotiations were being finalised and she wrote to Major James B Pond, of a commercial lecturing agency in America providing lecturers for literary societies and other local organizations, confirming that she would be travelling there on 27 December.[8] She formally accepted a 50/50 financial agreement: 50 per cent to the agency, 50 per cent to be retained by her. The agency dealt with entertainment as well as education. Pond replied that he had announced that she would be going to lecture in America.[9] They would charge fees of $50 upwards. He believed that high fees were necessary to cover expenses since he had made a 'heavy investment,' but not so high that she could not be afforded by groups that interested her. From his experience, he thought that she would do 'quite well.' He warned her that 'only sickness, accident or circumstances' beyond her control would prevent her becoming liable to him for non-attendance. It seems likely that she undertook the tour at least partly to earn money. Her cases were infrequent, she may have felt that she had no choice but to earn as much as possible by cashing in on her fame to fund the rest of her career at the Bar.

A passport in her maiden name

In order to travel she needed a passport. In autumn 1924 she applied for one in her maiden name. The Passport Office refused to issue one in a married woman's maiden name. Helena explained:

> 'I went to the passport office myself and the clerks confirmed what the tourist agents had told me [that she could not have a passport in her maiden name]. Then I went to the chief of the legal department of the Foreign office, who said that as I had won recognition from the Benchers of the Middle Temple to be a barrister at law in my maiden name I was entitled to a passport. I received it in due course and had no difficulty in getting the document visaed at the United States Consulate.'[10]

She added that her husband supported her claim to use her own name. 'Indeed when I had the difficulty in getting a passport at the Foreign Office he would have legally become Mr. Normanton temporarily to help me out, but it was not necessary.'[11] Maintaining her maiden name was obviously important to Helena, she rejected coverture, and believed that marriage was contract between equals.

American Interest in Helena Normanton

American women gained the vote in 1920 and engaged in campaigns and issues concerning gender equality similar to those in Britain. By November 1924 Helena's American tour was arousing much interest in the Press. The *Washington Herald* reported that

> 'England's most noted woman lawyer is coming to Washington to take up the fight started by the National Woman's Party over the right of married women to retain their maiden names.'[12]

This referred to a dispute that had arisen in August 1924, when the Comptroller General,[13] John R McCarl, handed down a decision that, in order to receive their pay, married women must sign their husband's names on the pay roll. Dr Marjorie Jarvis of St. Elizabeth's Hospital believed that not only had she a right to use her maiden name, but that her professional practice would suffer if she was compelled to take her husband's and she fought this decision. According to the *Washington Herald*, 'Members of the National Women's Party are in the best of spirits that Helena Normanton is coming to help them with the retrial. In fact they are jubilant as Normanton won the same sort of case in the UK.' The hope was that, as Dr Jarvis's case was based on common law (on which the US system was also based) they would also win. However, in December 1924 Helena received a letter from the National Woman's Party, in Washington, informing her of Dr Jarvis' resignation for personal reasons, which was the end of the case.[14] They concluded that, when Helena was in Washington, they expected to see her, she was 'good publicity' and they thanked her for her support. Evidently Helena had achieved public status as a women's rights activist and was viewed as a feminist role model.

We have some idea of the American lecture circuit at this time from E L Delafield's fictional (and ironic) *Provincial Lady*.[15] The Provincial Lady of the book was asked to go to America to promote her writing. She described her amazement at receiving such generous terms, but was nervous about what to wear on such a trip, as America was seen as very modern and forward thinking.[16] She recounted being taken by a tender to a ship that overawed her by its size. She, like Helena, travelled without her husband. Her journey began well, with a nice cabin and fine food, but it was overtaken by appalling seasickness.[17] On explaining to a fellow traveller that she was on a lecture tour, she met the comment that the type of women she would be lecturing to were 'club women,' 'large women with marcelled hair, wearing reception gowns.'[18] On reaching America, the Provincial Lady was enthralled by the sight of the Statue of Liberty. When she disembarked she was met by her publisher and taken to a hotel. She reported:

'Come to conclusion that everything I have ever heard about American Hospitality is an understatement. Telephone rings incessantly from nine o'clock onwards, invitations pour in, and complete strangers ring up to say that they liked my book, and would be glad to give a party for me at any hour of the day or night. Am plunged by all of this into a state of bewilderment.'[19]

She met her publicist (the equivalent of Major Pond) and gave endless rounds of interviews. The 'Provincial Lady' is obviously a comedy fictional character, but Delafield's account provides some indication of how Helena's tour of America might have been.

On 28 December 1924 Helena travelled to America. The fact that she was the first woman to travel on a passport issued under her maiden name was widely reported.[20] The *Westminster Gazette*[21] commented that she had succeeded where Ruth Hale, the Leader of the Lucy Stone League in America had failed.[22] The *Overseas Daily Mail* reported that she had said that 'her legal and only name in public and private life was Mrs Helena Normanton.'[23]

Her tour was advertised in the American press with comments such as 'she is a very able lady' who has 'a very business-like suite of chambers in Lincoln's Inn, and is building up a good practice.'[24] Publicity flyers[25] advertised that she would be available to speak on the following topics:

Women & the law
The English law of divorce
The common law of England & America
Has a married woman a right to her surname?
English women of today who are making history[26]

The flyers stated her availability as 'January to April'. Anyone interested was directed to the Pond Bureau for terms and dates. A magazine advertisement (totalling four pages) explained that she was in America and available for speaking engagements.[27] It provided a potted biography, describing her interest in history, and that she was related to

'Alice de Montacute who in 1407 won the right for noblewomen to representation in the English Privy Council. On her paternal side her great grandfather was banker to Napoleon! And financed the Battle of Waterloo. He was the original Robert Moore in Shirley.'[28]

It further advertised that she could speak on the following wider range of topics:

The common law of England & America
Has a married woman a right to her surname?
Women & the law
The English law of divorce
English women of today who are making history
The Economic Position of Women in Present-day civilisation
Women in the Council Chambers of the World
Humour on Political Life
British Political personalities
Will Britain Go Red
Benjamin Disraeli, Earl of Beaconsfield
India, Britain's Greatest Problem.

Arriving in New York

On 6 January 1925 Helena arrived in New York. She travelled on the White Star Liner, *Adriatic*, from Liverpool.[29] She was fearful of any breach of Bar etiquette as on 8 January 1925 she received a response to a letter she had written to Middle Temple about her conduct whilst in America. They wrote that they had no objection to her arguing a case in America if the court gave special consent; they also had no objection to her being called to the Bar in America (she was not); they added it would be objectionable for her to sit behind American Counsel, furnishing them with information as if an attorney's clerk. They would allow it if she was junior counsel, but advised her that it would be better to give the information in open court; lastly they said that there was no objection to her giving evidence.

Her first known engagement was on 11 January when she spoke on 'The Separation of the US and England' to the Association of the Bar of the City of New York.[30] She may have had other engagements in January 1925 but the evidence has been lost. Her next known engagement was 13 February at 3 pm. She was invited to the Astoria Hotel to speak to the National Women's Committee of the George Washington-Sulgrave Institution. A 'moving picture' was shown there on the same evening.[31] On 17 February Helena was the guest at the Dutch Treat Club, Hotel Martinique. Whose guest and whether she was paid is unknown. Another guest was Zathuretzky, one of the great violinists of the day.[32] Eleven days later she was guest of honour at the Portia Club annual luncheon, at the Hotel Astor.[33]

Appearance as a witness

At some point during her tour she appeared as a witness (sometimes wrongly referred to as her conducting a trial in America[34]) before the US Secretary of State as reported in the *Law Journal*.[35] The case involved Ruby Black (wife of the journalist Herbert A Little).[36] Black carried on where Dr Jarvis had withdrawn, demanding that she maintain her maiden name. She asked to be issued with a passport in that name. A regulation introduced by President Woodrow Wilson during war ruled that in the USA women could only be granted a passport in their husband's name. Helena's archives contain a copy of the *Law Journal* report annotated in her writing:

> 'Before this hearing, various courts in USA had refused to hear the case on the ground of lack of jurisdiction. Helena Normanton had nothing to do with procedure—was briefed to appear to state English Common law at the actual trial. It was finally decided that as the pleadings said a matter touching upon the prerogative of the President of the USA, the matter must be dealt with upon a petition to the President through the State War & Navy Department, the Secretary of State (Mr Kellogg) to sit as Judge & to report his finds to the President. This was done.'[37]

At the end of a long hearing, the Secretary of State ruled that the petitioner might have emergency relief, a passport in her own name, but that it was such an important matter that it should go to the president for a ruling in relation to the American Constitution and in particular the fourteenth amendment. In November 1925, the National Women's Party reported that several other applicants had been granted passports in their maiden names. The *Law Journal* reported that

> '...there has been left with the Secretary of State by the English Counsel who appeared, a bulky 'brief'(in the American legal sense of the word) containing the history of the English surname since the Norman Conquest. As during the hearing, the Secretary of State had avowed that "he knew we [i.e. Americans] were under the English Common Law in the matter," the conclusion reached affirming the legality of American married women's retention of maiden surnames is of great weight here, as it was an open secret in Washington that the Departments were so hostile in the matter that only a heavy preponderance of English Common Law and legal precedent was likely to prevent an adverse ruling.'[38]

Helena's intervention was important. Her appearance as an English barrister, commentating on English common law added credence and weight to the women's argument. She was clearly well-prepared and stated her case well.

Other engagements

Helena's tour continued into March 1924. On the seventh of that month she appeared at the Auditorium Hotel, where she spoke on 'Queen Elizabeth' in aid of the Elizabeth Garrett Anderson Hospital in London.[39] A lunch was given in her honour on the thirteenth by the Transatlantic Society of America at the Bellevue-Stratford.[40] She travelled to Canada to give further lectures. She was engaged by the Pond Bureau on 23 March to speak to the Montreal Woman's Club on 'British Women, etc.' for $150[41] and remained there until April.[42]

Return to England

Her tour was still being reported in June 1925,[43] but she left Quebec on the *Montrose* arriving in Liverpool on 23 May 1925.[44] She was obviously concerned that her conduct would be misconstrued, as she wrote a letter to Middle Temple whilst aboard which began: 'Upon my return to England I think it only respectful to inform you that...'[45] It is a long letter but essentially informed them that the first case in which she was asked to act in the US was settled and the second was a test case in which she was asked to act in conjunction with an American attorney, in which she gave a summary of the common law cases. The letter on the face of it seems rather pointless, but when placed in context it can be seen that she was anxious that her behaviour would not be misconstrued. She was trying to be open and transparent.

Gossip in Helena's absence

Whilst Helena was returning to England a letter arrived in London from a *Women's News and Views* journalist, enquiring as to whether she wore her wig and gown in the American courts.[46] Apparently this was a 'picturesque detail' which would add to an interesting account of the case Helena 'argued' before the American Secretary of State. The journalist stated that she been informed by another female barrister that Helena had applied to the Bar Council 'to tour America wearing her wig and gown' and that she had worn it on platforms. She said that the female barrister had seen it in the Bar Council minutes.

Helena's reply is revealing.[47] She politely thanked the journalist for 'asking before publishing.' She requested that the journalist not publish anything personal and omit Helena's name as she did not want any publicity. She explained that she had heard an account of the woman barrister's comments and advised the journalist to be 'very guarded.' Helena explained that she had seen a letter on the Middle Temple library door stating that any barrister appearing at The Hague should wear full robes, therefore she applied in order to find out if it was so concerning any foreign court. Her exasperation became evident: 'As to travelling and lecturing in robes, the poor woman must think I regard myself as a sort of circus.' She said that the Americans would have thought her insane. The Bar Council made clear that she did not have to be robed, much to her relief. Sadly she concluded that the comments were 'malicious gossip' that tried to infer that she enjoyed attention. She added a postscript that no woman sat on the Bar Council and therefore could not have seen the minutes.

'Privileged to have met you'

The media had followed her in America, and she had numerous engagements, including meeting women's groups. The Pond Bureau was a large and successful lecture circuit agency with a vested interest in her success. She was establishing her own network of international women lawyers. This could only strengthen women lawyers. Her tour contributed towards the continued momentum of the international women's movement. Her presence in North America presented women with a role model: an independent, successful, professional woman. The newspapers were enraptured by her. The *Chicago Illinois Tribune* reported that she was of

> '...medium height, though of ample proportions...Blonde with small regular features set in a plump, smiling face. She has a voice to woo the hungriest ogre from his daily meal: it is soft, musical, with delicate inflections and a delightful utterance. Added to this she is an extremely clever, witty, genial speaker, easy in manner, quite able to make her points, and leaving an impression of a mellow wisdom delightful to meet in a controversial, fretful world...'[48]

However, not everyone was so enthralled. In April she received a reply to a letter in which she appears to have accused American women of not having a genuine intention to fight for their own names. The National Woman's Party replied that American women did indeed: 'just that they haven't had an opportunity. Old style suffragists see the question of a name as trivial.'[49] It was not surprising that they were annoyed. Despite this her autograph book displays real affection on her farewell to America, including 'Goodbye and come back', 'An affectionate *au revoir*', 'Privileged to have met you.'[50]

CHAPTER 7

Back On Home Soil

'[W]e need a more complex understanding of the twentieth century, which recent research is beginning to make possible. A large part of the problem historians have encountered in interpreting events after 1918 relates to expectations. How soon could women have expected to overthrow thousands of years of male predominance in the political culture? Too much writing on this theme assumes that because there were not more dramatic changes in gender roles shortly after the partial attainment of the vote, therefore there were no significant changes. There is a danger of measuring impact of the vote by impossible standards, of expecting change to be unrealistically rapid, and of underestimating, by applying the values of later generations, shifts which were more significant in the context of the 1920s and 1930s than they appear with hindsight.'

Pat Thane, 2001[1]

By the summer of 1925 Helena was back in London. Legal life was by no means easy as cases continued to be intermittent. Prejudice was still prevalent within society and the culture of the legal profession.[2] Still she persisted in her task. This period saw more accusations of self-advertising. Her practice began to move away from the divorce courts and became dominated by criminal prosecution work. Helena also set her sights on joining the judiciary, an ambition that would never be realised.

Libel

Two months after her return from America, she considered bringing libel proceedings against someone, but there is no record of who this was, perhaps the female barrister who was 'gossiping' about her. This is relevant to her story because it adds texture to her working life and demonstrates the obstacles that threatened her career. She was advised that she had a 'good prima facie case' but told to omit from the pleadings a complaint that she had been described as having a 'manly appearance and that her collars are uncomfortable.'[3] Commenting on a woman's appearance is an old, disappointing and unpleasant form of bullying that still persists today. This wouldn't be the last such matter as in July 1937 *Punch* published a caricature of an obese 'woman' barrister examining a woman in the dock.[4] The caption read: 'Lady Barrister: What is your age?' Witness 'About the same age as you.' Helena commented in her Scrapbook, 'this caricature was sent me by M T Treasury who were of the opinion that it was meant to be me. HN'.[5] The libel action was obviously her attempt to try to stop untrue and unfounded rumours about herself circulating in the press as they were damaging to her career and made her the subject of disciplinary inquiries that carried the risk of her being disbarred.

Evidence of commitment: *Moody v Lee and Beaulah*

Despite the problems concerning her practice and the fact that her cases were still infrequent, she displayed absolute commitment to those on which she was briefed and to her clients. This was appreciated by solicitors who briefed her. In October 1926 she received a letter from one thanking her for her 'determined and persistent efforts' in a civil matter before the Court of Appeal where she represented William Moody (a painter and decorator).[6] The case involved a collision between a bus and Moody's motorcycle, in which he and his wife had been injured. Moody had suffered significant injuries to his head, hand, ribs, leg, knee and abdomen, had been in bed for 12 weeks and had to hand his business over to his sons. The original trial had been heard in March 1926 and the judge found in favour of the bus company. Helena appeared before the Court of Appeal in October 1926 and secured a retrial. The solicitor thanked Helena for her efforts and praised her for her success which he believed 'may save him and his family from severe losses.'[7]

Helena went on to represent Moody in the retrial[8] and Mr Mortimer KC represented the bus company. She was only four years since call and was pitted against a KC. During the retrial, the court heard that, in the war, Moody had been an officer's chef, but because of the accident was no longer strong enough to return to this occupation. Helena commented that cooking was highly skilled work, 'I always think so when I cook. Oh, I do. I see there is a lady on the jury, and she will, I suppose, be able to guide the jury on that point.'[9] The judge quickly returned, 'What has this got to do with the case-unless Mr Mortimer makes the suggestion that the plaintiff could very well be an hotel chef?' Mortimer KC disclaimed the idea that they were suggesting that Moody return to this occupation and his junior barrister remarked (causing great laughter), 'Nobody who ever saw an Army cook would ever make that suggestion.'[10] The hearing was adjourned for the day.

The report of Helena's courtroom style is troubling. Her comments were represented as trite and unprofessional. Yet, as a woman, she was aware that cooking was hard and skilled work and it was perfectly valid in a personal injury case that she examined her client's ability to work in a field in which he had experience. But since women's domestic work was perceived as valueless, she was ridiculed for making what could be perceived as a very feminine suggestion.[11]

Publicity and 'con-men'

The problems she faced both in the courtroom and out persisted as her career continued and were not just to do with publicity and the risk of being disbarred. For example in January 1927 Helena replied to a request from journalist and former peer Beatrice Honor Davy, for a photograph to illustrate an article she was writing about women at the Bar.[12] Her reply was a polite, but emphatically, negative. She wrote that she 'must protect herself against being accused of self-advertising.' The following year she refused to write an article for the Women's Union Society as it was dangerous to publicise a list of women barristers because there 'are con-men who targeted women.'[13] Apparently both Helena and her sister were the victim of one such man. This was no trivial concern as there is evidence that in 1938 she was accused by an art dealer of selling him paintings that had no value (he said they were not originals). She emphatically denied this and counterclaimed that he was, for want of a better description, a 'con-man.' Middle Temple, who the man wrote to, could not see how they could take further action and the matter ended.[14]

Ill health

Helena's troubles were not just confined to fears of self-advertising and con-men, in March 1927 her practice was affected by her health.[15] She offered it to another female barrister, Venetia Stephenson,[16] while she had an operation. In a letter Helena explained to Stephenson that because of her recent 'indifferent health' there was not much money in her practice, she had been 'avoiding work rather than encouraging it' but had not the 'heart to turn down Poor Persons work.' We do not know the reason for her operation but it appears to have been serious. She wrote 'I do not feel extraordinarily hopeful about my own operation. The surgeon has not given me a wonderfully good account of myself.' She left papers with Stephenson[17] 'in case I don't make it through the operation.'[18] It is unclear how long she was out of action.

Public service

Despite these problems Helena still continued with her desire to do public service and this included protecting the public. This is evident in the fact that she not only defended but also acted for the prosecution. In the case of *R v Gray*[19] she led the prosecution at the Old Bailey.[20] The facts are straightforward, Robert Fairbairn Gray, aged 31, was a painter from Kings Cross. On the night of 14 October 1927, a woman, Mrs Ellen Rock, the wife of a costermonger, was going home when Gray stopped her. She tried to hurry away but he grabbed her by the throat and snatched her bag and ran off with it. He was followed by another man and apprehended. Gray pleaded guilty to the charge of robbery with violence, and it was discovered that he had a string of similar offences in the past. He was sentenced to '20 strokes of the cat' plus three years penal servitude.

A job offer

The press interest in Helena did not relent but nothing could detract her from her career at the Bar. In 1928 she was written about in the newspapers and thought it necessary to explain to Middle Temple that the matter was being dealt with.[21] Despite this continuing behaviour and the infrequency of briefs, Helena was determined to practise at the Bar. This was her way of continuing the struggle to open the Bar to women. We can see this determination in May 1928 when she was offered work in finance.[22] This happened by chance whist she was visiting a newspaper office to look at their files, where she met a 'world famous financier' who offered her a five year contract with a salary in the thousands. She was, in her own words, 'surprised' and asked the financier why he thought she would leave the Bar. He replied,

> '[F]or the past seven years you have been sniped at almost every day of your life from behind your back, not of course by eminent people in the legal profession, but by people at the fag end of it, as you must know very well. And the process is still going on, isn't it?'

She answered 'Yes' and asked him how it was that he knew so much about her. He replied that he did not offer a woman work for a salary of thousands without knowing intimately about her. He had made enquiries and been in touch with all the editors in Fleet Street. He commented,

> '[T]here has been one point which pre-disposed me more towards you than anything else, which was that you were able to treat with silent dignity and contempt what would have caused 99 people out of 100 to scatter around any number of writs for libel and slander. I very much like your attitude of leaving things alone, although I cannot see what there is in the legal profession for you or for any really gifted woman for the next 20 years. It will be nothing but a few cheap county court and Sessions briefs, and why should you bother about that kind of thing? How can it possibly be worth your while?'

She did not accept the job as she was committed to the Bar.

The end of the 1920s saw her give up metropolitan living when, in 1929, she left her house in Mecklenburgh Square and moved to the suburbs, to Beckenham.[23] She also changed chambers the following year with a move to 3 Dr Johnson's Buildings, Temple.[24] Changing chambers was not unknown. Chambers were much smaller than now and sometimes just collapsed, for instance if the head became a judge, so her move was not unusual.

Fee book No.2[25]

Helena's archives contain her one remaining fee book for 1930–1939. The information it contains is often sketchy. It appears that in 1930 she dealt with 30 cases. Twenty-five of these were Poor Persons cases, so were not financially rewarding. The other five were paid. In 1931 she had 43 cases, 36 of them were Poor Persons. In 1932 she dealt with 43 cases, including 25 Poor Persons; in 1933 31 cases and 16 of these appear to be Poor Persons. In 1934 she had 29 cases, of which only three appear to be Poor Persons. In 1935 35 cases, and apparently all paid work; in 1936 21 cases; in 1937 she only appears to have dealt with nine cases. In 1938 she had 24 cases, in 1939 30, some of which appear to be Poor Persons. The information is not very clear. It shows she was being briefed but not very lucratively or frequently.

It is hard to ascertain the exact nature of every case. It appears that 83 of these cases were divorce matters. She seems to have acted for the prosecution in at least 20 cases and another ten cases were for the defence. She had five breach of promise cases, three involving wills, one libel, four child custody, and one employment case. The majority took place in London courts, but she also appeared to have a strong legal link with Leeds.

The 1930s were a difficult time for any barrister. The *Leader* reported, 'Very Little Bread and Jam for lawyers Today!'[26] It described how there was not enough work for the existing 10,000 barristers (not all practising) let alone newly qualified ones. It highlighted that this was because the public did not have direct access to barristers; it was expensive to qualify; self-advertising was prohibited; and the number had dropped by two thirds. The days of 'oysters and Chablis' had gone. They did not give a reason for this decline, but it was probably due to the depression.

Prejudice and lack of briefs were not the only difficulties in Helena's professional life. Fees were also an issue. In October 1934 she again asked for help from Mr Godson at the Bar Council.[27] Her problem arose because a solicitor[28] refused to pay her extra for dealing with an exceptionally large bundle of papers, as was normal.[29] The solicitor flatly refused to pay an extra fee when she rendered her accounts and she only received £3. 5s. 6d. The Bar Council was unable to assist her and the Law Society also refused to take the case further.

Accounts 1937–1938

For the financial year 1937–1938 we have a precise insight into Helena's earnings and therefore a rare opportunity to gauge the success of her legal practice in conventional and financial terms. We know that 1938 was a difficult year for her when her ability to work was affected by caring for her husband who was in poor health, underwent two operations and so she missed ten weeks of work. Helena acted as his carer.[30] Her earnings from *all* sources were £337 9s 6d (approximately £12,479.83 at today's value). She collected rent from tenants in chambers of £135 13s 0d, which suggests that she was head of chambers at 3 Plowden Buildings, making a total of £473 13s 0d (approximately £17,515.58 today). Her total expenses were £348.11s 101/2d/approximately £12,889.53, hence her net income was £124 10s 7½d, approximately £4,605.09. Her legal earnings for that financial year totalled just £37 0s 6d (for ten cases). From journalism and writing she made £284 14s 0d; from lecture fees £15 15s 0d and she spent £78 3s 0d on 'special historical books'. Her practice made her very little income compared with her other earnings.

R v Aynsley 1930

In March 1930, Helena became engaged in one of her most famous cases, *R v Lesley Aynsley*.[31] This was the first time that a woman had led the defence in a trial for attempted murder.[32] The hearing was held at Newcastle-upon-Tyne Assizes, before Humphreys J.[33] Aynsley was a 23-year-old plater's help (this was an assistant to a structural steel engineer). He was charged with the attempted murder of his wife, Ethel, aged 19, and father in law, John Hume. The prosecutor, Mr C B Fenwick,[34] alleged that this was a savage hammer attack. It was a difficult case for the lawyers as Aynsley's wife, and victim, refused to give evidence. The defendant was also clearly mentally unstable. There was a feminist issue in that the wife claimed to be devoted to her husband (or terrified of him) but he had caused her great harm and she needed protection, even from herself. The medical officer of Durham Gaol said that Aynsley had been in a state of 'maniacal excitement' at the time of the attack and he had apologised for hurting his wife, but in the 'way that you would if someone trod on your foot.'[35]

Helena was described by the press as 'unruffled and self-possessed...A matronly woman with a soft and silvery voice, conducted her case with ability and incisiveness.'[36] The victim's mother sobbed loudly throughout the trial. The judge believed that the he was in the early stages of insanity and kept pushing Helena into using this as a defence, asking whether she would ask the jury to find a verdict of insanity. She replied, 'I intend to plead with medical evidence that I can adduce, and I must leave it to the jury to find on that evidence what state Aynsley was in.' The judge persisted, 'You will have to do that in any case, Mrs Normanton. You need not tell me what your defence is. I was only trying to help you.' Helena retorted, 'I appreciate your kindness, but this is a borderline case, and I am in that difficulty.' The judge behaved in a kind but paternalistic way. He was 'helping' her, but she was a barrister of eight years call and 48-years-old. His comments could have undermined her credibility in front of her client and, most significantly, the jury.

The witnesses also proved problematic. The defendant's mother-in-law explained in examination-in-chief that she saw Aynsley strike her daughter with something grasped in his fist. In cross-examination Helena asked, 'You cannot say what Aynsley had in his hand?', to which Mrs Hume replied, 'No, Ma'am.' Helena persisted in questioning about a hammer produced in court, and the judge interrupted: '[T]he witness seems more accurate than you as to what is admissible in evidence, Miss Normanton. She did not see it, and prefers to say nothing about it.' Helena stumbled, 'I did not intend my questions as your Lordship appears to think.' She clearly wanted to test the evidence. The defendant was believed to have used a hammer which had been produced in court.

The only witness to the attack (the mother-in-law) maintained that she had not seen what he was using. Why not? Had she really seen the attack? How close was she? Was her view obscured? It was perfectly proper for Helena to ask the questions. She may also have wanted to plant seeds of doubt into the jury's mind as to the witness' reliability. The judge, on the other hand, viewed this as almost sharp practice. He believed that Helena was leading the witness excessively.

The doctor called by the prosecution admitted that he did not inquire too closely into the issue of insanity. Helena asked him in cross-examination: 'Look at the hammer doctor and please take off the label. [He did] If you had the intention to murder a person with that hammer, could you do it?' The doctor replied, 'It would depend on whether the person was passive or not.' Helena persisted, '[H]ow would you hold it?' The doctor replied, 'I must say that I have no intention …' and there was laughter throughout the courtroom. This made her sound incompetent. The doctor was an expert witness on the injuries inflicted by the hammer on the victim and the defendant's mental state. He could not answer questions as to what weapon a murderer would use or how best to hold it in order to cause maximum injuries. She was making a valid point: she needed to examine the weapon and the wounds that it could inflict, but this was not the correct expert to ask.

This case as reported does not sound like a triumph for Helena, but the result was. She asked the Crown to accept a plea of guilty to unlawful wounding, which was agreed, and the jury returned a verdict accordingly. Aynsley was not tried for attempted murder (which carried a life sentence) but pleaded guilty to a lesser charge. The news reports and references to the judge's comments and the court's laughter make her seem inexperienced and uncertain. Yet she stood up to the judge and stated her case. She asked relevant questions in cross-examination and planted seeds of doubt. The case was difficult, as she admitted in court. One of the victims was the defendant's wife. She refused to give evidence, wishing to 'stand by her man'; yet Helena would have been aware of the frequency of violence against women and vocal in campaigning for better protection for them, recognising that they often would not give evidence for fear of retribution from the man. In sentencing, the judge said that he did not regard Aynsley as an ordinary criminal because of his mental state and he would sentence him to 12 months imprisonment (second division), but if he was judged insane during his sentence he would be sent to a lunatic asylum, which was precisely what happened.[37]

A typical 'hotel case'

Not all her cases were criminal in nature. In 1930 she dealt with a typical 'hotel case' divorce. 'Hotel cases' were typical divorces, where the case was undefended and both parties were anxious to bring the marriage to an end. One party would confess to adultery and corroboration would be provided by a hotel receipt or calling a witness from the hotel staff in support of an extra-marital liaison. By the 1930s these cases were causing concern to lawmakers and were a factor in the implementation of the Matrimonial Causes Act 1937.[38] On 4 March 1930 Helena dealt with such a case. She was continuing the Parsonage divorce matter which had been delayed by order of the judge, Mr Justice Hill, from 3 February 1930. The judge had insisted that the adulterous husband should name his mistress. This was to be a warning to husbands as delay cost money as well as slowing down the ending of a marriage. Helena remarked in court that this was a typical hotel case. She was acting for the wife and informed the court that the other woman had been informed of the proceedings and served with notice to attend, but she did not. The judge had no choice but to order a decree nisi and said that he would continue to adjourn such cases and award costs against husbands who would not reveal the name of the other woman.

Another change of chambers

Helena stayed at 3 Dr Johnson's Buildings for only a year, moving then to 3 Plowden Buildings, Temple.[39] Such a quick move may reflect an issue with the clerks or other members of chambers. In July 1931, she was elected to the North London Sessions Bar Mess.[40] This was an association of and for barristers operating within the South Eastern Circuit (covering Snaresbrook, Harrow and Wood Green courts). Its purpose was to promote barristers' interests and standards.

Assizes and Quarter Sessions: More dock briefs

This period of Helena's life saw her mainly in what is nowadays the Crown Court, more often than not as a 'dock brief,' but she was not turning into a 'criminal hack' (a lawyer who only acts for defendants in criminal cases and at the junior level, such as the fictional Horace Rumpole)[41] as she took on more prosecution work. In August 1931 she acted for Annie Dunn,[42] a 25-year-old accused of converting £129 of holiday club money for her own use.[43] Dunn ran a holiday club for fellow employees at Messrs Rowntrees of York. Helena appeared both at the committal stage in the magistrates' court and in the higher courts. She argued strongly in the magistrates' court that the more serious charges of larceny be dropped and that the matter should be tried there and then in the magistrates' court. This would have been preferable as the magistrates had more limited sentencing powers. However, after much discussion, Helena advised her client to reserve her plea and be committed for trial. The suggestion was that this was in order for the real perpetrator to be brought to court.

The trial was held in October 1931[44] and Dunn pleaded guilty to three charges of fraudulent conversion. Helena's role was to present the court with a plea of mitigation in an attempt to lessen the sentence. The court heard that Dunn was treasurer of the holiday club and also pregnant and unmarried. The father-to-be had left for South Africa and Dunn stole the money to pay for her passage to follow him. She disappeared on the eve of the girls' annual holiday, but only travelled as far as Leeds, where she was arrested. She had only £17 16s 11d of the money left. She had no previous convictions, earned £2 4s per week and was desperately anxious to repay the money. She was spared a custodial sentence and bound over for six months.[45] This was an excellent result in a matter of theft. A condition of her bond was that she should repay the money. Helena announced to the court that Dunn would repay £80, but the judge, a recorder, said he only knew of £32 10s owing. This sounds typical of Helena: while defending her client she wanted to ensure that justice was done for the women who had been deceived. Her client had probably told her the truth about the amount of money taken, rather than the amount that the prosecution could prove.

As indicated, Helena's main employment appears to have been from dock briefs, and so we can presume that she was not earning a lot. To give a flavour of the experience: in September 1932[46] she was waiting in court at the Old Bailey with Venetia Stephenson when a prisoner was reported in the *Liverpool Post* to have said, 'I'll have that one.' The other defendant selected Stephenson. Neither defendant realised that they were women.[47] On discovering the truth, they did not change their minds and the recorder is reported to have commented, 'You have both made a wise choice.'[48] Helena remarked in her Scrapbook 'Every Little Helps!'[49] *The Evening News* commented, 'But now it has been repeatedly indicated that the prisoner is unable to tell if the counsel of his choice is a bloke or a woman barrister, the uselessness of the system is demonstrated'. They called for the system to be abolished as it was derogatory to both sexes. In April 1933, Sir Montagu Sharpe, chairman at the Middlesex Easter Quarter Sessions, agreed to allow prisoners with dock briefs to come to the front of the court to choose their counsel. He pointed out that, previously, prisoners had not been able to see the faces of counsel. He believed that it was now desirable they should do so-especially as there were women barristers present.[50] Why should it have made a difference if the barrister was a woman or a man?

Failed prosecution

Helena appears to have been fairly successful in her practice (in terms of winning). However, in January 1933 she lost her only case for the prosecution (it is difficult to see why it went to trial). It involved a defendant, Annie Bines, aged 49, who was on trial at the Old Bailey for bigamy.[51] Her first husband was a seaman during the First World War and she was informed that he had been torpedoed and killed in action. She remarried in 1918. Her father-in-law appeared as the main witness for the prosecution, arguing that the torpedo story was one of mistaken identification, although he could not provide any evidence that his son was alive. Indeed, it was never proved that the first husband was actually alive in 1933. Recorder Sir Ernest Wild KC, remarked that she should never have been prosecuted. Mrs Bines was so poor that the detective on the case, Mr O'Sullivan, provided her with money out of his own pocket to get home. On discovering this, the judge said that the detective should make sure that he got his money back, adding that he had behaved admirably. Helena remarked in her Scrapbook:

'Between 1923 & 1933 this was the only unsuccessful prosecution by HN. The principal witness for the Crown was very deaf and the Learned Judge soon got very angry with him and finally said he did not believe a word he had said. He was Mrs Bines's father-in-law and had (so he said) often shown her affection when his son was alive, he believed that the torpedo story was a matter of mistaken identification.'[52]

Helena's other prosecutions were more successful. In September 1933[53] she prosecuted two brothers[54] who entered the home of 'Mrs Edward James in Park Lane, [and] seized her German maid ...'[55] They pleaded guilty to assaulting the maid with intent to rob and were both sentenced to 12 months' imprisonment by Judge Whiteley.[56]

A proposed Association of Women Barristers
More than ten years after call Helena was still aware that the boundaries needed pushing back in terms of the Bar accepting women barristers so in January 1933 she proposed at the Annual General Meeting of the Bar Council[57] that women barristers should have an Association of Women Barristers. Her rationale was that this would entertain foreign women barristers and promote educational studies. She assured the council that there was no question of creating a rival to the Bar Council. It seemed a modest request. However, it was rejected by the majority of other women barristers who felt they would rather be governed and have their interests protected by the same authority that dealt with their male colleagues. She clearly felt that the way forward for women barristers was to unite and act together to promote their interests. Others felt that they wanted to operate within the current system. Helena may have had the right idea, given that discrimination remains rife within the legal profession and few women fill senior judicial posts. Certainly, in November of that year,[58] *The Queen* reported that a judge had said that he regretted that there were not more women practising. The magazine commented that plenty

of women were being called to the Bar, the problem was that solicitors did not use them. In its opinion, women conveyancing barristers were doing well, but those appearing in court were few, because there was strong prejudice against them.

Further accusations of self-advertising

It is perhaps unsurprising that two months after her suggestion for an Association for Women Barristers that Helena should be accused yet again of self-advertising. In March 1933[59] she received yet another letter from the Bar Council, this time asking her to account for articles written in *The Daily Sketch* in which she was described as the 'senior practising woman barrister in England.' Helena replied to Mr Godson at the Bar Council, 'No descriptions of myself are ever furnished by me to the press nor any interviews, nor any personal news.'[60] She continued that she neither saw nor furnished the paragraph complained of, in fact she was seriously ill in bed (the doctor was visiting twice daily) and under a sleeping draft. When it was published her husband saw it and rang the newspaper straightaway to complain. She maintained that she did not write for the newspaper, rather they paid her a fee to use extracts from her book. Rather belligerently she added: 'As a matter of fact I am not at all keen to be described as "the senior practising woman barrister at the English Bar," although it is mathematically correct.' She stated that this might have come from the late Dr Blake Odgers (a Council of Legal Education lecturer and renowned legal writer) who pointed out the rules of seniority at the Bar and he might have communicated this to the press via the Press Agency at the CLE when Ivy Williams announced that she had no intention of practising. Helena did not stop there, but continued that the title was not one she had adorned herself with and could see nothing in it (which she wrote she did not mean 'discourteously or flippantly'). She persisted that when she was invited by French colleagues to attend a women lawyer's event, the matter was raised by some other women barristers. The Bar Council looked into it and concluded that she was the most senior among practising women barristers. She continued that she could not order the press not to call her that, only ask them not to out of courtesy for her. The description she felt was not inaccurate, in view of the Bar Council's own ruling. Finally, she stated that she had done all she could to keep her personal life out of the newspapers, constantly turning down publicity that would be lucrative. If anything was written about her, it was not because she liked it, it happened despite herself. The Bar Council's reply to this rather long letter is brief,[61] stating that they had considered her reply and were glad to have her assurance that she was in no way responsible for the description. Helena was now more confident and disgruntled by the continuing allegations of self-advertising. She may have felt that she should not be expected to continue defending herself. She had told the Bar Council once and that should be an end to the matter. Her letter was perhaps rather tongue in cheek.

She was not quite so confident in August 1933 when she had cause to write to Mr Godson at the Bar Council again[62] excusing her behaviour in relation to an article she had written for the *Daily Herald* 'in haste'. She explained a boy was waiting for her to take the piece straight to the press office. The article was published with a photo of her, despite her instructions not to do so. They also referred to her as 'the most senior practising barrister.' She said that this never occurred to her and was beyond her control. They replied the next day noting her letter in case anyone wrote in and sympathised that captions were difficult to regulate and she had no doubt takes steps to deal with them.

Benson v Benson Divorce

We have seen that 1933 was a troubling year for Helena and it ended with one of her most difficult cases, which involved a campaign close to her heart. The case was heard in December 1933 and involved a divorce matter in which she represented the wife, a Mrs Benson. The case later caused her to break away from the Married Women's Association[63] and form her own group, The Council of Married Women[64] At the time of the action, the husband was serving seven years penal servitude for attempting to murder his wife.[65] The case took place at Leeds Assizes before Swift J.[66] Helena opened by asking for a divorce on the grounds of two counts of adultery and asked for custody of the child, aged eight, to be granted to the mother. The husband denied the charges of adultery, brought counter-charges against his wife and finally requested custody of the child. The judge is reported to have asked Helena, 'What do you imagine that he proposes to do with the child if I give him the custody of it? Is he going to take it to Dartmoor?' To which Helena replied, 'I would like to be there when he presents it to the Governor of the prison.' The judge said that this was ludicrous, granted a decree nisi and custody of the child to the mother.

Swift J added that the Benson case was tragic and if the wife had not been able to prove adultery before the husband went to Dartmoor she would have been bound to him for the seven years of his imprisonment. He commented:

> 'Cruelty and attempted murder and seven years' penal servitude are, in this country, no ground for the wife to obtain her freedom from her husband. But fortunately in this case she satisfies me that his activities as a man were not solely confined to wife beating and ill-treating and attempting to murder her but were directed to procreating children by other women. The custody of the child of eight who was the unhappy result of the union of these two people to be given to a man who has been sentenced to seven years' penal servitude for attempting to murder the child's mother would be a monstrous proposition and I shall not be a party to it.'[67]

Helena noted in her Scrapbook that '[T]he learned judge sent for H. N. to his room at the end of the sitting and warmly congratulated her on the mode in which she has conducted the Petitioners case.'[68] We saw previously that this was exactly the type of case that led Helena to campaigning for change in the divorce laws for women.

Indeed, shortly after this trial, she used this case to arouse public opinion to change the law. She used the press, not to advance her own career, but women's rights and for a change in divorce law, by writing in *The Daily Herald* on the state of the divorce laws in England and Wales.[69] In her Scrapbook she noted,[70]

> 'The Daily Herald was anxious for me to write a Divorce Law Reform article under the heading of the Benson case but as I had appeared for the

petitioner I asked to wait for a month until my own name as Counsel should have faded from the public memory. I also consulted the BAR COUNCIL in great detail about this article and fully complied with their views. HN.'

The article argued that the current law was 'outworn'. She illustrated this by arguing that if Mrs Benson had not been able to prove adultery before he tried to kill her she would have been left with no redress. She also used the 1922 *Rutherford* case[71] to illustrate her point. This involved a wife's appeal for a divorce from her husband which was rejected. The husband, Colonel Rutherford, had been found guilty of the murder of Major Setoff. He was found to be insane and was sent to Broadmoor. As he had not committed adultery there was no redress for Mrs Rutherford (who was quite young). At the appeal, Lord Birkenhead gave a judgment that appealed for a change in the law, stating that it was

'…unfortunate, that she should thus be tied for life to a dangerous and homicidal lunatic, after having for many years suffered both in body and spirit from his unfaithfulness and cruelty…She must look forward to a loneliness from which she can escape only by a violation of the moral law. To some this may appear a harsh and even inhuman result, but such, my lords, is the law of England. It rests with Parliament to end a state of things which, in a civilised community and in the name of morality, imposes such intolerable hardships upon innocent men and women.'

She called for an acceptance of Holford Knight's draft Bill which embodied the Majority Report of the Royal Commission on Divorce of 1912, which added grounds for divorce of desertion for three years, cruelty, incurable insanity, incurable drunkenness, and imprisonment under a commuted death sentence, all of which would apply to both sexes.

Breach of promise

Her cases remained in the junior division of work, as can be seen in 1936 when she conducted a breach of promise to marry case which was widely reported.[72] With Helena's assistance, her client was awarded £1,250. The case centred around Miss Stacey, Helena's client, who had been given three rings by her 'fiancé' (Mr Phillips), which induced her to move in with him.[73] However, once ensconced, he did not repeat the proposal of marriage but kept putting it off. It was reported that intimate relations took place, she became pregnant and miscarried. The partnership became unhappy, they slept separately and she left him, as she did not want just to be his mistress. She had been the victim of this sort of behaviour previously; in 1910 she had married a man who was found to be already married. The reason for the wide reporting of this case was Helena's involvement and because the woman had allegedly thrown a lighted lamp at Phillips, cut him with a carving knife, and threatened to shoot him, smash his window or scratch his face, yet she still won damages. Helena's success prompted the *News Review* to comment:

> 'Women barristers who usually spend time sitting in court watching and waiting for cases which never come their way, have been smiling sweetly on brother barristers.'[74]

Lady Emma Clark Beilby's will: A rare Chancery brief

Helena had a break from junior work with a rare Chancery case in May 1936,[75] which she lost. The action concerned a disputed codicil in the will of Lady Emma Clark Beilby[76] concerning the revocation of a gift of £2,000 to the National Union of Societies for Equal Citizenship (NUSEC). Helena appeared in the High Court on behalf for the NUSEC on one of whose committees she had sat during the campaign to open up the legal profession to women. This could have been a marvellous opportunity for her to break away from crime and divorce work.

Sustaining a practice

Although her cases were infrequent and perhaps junior in nature she remained in practice and had some interesting ones such as the Mrs Reader witchcraft case in September 1936.[77] Helena acted for one of the defendants, Mrs Reader, who had been charged under the Vagrancy Act. It was alleged that they used certain crafts, i.e., palmistry, to deceive and impose on certain of His Majesty's subjects. The police had used *agents provocateur*, who on visiting the defendant's apartment were charged 2s

6d to have their fortunes told. Helena fiercely defended her client, asking one prosecution witness: 'I put it to you that Mrs Reader told you once she was not a fortune teller and could not tell fortunes?' The witness replied, 'I cannot say that.' Helena continued, 'Some things she told you were not particularly flattering were they?' The witness replied, 'No.' Helena: 'I dare say what she gave you was, on the whole a description of your character and personality?' Again the witness replied, 'Yes.' Helena: 'And some of it was true?' Witness: 'Yes.' The witness then admitted that she did not believe in fortune telling.

Mrs Reader told the court that she could not make a living from this work, just £1 a week from her clients, and that she possessed insider power which enabled her to quickly sum up people (though she had failed with this client). She denied that she practised palmistry, stating that her power was similar to that of a water-diviner. She made no claim to be a fortune teller, and only put 'Palmist' up outside her house to attract people. In her closing speech Helena argued that the defendant's behaviour did not amount to an offence under the Vagrancy Act. This argument was not successful as all the defendants, including Mrs Reader, were found guilty and fined 10s each. The note in Helena's Scrapbook says that the fine was much heavier than had been expected.[78] This was probably part of a wider police campaign against fortune tellers.[79]

'A barrister's years as a junior are normally of immense interest to himself, but a little tedious in the narration'[80]

We have examined a selection of Helena's more interesting cases and it is evident that her work was sparse. It was not uncommon for barristers emerging from pupillage to expect a slow arrival of briefs and for their work to be confined to the county court and magistrates' courts, consisting of cases involving small debts, petty crime and Poor Persons' work. However, after a time, it was expected that a barrister's practice would become established and more lucrative.[81] Helena's practice never picked up. By 1934 the press had begun to speculate about her taking silk, which suggests that she still commanded a high public profile.[82] There were no women silks at this time. By this date she was 52 and 12 years since call. There appears to have been no time eligibility criteria for taking silk[83] (today there is an open application process which depends on excellence in advocacy and competence),[84] although the press mentioned the need to have practised for seven years.[85] Presumably there was speculation on this issue around the Bar also. Helena did not become a King's Counsel (KC) until 1949, in the final years of her career. She and Rose Heilbron became the first women to be awarded silk. If she had been made a silk in 1934 she would have raised the profile of women barristers thus attracting more women into the profession and providing a valuable role model for women and the general public. Her rise in professional status would have made her practice more successful in the long run, although she would have lost work at first, which in turn would have increased women's chances of succeeding at the Bar. It would also have encouraged solicitors to brief women. Instead of being made silk she was placed on the court brief list at North London Sessions[86] in July 1934[87] This meant that she obtained prosecution briefs as regular counsel. This procedure was mainly used for cases at the Old Bailey and was called the 'soup list', not quite the promotion that was hoped for.

Further disappointment: Passed over by the Bar Council

This was not her only disappointment. In 1938 the Bar Council decided that it should have one woman on its committee, but it passed over Helena and settled on another, Hannah Cross.[88] Not until September 1946 was she finally elected to the General Council of the Bar,[89] when this decision was widely supported.[90] Why was Helena passed over originally? She was the best-known woman barrister at that time. The answer may be evident from a sample of the correspondence between Helena and council. In 1933 she received a note from Mr Godson that:

> '…if a Judge addresses a male barrister they say Mr or just the surname. If it is a woman they say Miss or Mrs. But it is for the Judge to decide. The Council has made no move to accomplish conformity in this matter.'[91]

Presumably this letter was sent to many barristers, not just to Helena. She replied apologising for not replying sooner, because of heavy pressure of work, saying:

'The *Standard* says that there is a ruling that witnesses must call lady barristers, Madam. This is a nonsense. A witness may be of far superior rank to the barrister e.g. a Marchioness, who would be highly tickled to call a woman barrister "madam". In fact I thought that the compulsory use of Madam applied only if one were addressing the Queen in conversation; shop assistants when addressing customers; and domestic servants when addressing their mistresses…However I must own that I am not much given to pondering these social problems, so very likely I am wrong.'[92]

She added that she 'really wished' that the Bar Council would find a means to stamp out the too common practice of barristers giving interviews to the press under such generic descriptions as 'Woman Barrister', or 'Eminent Criminal Specialist'. She commented that the previous day the 'prettiest and most captivating' woman she had ever seen had tried to get her to express an opinion. She was too hardened to the blandishments of these delightful ladies, but she feared that a recently called young women might fall into the trap and the press would get an interesting copy for the paper without paying for it. Her reply is puzzling, she was not referring to a particular article or recent complaint, but rather to a general letter. What did she hope to gain? She was not 'playing the game'. The Bar Council was her governing body. If she wanted to succeed, she needed to cultivate them and pick fights only when necessary. Her letter was lengthy, quite arrogant in tone, discussing herself and the press, which was not the issue raised in Godson's note.

Later that month[93] she received a letter from Godson in reply to her letter of May 1933 regarding help for Jewish lawyers in Germany. She replied almost immediately[94] asking for advice on two further matters: an acquaintance asked for her opinion without consulting a solicitor, and she wanted to know whether she would she be within the etiquette in giving an opinion; and a woman had written to her enclosing a cheque, asking for legal advice: should she return the cheque? Godson's reply[95] conveys a tone of irritation and distance, referring her to the professional etiquette rules in the *White Book*[96] and stating that he would leave to her own discretion whether these actions fell within the ban. Again, in September 1934,[97] Helena wrote to him[98] pointing out that at the Annual

Conference of the NCW in Edinburgh, a resolution advocating reform of the matrimonial law would be debated. She wanted to quote the judge in the *Benson* case. As she was counsel and the case was widely reported she was concerned about any possible infringement of etiquette. Again he replied[99] with advice that it would be in order for her to refer to the law report, but not to mention that she was in the case or to any information that was given to her by way of instructions. Given Helena's problems with accusations of self-advertising, it is perhaps not surprising that she was cautious, especially as the rules were not published until much later. Were they available to her? He had referred to the *White Book*, implying that they were. Her letters to the Bar Council may have provoked hostility accounting for her failure to be elected to the committee.

'Shall we ever see a woman judge?'

In October 1934 the first rumblings of speculation began about a judicial post being offered to a woman. The *Daily Sketch* published a piece, 'Shall We Ever See a Woman Judge?'[100] This posed difficult questions, such as, what role did women play in the opening of the new sessions? What was the effect of women's lack of headway in the legal profession? It stated that prejudice remained and they could

> '...not be taken more seriously than as a handful of rather pathetic pioneers marking time, sowing a drill that others will reap. If you catch them off guard then they will be more deeply dissatisfied than you would guess. Some had said that if they had a daughter they would make her become a solicitor as she stands very little chance of anything except secondary cases and local courts. She would be of more use in a solicitor's office as she would be invisible working behind the scenes and women are good at routine work. Also it would be steady employment and she would not attract comment every time a case came along. The Press attach importance and publicise every tiny case that a woman does.'

This was not a ringing endorsement of the profession. However, the article declared that being a female barrister was 'difficult but not hopeless,' that more could not be expected for the first ten years, and it would be easier for the next generation:

'Male barristers have had the field to themselves for years, you cannot expect a woman to get a footing in the first few years of entering it. Another anonymous woman said that the legal secretary to the Solicitor General said: "My dear young lady, I do not believe that there is a prejudice against women barristers, though it may be true that solicitors are shy of taking their clients to women barristers. Women have not had time to prove whether they are good or not or how necessary they may or may not be. The law is the one profession that needs time and great patience. Why thousands of men never make a living at all! You hear of the few women barristers, but never of the thousands of men. The men who sit at waiting for years watching for the briefs that never come, expecting the worst, hoping against hope. A few, a very few make spectacular careers after years of hack-work by proving their eloquence and brilliance in criminal cases. It is a matter of years and years of waiting, I'm afraid, and for the fortunate ones a sudden turn of good luck."'

The article continued:

'Mr C. G. L. Du Cann[101] the well known barrister analysed the seeming failure of the women with clarity and deep understanding: "Women are good at passing examinations but they are not so good at using their knowledge practically."'

In her papers Helena red pencilled this saying, 'That's good of him!' Du Cann continued:

'It is not correct to say that women can do nothing at the Bar. The able woman, perhaps, doesn't come to the Bar yet. Take a woman like Miss Margaret Bondfield, who chose politics and would have made a first rate woman barrister. Miss Bondfield can argue a case as well as most men barristers and better than many KCs. It is not a matter of sex, but of ability. The solicitor wants to win his case. If a woman can win it she will be briefed. The Bar is possibly the most difficult of all jobs to get your footing in.

The really able woman is out for an easy living. Marriage or journalism or the stage or a business which brings in quick recognition and money. Also women are concerned with the deeper things of life. Woman's business is life, death, religion, and all the important manifestations of life. The little pedantic argument doesn't appeal to them. That is why women see a case emotionally and not technically. Believe me, the law is more a matter of mechanics than emotions. That is why women would be good in Children's Courts, such as they run so successfully in America, or a domestic court devoted to matrimonial disputes. But women will never try very complicated questions of law. It is unthinkable that they should ever occupy such positions of such supreme importance or that we shall ever see a woman judge. Women are interested in the trial, but not in the intricacies of legal argument. Put it this way: many women drive cars exceedingly well. But how many can mend one? Whereas a man — indeed, most men-take their cars to pieces for the sheer technical fun of putting them together again. The law, I'm afraid is rather like that.'

Gender stereotypes still prevailed. This article illustrates the discrimination women faced. It is no wonder that Helena struggled to be briefed, let alone become a KC or a judge. She complained about the article to the Bar Council and they informed her of their findings in December 1934.[102] They decided that no member of the Bar had authorised those comments. Helena replied to this decision in January 1935,[103] saying that she was not surprised that the committee found no evidence that any member of the Bar authorised the publication of the comments in the *Daily Sketch*. She believed that Mr Du Cann would never write such 'nonsense'. She said that she was rung by the press recently to comment on Miss C Colwill's[104] speech, or alleged speech, about her experiences applying for recordership, but that she never gave comments — they were against etiquette and believed that whatever was worth printing was worth paying for. She continued that before Christmas a solicitor begged her to speak to a young woman who had become a solicitor, to try to persuade her to come to the Bar, but Helena refused, saying everything was against women. She was grateful for the work the Bar Council did. She concluded by noting the list of barristers able to practise abroad, and asked if there could there be a list that says which barristers can speak a foreign language as she was able to assist Marshall Hall to some extent in the *Fahmy case*.[105]

Helena's ambition was to be a judge. In November 1937, tired of waiting to be asked, Helena wrote to the Rt Hon Sir Samuel Hoare, HM Secretary of State for Home Affairs,[106] asking him to consider her as a recorder for the North Eastern Circuit. She stated that she was a barrister of 15 years standing, with considerable experience, and provided two referees: Sir Holman Gregory (formerly a recorder) and Lord Merrivale, former president of the Probate, Divorce and Admiralty Division of the High Court. On failing to receive a reply she wrote again in December, enclosing a copy of her book, *The Trial of A A Rouse* (see *Chapter 8*).[107] She mentioned that the French in 1935 appointed a woman judge to preside over a commercial tribunal in Nice. She cited women appointed as judges in America, Russia and Turkey and added: 'PS *Daily Mail* has just asked me to write something about women judges.' Was this a threat? Was she intending a high profile campaign like that to open the Bar to women?

On the same day that she sent her second letter, she received a reply to her first.[108] This told her 'to apply for vacancies as they arise, difficulties arise in general applications.' The next day the Department of Home Affairs wrote to thank her for the book.[109] How would she know when vacancies arose? What did Helena hope to achieve by her letters? The Bar worked through a network of secrecy: judges recommended barristers for judicial appointments and silk to the Lord Chancellor, based on contacts and behaviour in court. There is no evidence that she wished to reform the judicial appointment system and perhaps she thought that attempting such a thing would permanently preclude her.

On the same day the second letter arrived from the Lord Chancellor's Department, an article appeared in the *Daily Mail*.[110] It reported that no woman barrister had been asked to serve as a judge, although women had now been at the Bar for 15 years. It pointed out that 300 women had become barristers. They reeled off the other countries which had appointed female judges: Germany had a female judge sitting in the Berlin Criminal Court; Sweden had its first woman judge in 1926; Poland's first female judge was sitting in the children's court in Warsaw;

in 1924 Belgium passed a law opening commercial judgeships to women; since 1935 France had a woman judge in the Commercial Tribunal in Nice; in 1930 Bulgaria sent a woman judge to Rome to represent its interests before the Italo-Bulgarian Tribunal; since 1927 Miss Soumay Tscheng had been sitting in the French court in Shanghai; and from 1928, Miss Daw Hme Khin had sat as a District Court Judge in Rangoon. In the USA, the Hon Genevieve R Cline, formerly the New York Customs judge, had been promoted to a federal judgeship and Judge Florence E Allen was likely to be promoted to the Supreme Court in Washington, and was currently sitting in the Federal Circuit Court of Appeals.

The *Daily Mail* quoted Helena as saying that there was an argument for female judges in England and Wales and that, although women had the same viewpoint as men, she argued why then would they make a difference:

> 'They will bring the wider variegation of personality which interprets the law and applies remedies and penalties to suit the persons before them. They will be especially valuable in dealing with women and young people and in applying the modern social and more humane legislation such as the new Matrimonial Causes Act.'

She finished by saying: '[T]he law is the only profession for women in which advancement has hitherto been denied, and England the only country to act so callously.' This was a dangerous move on Helena's behalf. She had already been accused of self-advertising, which could have resulted in her being debarred. Was she considering a new campaign?

England did not have its first full time female judge until 1945, when Sybil Campbell was appointed stipendiary magistrate at Tower Bridge.[111] In 1946 Dorothy Dix became an assistant recorder of Deal and Edith Hesling a deputy judge presiding over a county court.[112] It was not until 1962 that Elizabeth Lane became the first woman county court judge and in 1965 she was promoted to the High Court. Barristers, such as Helena, would have had to have practised for ten years to become High Court judges or seven years for the lower courts. She was, therefore, qualified. Applications were invited for the lower courts. They would be judged by their success at the Bar, Helena was not qualified on this point. The Lord Chancellor, Lord Sankey, was not sympathetic to women,[113] but stipendiary magistrates were at that time appointed by the Home Secretary. The first sympathetic holder of that office was Herbert Morrison (1940–1945). This however was not the judicial appointment that Helena sought. She possibly set her ambition too high. Helena's judicial aspirations were not helped by another trivial complaint against her.[114]

The country, apparently, was still unready for women in the judiciary. The *Daily Telegraph* reported in April 1938 a case concerning a disgruntled justice of the peace (JP) who had been found guilty of obtaining credit by fraud at a Folkestone Hotel.[115] George Easton, aged 69, a former deputy lieutenant of the East Riding of Yorkshire, appealed against his conviction for fraud. As a litigant in person he said that he resigned as a magistrate when the Lord Chancellor suggested that many JPs were too old. Of the four magistrates conducting his trial, two were women. He stated that he had the greatest respect for the fairer sex but that they were not worth much on the bench, as women had no opinions of their own. Did this case warrant a report? Although the accusation of fraud probably did, the headline did not, but it reinforced the point that women were unwelcome in a judicial role.

In May 1938 *The People* reported that 'Our Portias Now Want to be Solomons.'[116] This stated that English 'Portias' were angry because none of them had been appointed to the bench. The newspaper believed that the divorce courts would benefit most from their appointment. The Attorney General had recently announced in the House of Commons that there would shortly be more judicial appointments and women barristers felt that it was time for them to be included. At least they should become stipendiary magistrates. In her Scrapbook Helena noted,[117] 'Neither of these articles—other 9th July 1935 *Northern Daily Telegraph*—was written by or inspired by HN in any way. Any press work done by her is invariably under her own signature.' The newspapers also speculated on the lack of women barristers and silks. For example the *Daily Mail*[118] published 'Don't Envy the Woman Barrister'[119] and reported that, on call night, 95 men would be admitted compared to five women. The paper wished those women luck. It lamented that 19 years had passed since women were admitted to the Inns and that they were not admitted voluntarily. The article commented that there were still no women judges; only two or three women were in actual practice, whose combined earnings probably did not equal the earnings of a single busy male junior. Not one of them had come within sight of 'taking silk.' The paper believed that women passed the Bar examinations easily because they were industrious and conscientious, compared to men who were lazy and careless. That, it stated, was why women made excellent solicitors. Women barristers' weakness was to espouse their case without looking at the other side, although their appearance was a great asset in court, despite being handicapped by their hair and stature, which it reckoned made women look like a convict or beehives, and women's voices did not carry like men's. Helena was livid and demanded in a letter to the under treasurer at Middle Temple[120] to find out if the author was a barrister. They replied that there was no record of him. So she wrote to the other Inns who also had no trace of him. On 11 July she wrote a scathing letter to the newspaper's owner, Lord Rothermere, and asked if his father, a barrister at Middle Temple, would have approved of his son's newspaper constantly attacking women barristers?[121] He replied over two weeks later via his literary editor, saying that they would soon publish the case for women barristers and hoped that would dispel any illusions. She was a formidable opponent and defender of women at the Bar, as we will see.

The Saarinen incident 1938

Helena's exasperation at the negative portrayal of women barristers in England was evident three months later from her reaction to yet another *Daily Mail* report. This centred on comments made at the conference of the International Council of Women in July 1938 by a Finnish female judge, Judge Saarinen.[122] Saarinen was reported to have said:

'Women barristers in Great Britain will have to attain greater prominence before you get women judges. In Finland, women judges hold high repute.'[123]

Evidently, Helena read this report although she was not present. On a scrap of paper, she responded :

'English women barristers deeply resent the slander on them by Judge Saarinen. Please see that she publicly retracts it and full publicity is given to that retraction. Or else please arrange that the conference either declines to hear her or passes a suitable resolution that we do not recognise Saarinen a slightest authority on English Legal system. Only last week one women barrister was most highly commended by Mr Justice Humphreys in brilliant work in court. This is by no means exceptional occurrence.'[124]

This undated note was probably the draft of a telegram sent by Helena to Lady Ruth Balfour, President of the NCW of Great Britain. The telegram caused a great furore. Lady Balfour replied in a letter to Helena on 20 July, that the quote from Fru Saarinen was mistaken.[125] She was not fluent in English and never spoke of English lawyers, only of those in Finland. Lady Balfour pointed out that she had not heard or read the talk and it was too late to take any action, especially as it had only appeared in one edition of the *Daily Mail*, therefore to correct it would give too much prominence to the incident. She concluded by saying: 'I must add that I regret the tone of your telegram, which seems to me quite unnecessarily dictatorial.'

Helena replied the next day, remarking on Lady Balfour's delay in replying. She wrote that she would be happy to furnish her with a copy of the article as Lady Balfour was in a very responsible position. She continued that a group of English women barristers had met in chambers the previous day. If the tone of her telegram seemed unnecessarily peremptory she wrote that she was the first to regret it— 'but telegrams are very expensive.' She pointed out that the *Daily Mail* had a readership of two million and she therefore disagreed with Lady Ruth on retraction. She wrote:

'Legal women are defenceless as bound by etiquette…I, along with other legal sisters have for a considerable time been far from satisfied with the National Council of Women in relation to women in the legal profession.'

The issue of women judges was clearly extremely sensitive. Lady Balfour replied on 3 August, saying that she believed Helena had misinterpreted Saarinen's words:

> 'The National Council of Women, and I feel sure, all other organized women hope that this state of affairs will be changed (i.e. women not succeeding at the Bar) in the near future but I doubt whether attacks by their legal colleagues on women of other professions is likely to promote that good feeling and co-operation, which by implication in your letter you consider desirable.'

Helena's niece, Elise, who worked for *Good Housekeeping*, also wrote to her, addressing her as 'Auntie,' asking her to discuss the matter with Lady Ruth and hoping that her aunt would bring a satisfactory end to the controversy.[126] Helena wrote again to Lady Balfour in September, but not in quite the conciliatory terms her niece was hoping for.[127] She stated that she had reported the matter to the Bar Council who had approved her actions, adding that foreign delegates should not be given access to the press. It was an extremely long letter, rather patronising and superior in tone.

We can see from this incident and her letters to the Bar Council that Helena was often too wordy, which one sensed caused a negative reaction in the reader. This may have been true of her behaviour in court. In May 1939, she conducted a matrimonial case for a suspension of a committal order. It was refused after a reportedly long legal argument.[128] Helena noted in her Scrapbook: 'Bench unable to understand its [her argument's] effect'. Was her conduct in court too lengthy? Too academic? Or perhaps too Victorian? The times had changed since Marshall Hall.

Second attempt at a judicial post

In September 1938 Helena returned to her personal campaign for a judicial position.[129] She wrote to Sir Alexander Maxwell CB, Permanent Under Secretary of State, Home Office, explaining that she had written the previous year about a recordership and the Home Office had intimated that a woman might be considered. She noted that Storry Deans

KC, Recorder of Newcastle, had died and it occurred to her that a post might arise. She asked Maxwell to consider this her formal application. She received a reply from the Home Office[130] stating that the Home Secretary had asked her to apply for each vacancy as it arose.[131] Another letter arrived on the same day from Maxwell informing her that her letter would be placed before the Home Secretary.[132] Four days later Helena wrote again to Maxwell, almost pleading that she did not know when positions were vacant. She asked him 'please' to let her know when there were actual or pending vacancies.[133] The unhelpful reply from the Home Office was that the only advice that could be given was to look for notices in the press of the death, resignation or promotion of recorders on her circuit (as she had recently done).[134] In December 1938, Helena took a holiday to Rome, Naples and Sicily, apparently the first real holiday she had had for years.[135] She must have really needed it.

CHAPTER 8

Later Legal Work and Helena Normanton's Attitude To Practice

'The men, not at first very warm in their welcome, are now most kind and helpful.'

Helena Normanton, 1944[1]

Helena Normanton remained in practice until she was 68-years-old. This was a remarkable achievement given that so many of her peers were unable to remain in practice at all. We will see later in this chapter how she supplemented her earnings at the Bar with journalistic writing. She was extremely committed to her career and life at the Bar. She would never become a judge, which she really wanted, but she would become the next best thing: King's Counsel. However, the rest of her career was dominated by yet more accusations of self-advertising.

Another disciplinary inquiry[2]

Helena was subjected to yet another disciplinary committee following an article in *Girl's Own* entitled 'Some famous women of today' which highlighted Helena, amongst others.[3] It was an aspirational article for teenage girls, certainly not a vehicle for advertising services. On 1 March 1939, Middle Temple wrote to Helena saying that their attention had been called to it, i.e. someone had complained to them and explained that it could be seen as constituting an advertisement of her professional abilities. She replied the same day, saying that she never wrote articles about herself and never gave interviews to the press. Middle Temple persisted, two days later asking if she would categorically answer whether she had anything to do with the publications. This is quite extraordinary, and shows that they lacked faith and trust in her as she had already stated her case. Again, she replied immediately that the tone of the letters had caused her pain and considerable anxiety. She was unconscious of having done anything of the nature indicated by the question. Yet again, she enclosed letters from editors in 1923 saying she had never sought publicity, etc. She must have had sight of the publication for she wrote to Middle Temple on 7 March saying that she had just seen it and was in no sense party or privy to it. Nearly ten days later they sent a paper marked 'Treasurers instructions—take no further action.' It seems extremely unfair that an article written for teenagers should have been misinterpreted as a display of self-advertising. It is a wonder that she remained in practice. Their behaviour was intimidating and bullying, not to mention off-hand and impersonal. It certainly left her with no misunderstanding of their power to end her so hard fought for career.

September 1939

The Second World War was difficult for everyone. Helena was part of that war and was deeply affected by it. Almost a year after its start she related that, 'On the Saturday when the Surrey Docks were blitzed, I had gone there on legal business. A bomb came through the shelter and I saw a baby killed. I walked all the way home [to Beckenham] arriving at 8:30 in the morning'. Her work during this period was described by Margaret Paton Hyndman, an Ontario barrister and the second woman in the Commonwealth to be made a KC in an oral history interview.[4] She described Helena's work thus:

'And when the war came...she was made...Bailiff...at the Old Bailey [junior and secretary of the Old Bailey Mess], the chief criminal court in London, during the war when so many men had gone into the services, she was in this position and the position involved seeing that every criminal had someone appear for him or her if they wanted to be represented...That everybody has a right to be defended...And to get counsel for these people, these accused people, often meant taking the case herself, because she couldn't get anybody else because so many members of the Bar were serving in the forces. But she had a winning way with her, and she could in a serious case, command the very best legal counsel for an accused person.

And she worked night and day, she worked for her Inn of Court, which was the Middle Temple, she lived outside London, sometimes the trains ran, sometimes they didn't, sometimes she didn't try to find out. She was fighting fires around the Inns of Court and the Old Bailey and other legal buildings in London, and the Churches. And she worked like a slave …'[5]

It was not only the work that was difficult, tensions ran high during the war and this can be seen in the one complaint Helena made to Middle Temple about another barrister.[6] This concerned a Miss Lucy Smith who was also a member of that Inn. Her conduct was described at length by Helena as being anti-Semitic and generally slanderous, rude and malicious towards other women barristers. Miss Smith had also been heard demanding Nazi propaganda pamphlets which were dropped by air around the Temple. Passing on this material was a criminal offence. Helena was not the only one to complain. Others were Florence Earengey[7] and Margaret Hughes (whose daughter was a barrister who had been told she had a 'reputation' by Miss Smith, because she was seen talking to a man in the Temple). There is no record of the outcome, but the episode highlights the war-time atmosphere.

Missing fee book

Helena's fee book for this period is lost, but there is a case book[8] containing limited information. We can extrapolate from this evidence of her war-time work, in 1941 she dealt with 35 cases; in 1942 36 cases (including approximately three divorces and at least ten criminal cases); in 1943 she had 64 cases; in 1944 58 cases; and in 1945 64 cases. Clearly she was still being briefed whilst carrying out her war-time role but the cases were still not frequent, only a few each month. But after the war her cases became even more infrequent. In 1946 she had only 12. Of course, her case book may not be complete and she may have been assisting other barristers.

Wartime legal work

Details of her war-time practice are only available in fragments from newspaper reports. It was reported in 1943 that she defended Arthur

Wallace (his real name was Munday), aged 69, against the charge of being an habitual criminal. It was a disturbing case in which Helena had Wallace recite his life history in open court. It began in a workhouse in Leytonstone, having been abandoned there with his sisters by his drunken father. He said that he had always been hungry. His first period in jail began when he was 24 when he was convicted of stealing a lamp from a car. He was sentenced to two years in prison, not a bad result for this kind of case.[9] In addition to defence work she worked as a prosecutor for example in 1943 it was reported that she prosecuted a man accused of two counts of bigamy and the theft of objects from his own sisters. She was successful and he was convicted and sentenced to 21 one months for the bigamy and 18 months for the theft, to run consecutively.[10] Later in 1945, she prosecuted a young man accused of slashing the throat of a much older man. Again she won.[11]

When the war was over

After the war we can only assume that Helena's life continued as before. By this time she was 63. Her work was described by Margaret Paton Hyndman in her interview:

'Then when the barristers came back from the war, some of them had not been admitted and they [the Bar Council] were a bit lenient, they tried not to take people who were not qualified but people had been through a great deal and many of them, the experience they were getting, was through Helena Normanton in the Old Bailey, who wanted to do criminal work, said they did, thought they did want to, and then they would have a terrible time. Couldn't sleep knowing that they were going to go into court and defend somebody on some serious charge, and maybe it wasn't so serious. And she had to stand ready to go in, in case they just didn't show up on the day of the hearing or fainted at the last minute or during their defence. She would then have to rush around to get somebody to take the case or take it herself. She used to tell me stories about how they would come in, nice young men, and say, "Mrs Normanton, I can't possibly go into court, I can't possibly, and I was up all night, I had nightmares or headaches or diarrhoea or something" Well, she had the cure for that, she had Extract of Wild Strawberry in her cupboard, she had a cure for everything else, to settle them down enough to go into court. But she also would go over the case with them, and give hints as to how to handle it and so on. And they gave a big party for her at the Old Bailey and the Lord Chief Justice was there and the President or Treasurer of each of the Inns of Court, and it was going to be a great big splash. But I knew that one thing that they wouldn't have much of would be cake, and I have a recipe for a wonderful light fruit case [sic] and I think I made double the quantity and I sent it over to a very old firm of confectioners in London and they used to say that their icings…They used to say that Queen Mary's hats looked like something from the most famous confectioners in London who was famous for his icings on cakes created according to the occasion. So I wrote to them about it and they said, that, well, they couldn't possibly do their best, they needed so many pounds of icing sugar, they didn't call it that, they called it something else, but that is what it was, and so many pounds of butter, and they couldn't possibly get that, and so many eggs to make the icing. So I sent them all over by airmail, and the cakes, and they decorated them. And the Lord Chief Justice was asked to cut the cake, with the Sword of Justice, and they found it didn't have any edge to it, it couldn't cut. And they had to bring the chef in from the kitchen with his big knife to cut the cake. And that just brought down the house. I think I have Helena Normanton's letter on that, somewhere. But that is the story of the three tiered cake.'[12]

This was the 'Silver Wedding' party for the 'Portias' and was held at the Old Bailey mess.[13] Helena organized it to celebrate 25 years since the first woman was called to the Bar. She wore a flowing blue velvet gown trimmed with gold.[14] She had been the acting junior and treasurer of the Bar mess of the Central Criminal Court. The reporting of this lunch would become the subject of a later disciplinary inquiry by Middle Temple (described later).[15] She was quoted as saying: 'I may be a poor barrister but I can still cook.'[16] Was she really likely to have said this? Even if she did it was perhaps self-deprecating, not to be taken seriously. Was she not entitled to any celebrations?

1948

Nineteen-forty-eight began as something of a golden year for women. Florence Paton became the first woman MP (Nottingham) to preside over proceedings in the Chamber of the House of Commons and Eileen MacDonald became the first woman to sit at Liverpool City Sessions (she had been an assistant recorder in 1947 and was promoted on the sudden death of Edward Hemmerde). Helena herself achieved another first: she became the first woman to prosecute a murder trial. It occurred in Newcastle. A soldier called Sloan was accused of murdering his wife, *R v Sloan*. He was convicted.[17] Sloan was found to be insane so the death penalty was respited.

The year did not end so well. On 8 December Helena's husband died in a nursing home and was cremated at Croydon Crematorium on 15 December.[18] She inserted a notice in the *Daily Telegraph,* in which she wrote that he was dearly loved and mourned by herself: 'A verray parfait gentil knight.' A reporter for the *Sunday Telegraph* related how, when the reporter wrote his obituary, he rang Helena and asked her for help, and she invited him for tea. She is reported to have said at that meeting, 'Why don't you laugh? Is there any reason why obituaries should be dull and depressing? My husband and I had a happy life together.'[19] She told the *Beckenham Advertiser,* 'No woman ever had a happier marriage. Our only quarrel was over the correct way to carve a salmon.'[20] She was also reported to have said, 'To me he was perfect. I was never worthy of him.' These comments give us a rare insight into her marital relationship. She continued that he had no regard for wealth and could not resist helping genuine cases of hard luck (a trait she also shared as we shall see later in the chapter). He left her £1,325 (about £47,000 today).[21]

King's Counsel

Helena never became a judge, despite her letter writing. But in April 1949 the unexpected happened: she was awarded silk, aged 67. She must have applied for this the year before to the Lord Chancellor, Lord Jowitt (1945–1951), as it is unlikely that this was her first application, especially given the evidence that surrounds her direct approaches for a judicial appointment (sadly no records surrounding her application survive).[22]

Jowitt was a Labour politician who wanted to end social inequalities and was responsible for introducing appointments on merit. He accepted few applications and only after approaching other members of the Bar and judiciary for their opinions. She would have required two referees: it would have been interesting to know who supported her. The name 'silk' is taken from the fabric of the gowns that (nowadays) Queen's Counsel are entitled to wear and indicates that they are senior barristers (junior barristers wear gowns made of 'stuff', a kind of strong cotton). Originally they were appointed to assist the law officers working for the monarch. This duty was abolished in 1831 and they became the most senior practising barristers, the elite of the profession.[23] Becoming a King's Counsel would have prevented her from undertaking much of the junior work that her practice until then depended on, such as the preliminary stages of cases. She would now require a junior barrister to assist her in any cases, and was required to charge higher fees but as she was at the end of her career this would not have concerned her.[24] She and Rose Heilbron[25] became the first women in England and Wales to 'take silk.'

The event was widely reported, her archives contain a large file of press cuttings.[26] Letters of congratulations abounded.[27] The Old Bailey mess wrote to Helena having, unanimously decided to invite her to accept honorary membership, hoping that she would accept their invitation as some small expression of the regard in which she was held and of the gratitude of members of the Bar for her devotion to their interests.[28] For Helena this honour of becoming a KC came too late. It was of no practical use to her, as her career was almost over. Why it occurred is open to speculation. She was the most senior practising barrister in terms of being the first woman to be admitted to an Inn. It might possibly have been unacceptable to award Heilbron the title without acknowledging Helena's longstanding career in which she contributed much on behalf of the female members of the Bar. It was probably awarded in recognition of the longevity of her career and the fact that she was instrumental in opening up the Bar to women.

On 26 April 1949, Helena attended the House of Lords and was formally made a silk. She wore a style of dress formally approved by the Bar Council,[29] a full dress robe consisting of a court coat (made of black superfine cloth in the same style as the men's but not skirted,[30] but like a lady's everyday coat), ruffles at the wrist, a lace neck frill, a silk gown with a pouch attached at the back (used in the past for clients to drop money into which barristers were not allowed to discuss), skirt, white gloves, patent shoes with a silver buckle and a shoulder-length grey wig. She made her own stock bands and cuffs from a piece of seventeenth century French lace which had been worn at the court of Louis XVI, [31] because a shortage left only enough lace for one woman KC. Helena left that for Heilbron and made her own with the antique recycled lace. In his speech, the Lord Chancellor mentioned, 'Two years ago there were women among the clerks, now women among the K.C.'s — you can never keep a good girl down ...'[32] The choice of the word 'girl' is telling and its connotations. The following month found her 'resting' as she tripped over one of her cats and cracked her ribs.[33] She retired from her role at the Old Bailey and they gave her a diamond and pearl necklace.

Retirement

Two years later in 1951, aged 69, she gave notice to her chambers of her retirement.[34] Her resignation letter said that her health had 'given way', she could no longer conscientiously practise at the Bar and she had lost her husband. She wrote that her poor health resulted from damage to the ligaments of her left ribs[35] after an undated accident left her 'smashed' in a railway carriage (was this an excuse for the accident with the cat or another unfortunate injury?) and arthritis had painfully set in. She wrote that she was trying to raise money to go to Aix-Les-Bains for a cure, though the sum left in her will suggests that she did not need to raise money (although she did not know how long she would live for, or how much money she would need to fund her retirement). She announced her retirement in *The Times*[36] and it was widely reported. *The Advertiser* (Beckenham[37]) ran an article 'Beckenham Woman KC Retires' in which they commented that few people knew of her retirement until her vast law library was sold. They quoted her as saying,

'I felt that I had done enough. I was very sorry to retire, but I knew the time had come. I did not want to be like a concert singer who carries on when she has lost her voice.'

She commented that she had spent the last seven months moving out of her chambers, 'there is a lot of work attached to retiring. It cannot be done in ten minutes. Now I shall stay at home in Beckenham and concentrate on a Shakespearian book I am writing.' Not all the reports were so kind. The *Daily Telegraph* reported (wrongly) that she had retired at age 58 and not at 60 as men normally did. They commented that this was hypocritical when she had been an advocate of equality. Why this hostility at the end of a pioneering career? She was in fact 68.[38] Others reported that she had given up a £5,000 per year career for housework.[39] What was their point? That working women really only wanted to revert to their traditional or 'rightful' role/work? Others, however, noted her considerable achievements.[40]

It was not only her health that led her to retire. A week before she announced her retirement to chambers she received a letter from Middle Temple[41] regarding the conversation in her own house during a lunch party. The lunch was reported by the *Evening Standard*[42] some three months earlier, alleging that she had described herself as 'the most senior female barrister in England' (wasn't this true?). This was to be the final accusation of self-advertising. The General Council of the Bar asked Middle Temple to deal with this complaint. The letter advised her there would be a hearing about her conduct on 24 May, before the benchers of Middle Temple. They also wrote about a complaint concerning the reporting of the 1947 'Silver Wedding' anniversary party described earlier in this chapter.[43] She was invited to appear or to send a representative. She replied that she could not instruct a lawyer as her health was in a very poor state:

'…If I were well there is no reason why I could not meet them with any confidence, for I have never courted a syllable of publicity in my life for myself. From my angle I have been the victim [of] rather sharp practice.'[44]

She wrote that in a previous letter she had given a full explanation of the article in the *Evening Standard*, which she had heartily disliked. She begged the treasurer to accept her explanation and to drop the matter:

'The reproduction of small talk at a lunch at my home cannot possibly injure the Bar of England and as I have refused all legal work for over two years because of the state of affairs described to Mr. Gilbert, and now find I cannot return to work I was obviously not touting for the attention of solicitors.'

Mr Godson of the Bar Council, she entreated, would have dismissed this matter as 'trivial rubbish.' She stated that if the treasurer wanted to take it seriously she would not shirk from it, would notify him as soon as she felt well enough and would bring a silk and a junior. She explained that she had two public engagements she hoped would not seem inconsistent with her claim of ill-health as they were made long ago and were pleasant duties, presenting no strain. She wrote again on the day before her hearing saying that she hoped to be in attendance, but was suffering crippling pain.[45] If she did not attend she hoped they would realise that it was due to her disability. Furthermore, she had been too unwell to get counsel and could say no more than in her letters. Despite this, the hearing took place on 7 June 1951 in Middle Temple Hall, before the master treasurer, Ralph Thomas J. Helena appeared in person. They decided, because she had ceased to practise, to take no action. She said that did not satisfy her, she had never sought publicity and it was painful for her to end her career in this way. They replied that she had not been punished and that she should have avoided situations where she could be written about. This could not have been how she wanted to end her career at the Bar. What a cruel end to this pioneer's career. This incident evidences the climate in which she worked and also why she stayed in practice for so lone: to force open the Bar to women and to break down the discrimination that still existed.

This hearing had a profound effect on her. Despite having retired she wrote to Middle Temple on 30 November 1952 to inform them that she had been accused of fraud against a client. There is no evidence of this in her archives and the letter is long and rambling. She commented in passing that 'for some years now the publicity obtained for Miss Rose Heilbron has frequently been conducted by ways of a parallel to myself, in which I am depicted as her feebly incompetent fore-runner…'[46] This is a clear indication that she felt that history was not judging her well. We may wonder why she did not write an autobiography to set the record straight about her contributions, but, given the controversy and hearing after the reporting of her lunch party, it is understandable why she did not (although she could have made plans for it to have been published posthumously). Again on 2 October 1952 she wrote to Middle Temple that she had complained to *Britannia and Eve*[47] magazine that she had been described as a barrister when she had in fact retired.[48] She emphatically denied that she had anything to do with the article. Again she commented that it was generally understood that her practice consisted of dock briefs or Poor Persons cases.

Her sense of injustice and struggle is echoed by one of her contemporaries, Enid Rosser[49] who wrote about her career, and thus commented indirectly on Helena's:

> '…Looking back on those years I realise how spoilt I was. Women were still regarded as interlopers in the professions and in higher branches of the civil service…To the Bar a few, perhaps 30, had been called but they did not number in 1927 more than half a dozen who practised…Helena Normanton, later who became a KC was still struggling and having a fight with her Inn, the Middle Temple, to retain her maiden name professionally.'[50]

Helena's feelings described above, as being remembered as a feeble forerunner for Rose Heilbron, or that her practice only consisted of Poor Persons work or dock briefs, did not come from an inflated view of herself or her standing. Rather, the comments failed to acknowledge that she was the 'first,' she was the trailblazer. Without her contribution there could have been no Rose Heilbron. Her work may have consisted of Poor Persons work and dock briefs, but her practice broke down barriers and paved the way for later women.

'Professions produce services rather than goods'[51]

Barristers in 1919 were advocates and specialists. They were a powerful profession, an elite who understood the intricacies of the law. Their function was to provide advocacy and specialist, expert legal services. Law is man-made, with language constructed to serve a particular purpose: certainty. That language also ensures that only those with a particular training can understand it. Control of the profession in 1919 was by self-regulation and therefore by its members.

Helena saw the operation of the Bar as essentially masculine and wanted to feminise it: making it accessible to all. She had mail from women requesting help and their principal complaint was that men did not listen or did not understand.[52] She believed that women did not have access to basic legal training as men did (but in reality probably did not). This is evident from her book, *Everyday Law for Women.*[53] She wrote this in 1932 with a view that all women should be able to understand the law. This idea of helping and advancing women began with the treatment of her mother by the solicitor when Helena was 12-years-old described in *Chapter 1*. She was aware of the problems that women faced, she had experience and, importantly, empathy.

Everyday Law for Women was published on 15 December 1932. Its dust jacket boasts that is was written by 'the first English woman barrister.' Its purpose was to summarise all those parts of English law which had a practical bearing on the lives of women. It was supposed to be written in 'simple, clear English, without technicalities' giving information on the legal aspects of a woman's life from the cradle to the grave. It considered a woman as a 'fiancée, wife, mother, voter, magistrate, widow, beneficiary under a trust or a will and above all as a householder.' It gave helpful information on women engaging upon commercial activities such as being a partner in a business or a professional partnership or a company director or shareholder. It gave 'explicit' guidance upon the recovery of debts, the law concerning agency and a 'thousand other helpful matters.' It was supposed to give 'preliminary' guidance to a woman seeking legal advice. 'Rightfully employed' the book would prevent a woman from 'harassing legal complications giving her a broad outline of her rights in a thousand perplexing situations.' It attempted to be a comprehensive bible of women's rights. Helena intended that it would educate women to the same standard as men and prevent them from suffering injustice.

Publishing: A means to survival

Everyday Law for Women might also have been viewed by Helena as a means of supporting her through private practice. It was, however, not a best seller. Her publishers issued a publicity review pamphlet about it, quoting numerous sources. The *Law Journal* described it as so complete that it would be welcomed by all; the *News Chronicle* commented that it should be standard reference for all; the *Queen* said it should be in the possession of every woman; the *Morning Post* said it was worth more than its price; less convincingly the *Christian Science Monitor* described it as 'readable'; but *The Times* thought the male reader would find that it applied to him, and the *London Teacher* enthused that it was written with few technicalities.[54]

Helena had begun work on the book in October 1931. She requested permission to dedicate it to Queen Elizabeth and received a polite but firm letter from Buckingham Palace in September 1932 regretting that this was not possible. She wrote to her publisher, Ivor Nicholson, on 26 January 1933 expressing her dismay that they had not had it reviewed in all the newspapers as promised. The letter is polite but slightly threateningly, as she relates that, 'I have had a tentative offer from another publishing house to write for them a parallel book *Everyday Law for Men* 'At the moment I cannot tell you their name because they have made me promise to keep that quite confidential otherwise I should tell you.' What was she trying to achieve? A further contract or was she pushing for a harder sell of her existing book?

Ivor Nicholson replied on 27 January that the newspapers had received the book but were often slipshod. He doubted *Everyday Law for Men* was a good idea as there were already two such books. He met fire with fire by concluding that he was thinking of an 'Everyday' series on topics such as health! Helena then bombarded him with letters about advertising, including where to send it for further review. She even complained that it was not displayed in the window at Newspaper House, to which they replied that it was, in the corner.

By January 1934 the book was selling at a reduced price. She was informed that she would have to wait for royalties until income from sales passed the £120 already advanced to her. The director of Nicholson wrote that they were disappointed that it did not sell. She replied with new ideas of publicity, such as marketing the book targeted at magistrates. The final letter from Ivor Nicholson, in October 1934, stated, 'I think all your suggestions are excellent and they are being adopted.' The correspondence then ceased.[55] The book therefore had a dual function: to provide women with a readable understanding of the law and as a way of supplementing her income at the Bar—a way of remaining in practice.

Famous Trials series

Everyday Law for Women was not Helena's only effort at making an income from writing. She was a prolific writer. She wrote two books in the Famous Trials series, neither of which concerned her own cases. The first was *The Trial of Alfred Arthur Rouse*[56] also known as 'The Blazing Car Case.' They are what we would describe today as 'true crime' books. She acted as editor, taking a transcript of the cases and putting them in a readable form. In her introduction, she thanked her niece Elsie Cannon, for 'valuable secretarial assistance.' The Rouse case was an infamous trial conducted by Norman Birkett KC for the prosecution and a Mr Finnemore for the defence. Mr Justice Talbot presided. The crime had occurred on Thursday 6 November 1930, when the unknown victim was burnt to death on a lonely road near Hardingstone, Northamptonshire. It was suggested by the prosecution that the defendant, Rouse, had committed it to obscure his identity, as he was in embarrassed circumstances. He was seen at the scene by two witnesses. His defence was that the car had been accidently set alight by the dead man whilst Rouse was out of it. He was found guilty, sentenced to death and executed in Bedford Prison on 10 March 1930. His confession was published by the *Daily Sketch* the next day.

Her second book in the series was *The Trial of Norman Thorne, the Crowborough Chicken Farm Murderer.*[57] The defendant pleaded not guilty and maintained his innocence to his execution. The case was prosecuted by Sir Henry Curtis Bennett KC and defended by Mr J D Cassels

KC. The facts were simple: the victim, Elsie Cameron, left home on 5 December 1924 to visit her lover, Thorne, who kept a chicken farm in Crowborough. She arrived there, but was never seen again. A search went on for six weeks, with Thorne assisting. They found her dismembered body buried on the chicken farm. He maintained that she had committed suicide or had been murdered by someone else whilst he was out. He was found guilty and hanged. There is no evidence as to how these books sold or were received. She also wrote a romantic detective book called *Oliver Quendon's First Case* under the *nom de plume* Cowdray Browne.[58] She was an extremely driven woman.

Articles

Helena was also a prolific writer of articles for magazines. At one point her clerk commented that he could not keep up with the accounting for her contributions because there were so many.[59] She wrote for the *The Quiver* (a Victorian journal) between 1927 and 1935, on a range of topics: children, education, divorce, child offenders, legitimacy, widow's pensions, surnames, holidays, reading.[60] They approached her in October 1922 requesting that she contribute saying that it was not the 'old fashioned Sunday magazine it used to be years ago.'[61] She also wrote for the *Pall Mall Gazette* (an evening newspaper) between 1926 and 1928,[62] again on all sorts of issues from marriage and the trial of Roger Casement for treason, to the suspected murderer Madeleine Smith. Likewise, she wrote for *Woman* magazine between 1924 and 1926 on an abundance of issues: dissolution of marriage[63], Christmas and the Child;[64] 'Marriage as a Mausoleum';[65] 'The Earl of Birkenhead Friend or Foe to Woman's Interests?'[66] She also wrote for *The Queen* between 1934 and 1936. She wrote to them in September 1933 offering her services. As a result she earned £5 5 0 for each article.[67] She also wrote for *Good Housekeeping* for many years.[68] Her articles sometimes provoked complaint, such as one she wrote for that magazine on the USA on 13 July 1925.[69] They passed the letter to her saying she was not 'what you might call a very polite person.'[70] But often people wrote to say that they had enjoyed her articles, for example her piece on pensions.[71] Some of the letters were strange, such as one concerning her article 'Lonely Woman is the Post war Tragedy.[72] A man wrote that he would marry one such woman and gave his age and personal details.[73]

She also made one off contributions to publications such as *Child Education* journal in November 1926, on 'Teaching a Child Race.' This is a difficult essay for modern eyes, as she describes how the biggest problem for the USA after the Civil War was the future destiny of her coloured population, 'two decades since they were "raped" from Africa.' She describes the African race as a child race; who needed manual qualifications to fall back on if they could not succeed in the professions. Why did she differentiate between Africans and Indians?[74] She wrote for the *The Englishwoman*,[75] *The Coming Day*,[76] *Teachers World*,[77] *The Nation USA*,[78] *The Nation*,[79] *Advertising World*,[80] *Coming Fashions* magazine,[81] *The Journal of Careers*,[82] *The Daily Review*,[83] and for *Popular Motoring* under the pseudonym 'Hortensius' on personalities such as Justice McArdie.[84]

A meeting with Wallis Simpson

Helena was extremely sympathetic towards the plight of Wallis Simpson and Edward VIII. This is not surprising given her views on marriage and divorce. She wrote to Simpson in 1937, whilst she was in France, as she understood that they had a common ancestor, Alice de Montacute.[85] They met at a time (unknown) when Helena described Simpson as 'melancholy and distressed by the stories against her.'[86] At that meeting Simpson agreed to Helena writing a sympathetic article about her. The typed manuscript bears a signed inscription by Simpson, saying that she was pleased with it and wanted no alteration. It was relatively short, describing how people viewed Edward VIII's abdication as simply a way for Mrs Warfield [Simpson] to marry a third husband. Helena argued that it was Simpson who applied for both her first two divorces. It was she who was unhappy and had been wronged. She was innocent of any wrongdoing and deserved sympathy. Simpson was not a Nazi agent, just portrayed as one to misrepresent her (perhaps Helena felt a connection with Wallis Simpson because she was so often also misrepresented by the press, her contemporaries and legal governing bodies). There was, naturally, huge publicity for her article. It was sold for £3,000 by Curtis Brown, to the International Publishing Bureau,[87] who suggested that Edward, now the

Duke of Windsor, should use her as an 'official line of communication between them and the public.'

On 29 April 1937 Simpson had photos taken by Cecil Beaton to accompany the publication of her article in England. It was published in America only by the *New York Times* on 31 May 1937.[88] Helena believed at this point that Simpson would become HRH The Duchess of Windsor.[89] There was huge publicity and stories began to circulate about Simpson, so by 1 June Curtis Brown wrote to inform Helena that article was not to be published in England. The article was postponed on the grounds that it could be libellous. By 7 June 1937 the Duke did not want the article to appear. Helena was very upset. She was planning to write a book about the change of the law on succession. She instructed solicitors to record that she had acted in an honourable way. On 24 June 1937 she received a cheque for £1,350 for her work. *The Star*, who had purchased it, did not publish it but wrote two articles incorporating it.[90] Simpson was not the only controversial person that Helena met, in 1935 on a visit to Italy she met Benito Mussolini. There are no details of this meeting in her archives or newspaper reports.

Public speaking

Helena also gave many public lectures, as another means of supporting herself. She had always done this, for example in 1916 she lectured on 'Frederick the Great' in Hampstead,[91] and 'Everyday Law for Women' to the Wolverhampton Women's Luncheon Club.[92] Her archives contain many undated flyers for public talks on a host of different topics, such as history, film and women's rights.[93] For her lecture tour of America see *Chapter 6*.

1957: Final writing

Even in the year of her death, she was still writing. She attempted to publish a book called *The Detection of Willobie's Avisa*. She wrote two chapters and her niece sent them to a publisher.[94] It was rejected on the grounds that it was neither scholarly enough nor popular enough for the general public.[95] They did, however, say that they looked forward to her autobiography. We can see that her journalistic efforts were enormous.

Writing provided a way for her to continue practising at the Bar. She had a very busy work life.

Prisoners

Helena believed in justice for all, including defendants. We have seen that she both prosecuted and defended cases. She had strong views on justice. She believed absolutely in British justice. In 1925 she remarked:

'The judges in the courts are a fine type of men and do not make a discrimination in their dealing with cases that come before them. The poor man gets justice and when he wins a verdict against a rich corporation the latter has to pay and cannot swing the case from one court to another until the unfortunate plaintiff is ruined or dead.'[96]

She firmly believed that justice should be open to both men and women equally. She had great empathy for her clients and tried to do her best for them in and out of the courtroom. She did not see her role as just applying the 'cab rank' rule. She did not only view her job in life as opening-up the Bar to women but also as feminising the criminal justice system. Given these strongly held liberal views it seems strange that she was less certain about capital punishment. She had previously been on the list supporting the abolition of the death penalty, but in July 1939[97] she wrote to Mr Pritt, of the National Council for the Abolition of the Death Penalty, requesting that he took her name off the list, 'as it is unfair to waste your stationery and postage. I have oscillating views on the subject. I don't like the death penalty but also don't like the arguments put forward for abolition.' By 1957 she had formed a view that the death penalty should be kept for murder during rape.[98] Capital punishment is about retribution and vengeance, yet Helena's behaviour towards her criminal clients bordered on the ideal maternal model, full of forgiveness and compassion. Some of the letters from prisoners in her papers demonstrate that she felt a duty of social work towards her clients. But this feminising of the law did not mean sacrificing justice.

In May 1937 the *Daily Express*[99] reported that George Cheshunt,[100] aged 38, 'thanked Miss Normanton for fighting so skilfully such a hopeless case'. Cheshunt had pleaded guilty to fraud and was sentenced to three years penal servitude and five years preventive detention (he also had two years of a previous sentence to serve). Apparently his method of fraud never varied: he would ring up a nurses' association and ask for a nurse to look after a member of his family who was ill in a distant town. He would then get rid of the nurse for a few moments at the railway station, steal her luggage and disappear. He would sell or pawn the luggage and use it to swindle others.

The day after he was sentenced, Cheshunt wrote to Helen.[101] His letter was extremely emotional. He thanked her from the 'bottom of his heart' for the effort that she gave to his case. 'It was a colossal task,' he wrote

'and you are the only being who ever really cared whether I got out of my difficulty or not. The decision went against me. But that was not your fault Mrs. Normanton. Your final address to the jury was magnificent…'

He continued that he had no doubt that the judge summed-up with a bias against him. He was confused as to whether to appeal against conviction and asked her professional legal opinion. Further, he wrote,

'I have naturally been hard hit by the verdict. You are right. I am not what I have become, by my own personal wish. I am part invalid. If I could be treated I would wish for no greater happiness than to then be able to justify your faith in my condition. Do you really mean what you said, Mrs. Normanton? Would you really try and obtain a job for me when this over? Oh—if only I could look forward to this as a certainty, then I would never let you down. It seems too good to be true. You see I have had such a long and hopeless experience of employment without a reference that am almost afraid to build my hopes upon anything now. But I really have faith in you…'

He then asked for permission to write to her, 'If you tell me I may hope then I will crush this sentence.'

Helena had her clerk reply to him.[102] The clerk informed Cheshunt that she, Helena, would do whatever she could and then communicate with him. He was told not to lose heart and to take every opportunity to take up the studies available to him. Helena would not lose sight of his case. This was a kind letter, but one that set distance between her and her former client (it also demonstrated that Helena had a good relationship with her clerk). But Cheshunt persisted. Two days later, he wrote to her again[103] asking whether or not he should appeal. He flattered her with words about her expertise, but she would have been well aware of his mode of operation. He was insistent, but too pushy, commenting that he had not had a reply to his letter, and suggesting that perhaps there was a delay in prisoners receiving their mail. He said that he remembered her kindness to him in making a personal offer to help him put 'this sort of a life' behind him. He continued that he felt that he could count on her word and that her fight in court for him was in reality successful. He was certain that the jury agreed with her and convinced that the judge used undue influence over them. He wrote that he was anxious to hear from her as he only had ten days to launch an appeal. He was obviously concerned about his appeal and was using flattery, but underneath all of that there is a sense that he believed that she really connected with him.

Again, Helena distanced herself from him by getting her clerk to reply.[104] This was a considered and cautious reply. The clerk explained that Helena had been 'overwhelmingly engaged' since his case (we know that her practice was not that busy) and that she feared that if they appealed and lost the Court of Appeal might increase his sentence. The clerk informed him how to appeal as a litigant in person, clearly indicating that Helena did not believe that there was much chance of success and would not act for him, finishing by adding that Helena had not forgotten 'the other matters' and that, as soon as he arrived at the prison where he would serve most of his sentence, he could write to her and, if his general record warranted it, she would try to shorten his preventive detention, as this was reviewed from time-to-time. She would not be manipulated by him, but set clear boundaries.

We might expect this to be the end of the story: he was a convicted con-man who had not managed to exploit her. However, in December 1937, Cheshunt wrote further to Helena from Parkhurst.[105] He described himself as being in 'good health' and that his spirits had returned to how they were in his college days, 'I have made an appalling waste of my life.' He wrote that he had experienced in the few months at Parkhurst more real introspection than he had in all his life: 'the result? — I'm through with all this nonsense. I shall yet get to the top of the ladder.' He described how he had learnt four languages in prison and was reading copious amounts of literature. The 'black sheep,' he continued, was not broken, 'he is captive only.' His letter explains his determination to turn his life around and that he would win whether he had anyone who cared for him or not and he would not forget that she wished him well. She clearly had made a major impact on his life and he told her that if he never saw her again he would not forget that she wished him well and would not forget their 'long talk.' He described her as not being like the other lawyers, not after money; rather she was doing some good in life. He finished by wishing her a Merry Christmas and saying that he was not bitter, rather paying his bill as he had been wicked.

We have no direct evidence of what was said in that 'long talk.' In a letter to Sir Alexander Maxwell, Principal Under-Secretary of State at the Home Office,[106] Helena explained that Cheshunt had asked to speak to his lady counsel after he was sentenced, as he had no family in the world, and he had urged her to tell him how he was to bear his sentence. She advised him to learn languages, never thinking that he would take her advice. The following year,[107] Helena wrote to the Governor of Parkhurst, asking if she could send Cheshunt a card and also give a foreign language book (for him) to the library. This must have been allowed as Cheshunt wrote[108] thanking her for her continued kindness. He felt she had kept her word. He recounted that his languages were improving (Italian, French, German and Spanish). Poignantly, he added that her cards and books cheered him up, 'You are unlike most women, you are rather more to be compared to a man. For your word is not an empty one.' He said that the Governor knew her reputation and granted all she asked for. She must have been sending him money, as he says that he did not want to spend her money as her 'friendship is enough.' She replied almost immediately[109] that she was glad to receive his letter and was sending a parcel of books.[110]

In February 1939 Helena wrote to the Governor of Parkhurst[111] almost in her capacity as a teacher. She was concerned that Cheshunt needed to further his studies by translating English into the other language. She had been unable to find a suitable book and so was sending a calendar of 'Great Thoughts' by separate post addressed to the Governor. She felt that if Cheshunt could translate the sentence for each day into a language he was learning it might be useful. She asked if Cheshunt 'may have' the calendar? And if it was not too much trouble could the Governor write to her and tell her if any help is given to convicts to gain the right pronunciation? She ended with a request for information. 'I am certainly somewhat impressed by this man's perseverance; that is to say if he is telling me the whole truth, but as his record was an extremely bad one I cannot give full credence to what he says without some word of confirmation from yourself.' The Governor replied two days later[112] informing her that they had a complete set of Linguaphone records. He admitted that he did not know how much private study Cheshunt did, but had advised him to see the chaplain. He obviously recognised Helena's desire for an account of Cheshunt's behaviour as he finished with 'Cheshunt is going on very well. He is well behaved and in a position of trust.' The letters continued in much the same way, but we have no knowledge of what happened to Cheshunt on his release.

Cheshunt was not the only client with whom Helena kept in touch. The *Daily Express*[113] reported that two women played parts in a drama at the Old Bailey during a case regarding James Barney (Mason)[114] who pleaded guilty to breaking into a shop. He had been released early for a previous crime and was sentenced to a nominal day's imprisonment for this offence and 20 months in Dartmoor for the unexpired sentence. Apparently both Helena, as his barrister, and Barney's wife pleaded for him, to no avail. The wife said that this was the first time that he had been given a chance. She related how they had met in Dublin and he had been honest with her about his criminal past. He went 'straight' for six years but, on his return to London, he met some of his old friends and returned to crime. In their 16 years of marriage she had only been with him for seven years. He had promised her, this time, to put his life of crime behind him.

Two years later Barney wrote to Helena explaining that he was at the end of his sentence and needed her help to win an early release.[115] Apparently she had told him previously that she might know of a builder who would employ him. Helena replied immediately saying that there was no hope of the builder but that she would try to help.[116] He desperately related his past work experience[117] in another letter.[118] Helena sadly replied that she could not make arrangements for a man who was not free and wished him luck.[119] He wrote to her again[120] thanking her for her help and saying that he understood that she could not do more in this 'hopeless matter' and that it was the 'difficulty of first getting a job that gets prisoners down.' He said that he would honestly go straight and that he would peddle newspapers first.

They must have kept in touch as Helena received a letter from Barney in September 1939[121] thanking her for her endeavours on his behalf. He wrote that he wished that he could do more to help her. He said that he was not a competent typist but could use a machine. He wrote that he was willing to work at anything—hard manual work, housework, clerical, organizing or executive. He wrote of the difficulties that prisoners suffered when trying to find a job with a criminal record and no references. He said that he would work day or night to make good, he just wanted to go straight and be a normal citizen. He said that he would be pleased to tend her garden, clean her car, windows or scrub the floors, that he was a good plain cook and 'housewife,' he could redecorate a room, glaze, paint a window or do odd jobs. He must have gone for a job interview because he wrote to her a week later informing her that he did not get the job because of the economic situation.[122] He said that he had seen someone at the Old Bailey and showed him her recommendation, but all that could be done was to send him to the Prisoners Aid Society, who gave him a letter to the Public Assistance Board. They too were unable to help him. He said sadly that he was 'now back where he started—nowhere and am on the verge of destitution. But I am strong, healthy, willing & anxious to exist in freedom.' He said that he now faced eviction, 'Do people realise how hard it is for men like me to come back?' He thanked her from the bottom of his heart and wished that he could show her that he was not a 'slacker'.

She clearly helped him by providing references as he wrote to her again with 'good news.' [123] He had been employed by the Church Army. He ensured her that he would not let her down and with her references he was an 'armed man'. He enthused that what she had done meant a new life for him and his wife.[124] That was not the end of the story as he wrote to her one final time saying that he had 'better news,'[125] he had a job in Pimlico at £3 per week (in this financial year she made just £10 from her practice) with food vouchers. He returned the money that she had sent him (2/6d) with sincere thanks.

Cheshunt and Barney were not the only prisoners that she helped and wrote to. Her files at the Women's Library contain many such letters from prisoners.[126] Why did she reply to them and take such an interest in their futures? Why did she write letters of recommendation and send money? This was not the job of a barrister where the cab rank rule applied. She obviously spent time with her clients and tried to sort their lives out, not just their cases. She was working in a social work role rather than just that of a barrister. This perhaps did not seem very professional to solicitors. She was not behaving as a typical lawyer. Her behaviour may have been interpreted as too feminine and 'motherly' to make her a credible barrister.

The Bar: A career for a woman?

Helena was very much the pioneer for the whole of her legal life. The numbers of women called to the Bar illustrate that there was not a great clamour of women attempting to join the Inns, the floodgates had not been opened. Many women were aware of the difficulties of life at the Bar. For example, Beatrice Honor Davy wrote, 'for a woman who must earn her own living the Bar is the very last profession in the world'.[127] She became a solicitor. Similarly, Winifred Holtby wrote that 'It is still impossible for many able women to make a living from the law.'[128] D W Hughes wrote that any woman choosing to go to the Bar 'needs to be a woman of exceptional determination.' In a careers guide, Willes (1938) advised boys to go to the Bar, but wrote, 'I cannot fairly and honestly state that at the present time (whatever may come to pass or lie hidden in the future of a "progressive" or rapidly changing world) practice at the Bar, in this country is a career which a woman or girl, even though possessed of exceptional ability, could be advised to adopt without serious misgivings.'[129] Another careers guide in 1955 stated 'the chances of any woman following her [Rose Heilbron] as a successful barrister are fairly remote.'[130] It advised them to be solicitors instead.

Helena herself wrote in December 1932[131] that she had just read an article by Lady Oxford who said that the Bar was not a suitable profession for women. Helena pointed to examples such as Florence Nightingale and Jane Austen (who had to hide her manuscripts). She railed that the whole article was years out of date. She felt it a great pity that, just because a woman has title, she is used as an authority. She finished by arguing that Lady Oxford's husband, as Mr Asquith, did not earn as much money in his early years at the Bar as many women were making in their early years. 'She was clearly trying promote a positive message about women at the Bar.

Helena would have been aware of the pitfalls of practice, she would have been aware of the hurdles facing her. This would have been a common understanding amongst the women who tried to practice, Enid Rosser for example, explained:

'Most of the distinguished gentlemen who encouraged me to try my luck warned me that I could never expect to rise to any height in the profession as woman ever would. Malcolm Macnaghten, who was one of the most enthusiastic, said it was worth doing because the world for some inexplicable reason thought too highly of the qualification of having been called to the Bar so that it opened the way to many forms of work especially if you could manage to be in chambers of repute for a few years and be able to call our self a practising member of the Bar. As he rightly and cynically said no one except your clerk knew what your practice was worth financially. They all urged me to start at the criminal bar because there was always work to be picked up if only dock briefs and minor prosecutions which came your way by virtue of being a member of the Bar Mess attached to the Old Bailey and the Quarter Sessions of whatever circuit you joined.'[132]

The Bar was equally a precarious profession for men, but Helena's tenacity and determined attitude to practice as a barrister meant that she remained in practice.

CHAPTER 9

Campaigns

'Anne Boleyn did not change her name even though she married the King. He at least had the decency to leave [her] with her own name even though he took her head.'

Helena Normanton, 1954[1]

Helena remained married to her husband until his death in 1948 but she was well aware that other women's experiences of marriage were less happy.[2] Her archives contain many letters from women begging for help because they were trapped in difficult marriages.[3] Although her ambition in life was to open up the Bar to women she also campaigned fearlessly for other feminist causes, such as equal treatment with regard to divorce, the right of British women married to foreigners to keep their name and citizenship[4] and tax reform.[5] This chapter focuses on her campaign to equalise divorce law, as this was central to her practice.

In 1921 (the year of her marriage) the only way for women or men to seek a divorce in England and Wales was through the Matrimonial Causes Act 1857.[6] Previously, divorce could only be obtained through a Private Act of Parliament.[7] Before 1857, a man wishing to divorce his wife had to show that the wife had committed adultery, that he had not and that there was no collusion between the two parties. There was a sexual double standard as the wife, on asking for a divorce, had to prove aggravated adultery.[8] Divorce was a lengthy process as, first, the party asking for it was required to petition the Ecclesiastical Courts for a *mensa et thoro*[9] in order for the couple to live separately, then they had to seek a judgment in their favour for *criminal conversation* and, finally, apply for a Private Act of Parliament. This was expensive and time-consuming.[10]

The 1857 Act significantly improved the process of obtaining a divorce, but largely maintained the previous limited and unequal grounds. The legislation did not arise primarily from concern for divorce reform, rather it was a result of a need of an industrialised country to reform the laws regarding probate.[11] In 1857 the Ecclesiastical Courts were dissolved in respect of divorce and probate. The new courts of Probate and Divorce and Matrimonial Causes were created. The 1857 legislation followed the old grounds for divorce exactly. A man could divorce his wife if he could prove she had committed adultery (Sections 27 and 31). A wife wishing to obtain a divorce had to prove under section 27 that her husband had committed aggravated adultery; this meant adultery plus incest, bigamy, desertion for two years, cruelty, rape, sodomy or bestiality.[12] Even this somewhat more accessible procedure was subject to a key practical constraint: the divorce court, created by the Act, only sat in London. This further added to the legal costs and other costs of those living outside London. The underlying policy was that marriage should remain sacrosanct although the law should not be so harsh that it would lead to the formation of illicit unions.[13]

In 1892 a Bill was introduced by Dr William Hunter[14] who wanted to extend the grounds for divorce. There was no intention by him to create any kind of equality between the sexes. It was rejected.[15] In 1902 a second Bill was introduced by the Second Earl Russell in which he proposed divorce should be allowed on the grounds of adultery, cruelty, living apart for three years or living apart for one year if both parties agreed, a prison sentence of more than three years or insanity. This was rejected and when he proposed it the following year it was again rejected. It was claimed that such an Act would 'abolish marriage'.[16]

In 1909 the Royal Commission on Divorce and Matrimonial Causes (the Gorell Commission) was asked to consider divorce reform, but they failed to agree their findings. The majority report suggested that divorce be allowed in cases of adultery, desertion for three years, cruelty, insanity, habitual drunkenness and imprisonment under a commuted death sentence. No new legislation was proposed because of a lack of consensus. In 1918, Lord Buckmaster introduced a Bill that would allow divorce on the basis of five years desertion, this was also rejected. He would reintroduce his Bill in 1924 designed to relieve human agony, but again it would be rejected.

In 1923 the National Union of Societies for Equal Citizenship[17] (NUSEC, a group for which Helena sat on the Legal Profession and Sex Disabilities Special Committee until 1920, when it was disbanded) introduced a Bill which proposed equal grounds for divorce between husbands and wives. This became law on July 18 1923 by virtue of section 1 Matrimonial Causes Act 1923.[18] Women could now also divorce their husbands on the grounds of his simple adultery. This satisfied NUSEC's desire for equality but did nothing further to reform the law. Without adultery there could be no divorce. This was a blow for reformers. Divorce continued to be expensive and adultery the only ground. It did nothing if a party had been deserted or treated cruelly. Many couples had to remain married or co-habiting with a new partner as one or both could not afford a divorce.[19] In 1858 there were 244 divorce petitions, in 1914, 1,000 and more than 10,000 in 1942, following further changes in the law.[20]

Helena had an ally in her fight to enter the Bar, Holford Knight. He, like Lord Buckmaster tirelessly campaigned for women's admission to the legal profession. Also, like Lord Buckmaster, he was a divorce reformer. He identified a factor that the Gorell Commission had drawn out: that insanity was a large problem in the failure of marriage. In 1930 he proposed a Bill which would have allowed divorce on the grounds of insanity for a period of five years.[21] His Bill failed on two occasions. He tried again in 1934 to introduce the majority proposals of the Gorell Commission and again failed.

Helena was very involved in this issue. Her strong views on divorce can be found in a letter to a Mrs Gray dated 15 April 1935 where she argued that the grounds for divorce should be extended.[22] She was concerned about the irregular partnerships that arose where people could not get divorced and about the high cost of divorce. She felt that the law was corrupt and encouraged immorality because people who realised that their marriages were over had to commit adultery or pretend to be adulterous (say by being photographed outside a hotel in compromising circumstances: *Chapter 7*).[23] She pointed out that even the Orthodox church of Bulgaria allowed extensive grounds for divorce including infidelity, gambling, attempt to murder, or cruelty to children. She was radical (but not alone[24]) concerning divorce. Her involvement in divorce reform was formalised in 1932 when she was appointed as honorary secretary and legal adviser to the newly created National Council for Equal Citizenship.[25] She was required 'to survey the whole field of inequality in the law between men and women, and to provide for an expert legal examination of Bills dealing with these subjects which come before Parliament.'[26] This committee was asked to consider the marriage laws and the question of testamentary provision. This gave her an official reason to consider divorce reform, rather than in her role as barrister, a role, which we saw earlier, involved her being wary of self-advertising.

She wrote an article for the *Daily Herald*[27] in January 1934 describing the divorce laws as 'outworn.' She discussed a disturbing divorce case in which she had acted for the wife[28] who petitioned for divorce from her imprisoned husband (for attempting to murder her); he was counter-claiming custody of their sole child. The wife was only able to gain a divorce as she could prove his adultery before he tried to kill her. If he had not committed adultery she would have had no redress. Helena lamented Holford Knight's failed Bill, an embodiment of the Majority Report of the Royal Commission on Divorce of 1912. Her Scrapbook noted:

> 'The *Daily Herald* was anxious for me to write a Divorce law Reform article under the heading of the Benson case, but as I had appeared for the petitioner I asked to wait for a month until my own name as Counsel should have faded from the public memory. I also consulted the BAR COUNCIL in great detail about this article and fully complied with their views. HN.'[29]

Also in 1934, A P Herbert published a novel called *Holy Deadlock*[30] which highlighted the difficulties of the divorce law. It sold 90,000 copies.[31] The following year he stood for election as an independent for one of the two Oxford University seats in Parliament. University graduates were allowed to vote in their home constituency *and* in their university constituency. He was elected and immediately introduced a Divorce Bill, along the lines of the Gorell majority recommendations, but with some differences: no divorce for the *first* five years, but grounds for divorce after three years included cruelty, insanity, drunkenness and a commuted death sentence. Helena was furious about the clause prohibiting divorce during the first five years of marriage. This would become a great source of controversy. She declared that this was a 'cowardly capitulation to reactionary ecclesiastics, who would rather never see young people free to marry.'[32] She was being unrealistic: some compromise was necessary since there was strong opposition to modification of the law.

The women's movement was active. In July 1934[33] Helena received a letter from the National Council for Equal Citizenship (NCEC)[34] informing her that their resolution on reform of the matrimonial law had been placed on the National Council of Women's agenda for their annual meeting in Edinburgh. It did not mention anything about the proposed provision that there could be no divorce within the first five years of marriage. The resolution read as follows:

'This Council holds that, as divorce cannot now be obtained unless adultery (or, on the part of the husband unnatural conduct) be proved, the present law both encourages immorality and leads to much individual hardship. This council therefore urges the Government to carry out the recommendations of the Majority Report of the Royal Commission on the Divorce Laws 1912 or to support legislation such as has been twice passed by the House of Lords by which the grounds for divorce for both husband and wife shall include adultery, desertion after three years, persistent cruelty, habitual drunkenness, incurable insanity after five years confinement, or imprisonment under the commuted death sentence. It further urges that all the inequalities between men and women be removed.'

Helena was asked to attend the meeting and propose the resolution. Ever fearful of being accused of self-advertising, she wrote to the Bar Council[35] informing them that she would be proposing, at the Annual Conference of the National Council of Women, in Edinburgh, a resolution advocating reform of the matrimonial law upon the lines suggested by the Royal Commission of 1912. She asked for permission to quote a judge in the case of *Benson v Benson* where he commented upon the deficiencies in matrimonial law. They replied that this was acceptable but that she must not mention that she was counsel.[36]

In early October 1934, she addressed the conference in Edinburgh.[37] Her notes outline her argument. This was that it was very difficult to advocate reform of the English matrimonial law for three reasons: extreme theologies, the professors who believed that to change the law would render England a replica of Hollywood or Reno, and because there were vast numbers of apathetic people-either single or happily married, who could not visualise the suffering of others. She then outlined the *Benson* case. She finished:

> 'The Christian ideal connotes monogamous union of complete fidelity...it is difficult to see how this ideal can be carried out where habitual drunkenness, incurable insanity or life imprisonment is in fact separating the parties and it might be far kinder to set the unhappy free so that they could enter into other and better unions where it might be possible to try to attain the highest ideals.'[38]

The resolution was passed, even though the Mothers' Union (not surprisingly perhaps) strongly opposed her suggested reform, arguing that marriage was indissoluble.[39] Parts of the resolution were incorporated into a modified version of A P Herbert's Bill.

The success of the resolution was not a foregone conclusion, Helena was fearful that her resolution would not be passed. She wrote that:

> 'I was little depressed by the reception on Monday evening [after her speech] as no one I spoke to seemed to think that the resolution would go through, as the Mothers' Union had been doing hard work against it. I also had information to this effect before I left London and you may have seen the attack in the Queen upon the resolution by the Countess of Selbourne. However that attack will be virtually replied to by an article by myself in this or next week's number...'[40]

She expressed her relief that it was passed, '...It went through by a very large majority and Lady Nunburnholme did not even think it necessary to have a count to see if the necessary two-thirds had been obtained.' She admitted that she had deliberately avoided being provocative. She commented that she had not attended the conference for years and thought that the standard of intelligence 'has gone up enormously from what it used to be.' She felt it evident that the NCW had become a far more progressive body than it used to be. Her proposal was seen by some as a 'triumph'.[41] However others were not so enamoured, for example the *Scottish Guardian* (a church paper) said women like Helena recalled

'the stirring times before the war, and the atmosphere of violence and law resistance by which the way was prepared for Communism and fascism ... Mrs Normanton who pontifically directs the reading of the great body of women who peruse the popular magazine *Good Housekeeping* ... presented the case for easier divorce ... Mrs Normanton, promoted to the rank of General Council for the Catholic Church ...'[42]

She threatened them with an action for libel.[43] Lady Nunburnholme wrote to Helena advising her that the NCW would not be taking the newspaper report further, rather they would be writing to the Bishop of Aberdeen and Orkney about it.[44]

She campaigned for reform as ferociously as she had done for the opening of the legal profession to women. For example she was invited to by the NCEC[45] to speak at their conference on Marriage Law Reform,[46] to which she agreed[47] saying that the task of marriage reformers was heavy because the 'enemy is vigilant and unscrupulous.' In January 1935, she agreed to speak to the Portsmouth Women Citizens' Association on Matrimonial Law.[48] These women's groups were pressuring for divorce reform. In March 1935 at the annual council meeting[49] of the NCEC it was noted that the law on dissolution of marriage was unequal and the grounds too narrow, the fact that divorce was only allowed for adultery led to unavoidable immorality, and the law inflicted great hardship. They were of the opinion that the sanctity and dignity of marriage were assailed by large numbers of irregular unions, respect for the law was undermined and they demanded the reforms proposed in the Gorell majority report.

Helena did not believe that the Herbert Bill was the way forward. She wrote detailed 'observations'[50] on it, which must have been her private views on the Bill. This is a long document that goes through the Bill in minute detail. To give a flavour, she commented:[51]

'The Bill's drafting is extremely defective, and if placed upon the Statute book without drastic amendment would cause more troubles than it would ever cure. It is also notable that it entirely omits any dealing with the injustices which arise under Variation of Settlements, Permanent Maintenance, and Alimony. These however are not very numerous and rarely serious.'

She believed that allowing no decree of divorce until after five years of marriage was a 'cruel piece of tyranny,' that the grounds for divorce were 'prima facie fairly satisfactory' but on jurisdiction and domicile the clauses were 'a miserable and nibbling attempt to deal with this issue.' She wrote to the NCEC that she was very worried about the Bill and the NCEC resolution on it.[52] She added that she should receive 10–15 guineas from the NCEC for her work on her legal opinion, she did not want the money but did want to hear that it has been 'considered and suitably used.'

Helena's strong views can be found in a letter in April 1935[53] in which she argued that the grounds for divorce should be extended due to irregular partnerships which arose because the law denied people divorce. The costs of divorce also concerned her, but Christian arguments did not as she countered that even the Orthodox church of Bulgaria advocated extensive grounds for divorce (above). Almost a year later in March 1936 the NCEC held its annual council meeting in which they proposed that the majority report of the Gorell Commission be enacted. That was uncontroversial, but there was much discussion over whether additional clauses should be inserted such as:

1. Divorce where there was mutual consent after waiting five years, or
2. A stipulation that there be no divorce until two years had elapsed and that the marriage had lasted for more than two years or less than 20.[54]

In November 1936 Herbert's Bill had its second reading in the House of Commons. Very few voted for or against it, but it passed. His strategy of not making divorce too easy by providing that it would be impossible within the first five years of marriage was effective.

In January 1937, Helena became increasingly concerned about the NCEC discussions and asked them to ask the Government formally to appoint a commission to consider what extensions were necessary to the grounds for relief under the 1923 matrimonial law of England in respect of cases of irremediable collapse of a marriage upon medical, psychological, and similar grounds; and what, if any, safeguards were necessary for providing for the dissolution of such unions.[55] She informed the NCEC that, if they were not prepared to do this, it would her duty to move the question and she would rather not be put in that awkward situation.

Meanwhile Herbert's Bill was moving through Parliament. In June 1937 it reached the House of Lords. There was great opposition and Herbert inserted a clause that there could be no divorce petition presented in the first three years of marriage.[56] This enabled the Act to be passed on 30 July 1937. It came into operation on January 1 1938.

It seems clear from Helena's correspondence that she was deeply unhappy that the divorce law was too conservative. Further evidence of her beliefs can be seen from her membership[57] of the Divorce Law Reform Union.[58] In November 1938 their literature warned of people thinking that the law had been reformed, when it was inadequate. However, she wrote two private letters to Marie Stopes that seem to contradict her campaigns. In January 1939,[59] whilst discussing the marriage bar, she wrote 'that a married woman cannot honourably contract two incompatible contracts at the same time.' What did this mean? That married women had to carry out their household duties before work? Stopes replied evenly:

'As women I do not think we ought to sit down under the idea that the "legal contract" of marriage should be incompatible with any other contract. Indeed it is not, and I do wish that we could all get together and get something effective done about this question, particularly in connection with schools where it has a very bad social reaction that marriage should be considered a bar.'[60]

Helena answered immediately saying that she had not made herself clear in her last letter as she was under great pressure and wanted to be clear that she did not mean that the law alone makes the marriage contract incompatible with the contract of employment:

'For instance, a marriage contract in itself implies that each partner will give companionship to the other, but at the same time it does sometimes happen that a wife accepts some other sort of engagement which makes it impossible for her to fulfil the obligations of companionship. For example, she may be an opera star and plan to take a long tour, whereas, her husband is a Civil servant and may not be able to accompany her on this tour unless he loses his job. Where each is agreeable to this mode of life, of course, no particular harm is done and some sort of affectionate relationship may possibly exist over long absences and distances. But if there is no consent then probably the first contract would be considered to have priority over the second and the second would probably be considered as infringing the first; whether it were the marriage or the tour…What I really meant was that no honourable person ought to plan his or her life so that incompatible contracts were not made simultaneously…When a woman's marriage does not make a continued gainful career an impossibility, and where she can do adequate justice to the marriage, of course I am quite with you in saying that outside compulsion on her to abandon her career is wicked and tyrannical.'

What was she trying to say? It is clear that she applied these principles to men as well as women. Did she mean women could have a career only where the husband agreed? Was the reverse true? That women were obliged to be a companion to their husbands, again, was the reverse true? Could women only work if there were gainful employment? Could women only work if they could do adequate justice to the marriage? What did adequate justice mean? She herself went to America three years after her marriage and was not 'gainfully' employed at the Bar. Would she have stopped working if her husband demanded that she were not being a proper companion? It contradicts the views she expressed to the NCEC.

Despite the Matrimonial Causes Act 1937, there were still extreme difficulties in obtaining a divorce, such as when one party refused to co-operate[61] and divorce remained extremely expensive. Not until legal aid was introduced in 1949 did it become easier for wives to access the courts on the same scale as their husbands[62] (although cost had been a problem for many men, and the problem of gaining a divorce if one party refused continued). By 1945 there was a divorce crisis because the courts could not cope with demand.[63]

By 1952 Helena was President of the Married Women's Association (MWA).[64] The MWA had been set up in 1938, after the failure of the Six Point Group[65] to persuade the League of Nations to incorporate an Equal Rights Treaty that would promote legislation in England and Wales for equality for married women.

The MWA's objective was to secure the rights of housewives, including by promoting legislation to regulate married couple's finances and create equality between those parties. Further, they wanted to ensure that both husbands and wives had equal parenting rights and that married women gained a right to the matrimonial home.[66] Various groups such as the British Medical Association (BMA) and the MWA gave evidence to a Royal Commission on Marriage and Divorce (1951–56), which reported in 1956.[67] Helena, as president, and as passionate believer in divorce reform was extremely active in promoting reform.[68] She prepared the evidence that the MWA submitted.[69] This caused great controversy and ultimately a split in the association.[70] She proposed that the husband and wife should have a fairer financial partnership, by virtue of the husband paying the wife an allowance either agreed by them or adjudicated upon by the courts. If the wife was guilty of wilful neglect (of the money) she should be answerable in law for this.[71] Members of the MWA complained that this had been submitted to the Royal Commission[72] without consultation or circulation, and they felt that this made wives subordinate — being paid pocket money and it was not a true partnership. Further they felt that her proposals only benefitted privileged women and other women remained at a disadvantage.

As a result Helena withdrew her report and pronounced that the MWA suggestion that couples should pool resources was 'nonsensical rubbish', that it was 'dangerous for a wife ... and unfair to a husband.'[73] This demonstrates her notion of social duty and responsibility and desire to equalise the relationship between husbands and wives. She believed in individual property rights and that neither spouse was entitled to the earnings of the other spouse. She was liberal in her ideology and fell short of a more radical approach that recognised the experience of other women who were unpaid within the home and had been restricted for generations by law and custom.

As a result of this disagreement Helena founded her own breakaway group, the Council of Married Women (CMW).[74] She was joined by the chair of the MWA, Lady Doreen Gorsky, the MWA's deputy chair, Lady Helen Nutting, and the MWA's honorary secretary, Evelyn Hamilton.[75] They took up identical positions in the CMW.

The CMW sought to support and promote marriage, but wanted to ensure that married women were equal to their husbands.[76] They wanted to propose a Bill in Parliament that would ensure that wives were given a portion of the family income after all the household expenses had been paid. The idea was that a wife's role should be recognised by society as a job and therefore as valuable as a working husband's. It was intended to promote and enhance a wife's standing in the public sphere; her work should be considered valuable. Helena sought to equalise the relationship between husbands and wives.

Not until 1969 would there be a new rationale behind divorce.[77] Helena died in 1957 and so did not live to see this reform, one she had campaigned for at great personal expense. Through the 1960s the CMW encountered financial difficulties and the organization's work largely devolved upon Lady Nutting alone. The body was wound up in 1969.

Other interests

We saw earlier that Helena was part of a network of women calling for equality such as in relation to divorce, the right of British women married to foreigners to keep their name and citizenship[78] and tax reform.[79] Her life was surrounded by political campaigns and agendas as well as her work to support herself. She was treasurer of the Bar mess of the Central Criminal Court and arranged social functions for the barristers who practised there.[80] She was Grand Dean for Europe of the International Sorority of Women Lawyers (Kappa Beta Pi),[81] chair of the International Federation of Business and Professional Women,[82] as well as an executive member of the NCEC, executive member of the State Children's Associations, first secretary of the NWA, founder and honorary secretary of the Magna Carta Society and founding member of the Horatian Society. In 1925 she was elected a member of the New York Women's Bar Association.[83] She had a *Diploma Ami de la Cite de Paris*.[84] Bridgeman[85] noted that Helena marched against the atom bomb in 1953.[86] She had a keen love for Shakespeare and enjoyed cooking and gardening.[87]

Social justice and firm beliefs

We have seen from this chapter that Helena had a strong notion of social justice, rights accompanied by their corresponding duties. Clearly some other women perceived her divorce campaign as anti-feminist, but Helena merely promoted equality. On the one hand she wanted to protect women from husbands who did not provide for their families and to equalise this she proposed that women should be responsible if they misappropriated the housekeeping money. She strongly believed that neither party to a marriage was entitled to the other's wealth. She did not believe in the pooling of resources but rather equal parties with their own finances. Sadly, this did not take into account many women's real social and economic position.

CHAPTER 10

Helena's Death

'In her last letter she was quite philosophic about death, she knew it was imminent, and it was wonderful to see her stoicism ... I tried so hard to get her to write her life, so rich, so full—but in vain.'

Extract of a sympathy letter from Herbert Marshall, November 1957[1]

Helena Normanton's niece, Elsie Cannon, wrote about the events leading to Helena's death.[2] She described how being made King's Counsel came too late for her, as she was already suffering poor health and her husband had died: 'She was too old and tired to forge a new career as a Silk. She virtually ceased to practise, but didn't officially retire until about 1951'. Then, in 1954, Helena had a coronary and became less active. This led her to consider her will and she made a new one, which centred on the idea of establishing a university in Sussex.

Helena's health declined. Cannon described her as 'lonely and life became difficult.' The Beckenham house was too big 'but crammed to overflowing with furniture, pictures, books, papers and so on, she lacked the energy to organize a move' and refused to allow anyone to help. During the summer of 1957 she became worse. On 14 October 1957 she died 'peacefully' in a Sydenham nursing home.[3] She had a private funeral and cremation at Croydon Crematorium on 18 October. Her ashes were buried with her husband's in November 1957 in Ovingdean Churchyard, Sussex. It was a simple ceremony attended by friends and family.

Her will left £22,919 in total[4] (over £500,000 today). It determined that the interest on the capital of her estate would be split between Elsie and her mother (after payment of bequests) for their lifetimes, and the capital itself be given to the University of Sussex if it came into existence (as it did in 1961). Helena had a happy and positive experience in

Sussex: she was schooled in Brighton and she and her husband had spent many holidays there.[5] She wrote in her will that her estate should pass to the University College of Sussex 'in gratitude for all that Brighton did to educate me when I was left an orphan.' It had been her ideal to establish a university in the county; she sent the first cheque towards its foundation.[6]

Ultimately her legacy was far greater and not confined to her property money or estate. By fulfilling her childhood ambition and playing a key role in opening up the Bar to women she paved the way for generations of women to come. She also helped change the law through her writings and involvement in a range of campaigns, her membership of (mostly feminist) groups and organizations across a long and active career and due to her personal determination. As Helena herself modestly concluded:

'I felt that I had done enough.'[7]

Endnotes

Notes to Foreword

1. Carol Sanger, 'Curriculum Vitae (Feminae): Biography and Early American Women Lawyers', 1994, 46 *Stanford Law Review,* 1245 at 1257.
2. Joan Wallach Scott, 'American Women Historians, 1884–1984' in Scott J. W. *Gender and the Politics of History*, New York: Columbia University Press, 1999. p 178 at p.179.
3. Paula Backscheider, *Reflections on Biography*, Oxford: Oxford University Press, 1999, at p.59.

Notes to Introduction

1. This was argued in Riley, D. *Am I That Name? Feminism in the Category of 'Women' in History*, Basingstoke: Macmillan, 1988, pp.67–95.
2. Purvis, J. 'Doing Feminist Women's History: Researching the Lives of Women in the Suffragette Movement in Edwardian England' in Maynard, M. and Purvis, J. (eds.), *Researching Women's Lives From a Feminist Perspective*, London: Taylor and Francis, 1994, p.167.
3. Alpern, S. et al. *The Challenges Facing Feminist Biography: Writing the Lives of Modern American Women*, University of Illinois Press, 1992, p.3.

Notes to Chapter 1

1. Normanton, Helena, *Everyday Law for Women*, 1st edn., Richard Clay & Sons, 1932, p.6.
2. See *Chapter 2*.
3. There was a strong philanthropic movement in the late 19th-century that she would have been aware of and may have been part of to further her mission to help other women, see Prochaska, F. K. *Women and Philanthropy in Nineteenth-Century*

England. Oxford: Clarendon Press, 1980.
4. *Code of Conduct of the Bar of England and Wales and Guidance*, General Council of the Bar of England and Wales, 2000.
5. For example Chrystal Macmillan, Sybil Oldfield, 'Macmillan (Jessie) Chrystal (1872–1937)' *Oxford Dictionary of National Biography*, Oxford: University Press, 2004. Macmillan was a Scottish mathematician who qualified at the Bar in 1924 and was a member of Middle Temple. She saw her role as one of promoting women's rights and world peace. Her life and career have been researched by Rose Pipes, who informed me that the Bar was a means of philanthropy rather than a source of income for her.
6. England and Wales, Free BMD Index, Jan-Feb-March 1883, Vol 4a, Page 14.
7. The spelling of his surname varies in different records.
8. *The Times*, 16 October 1957.
9. Her birth certificate and the census records for 1891 and 1901 state that her place of birth was Stratford in the District of West Ham, Essex.
10. Although the inquest report into his death states his occupation as a pianoforte tuner. He was recorded as a piano maker in the 1881 Census, as was his father.
11. England and Wales Free BMD Birth Index, Jan-Feb-March 1851, West Ham, Vol.12, p.338.
12. Death certificate dated 3rd July 1886.
13. Notes on inquest from *Lloyd's Weekly Newspaper*, Issue 2276, Sunday 4 July 1886.
14. See Elsie Cannon's notes, Women's Library (hereafter WL) 7HLN/C/09.
15. Thane, P. *Happy Families/ History and Family Policy*, British Academy Policy Centre, 2011 and Thane, P. and Evans, T. *Sinners? Scroungers? Saints?: Unmarried Motherhood in Twentieth Century England*, Oxford: Oxford University Press, 2012.
16. Shanley, M. L. '"One Must Ride Behind": Married Women's Rights and the Divorce

Act 1857', *Victorian Studies,* 25, 1982.

17. According to Elsie Cannon, in Willington Street. This cannot necessarily be relied on, but there is no suggestion that she intended to deceive; rather that recollections cannot always be trusted.

18. This would have been between 1891 and Helena's entry to Varndean in 1895.

19. Masson, J., Bailey-Harris, R. and Probert, R. *Cretney's Principles of Family Law,* 8th edn., Thomson Sweet & Maxwell, 2008 at 3–002 and 3–006. This is dealt with in *Chapter 2.*

20. Earning a living as a single mother was difficult: Hudson, P. and Lee, W. R. *Women's Work and the Family Economy in Historical Perspective,* Manchester: Manchester University Press, 1990; and Thane, P. 'Women and the Poor Law in Victorian and Edwardian England', *History Workshop Journal,* 6(1): 29–51 (1978).

21. Royal Infant/Orphan Asylum, Wanstead. Information supplied by Elsie Cannon, WL: 7HLN/C/09.

22. Ibid.

23. Ibid.

24. Ibid.

25. See Gleadle, K. *British Women in the 19th Century,* Palgrave Macmillan, 2001; and Purvis, J. *Hard Lessons: The Lives and Education of Working Women in Nineteenth Century England,* Cambridge: Polity Press, 1989.

26. Cannon, op cit.

27. This was true for many families, see Thane, 2011, op cit; Davidoff, L. '"Mastered for Life": Servants and Wives in Victorian and Edwardian England' in Davidoff, L *Worlds Between: Historical Perspectives on Gender and Class,* Cambridge: Polity Press, 1995 and Gillis, J. R. *For Better, For Worse: British Marriages, 1600 to the Present,* Oxford: Oxford University Press, 1985.

28. Sachs, A. and Wilson, J. H. *Sexism and the Law: A Study of Male Beliefs and Legal Bias in Britain and the United States,* Oxford: Martin Robertson, 1978.

29. For example *Jex-Blake v Senatus of Edinburgh University* (1873) 11 M. 784 at 790–795.

30. *Chorlton v Lings* (1868) LR 4 CP 374 at 388. In this case Mary Abbott challenged the fact that she was not on the electoral register. It was held that the word 'man' had been used deliberately in the Representation of the People Act 1867 to exclude all except men. This was supposedly because it was a privilege of the female sex not to vote.

31. Thane, P. 'Women and the Poor Law in Victorian and Edwardian England', *History Workshop Journal* 6 (1978); Dyhouse, C. *Feminism and the Family in England 1880–1939* New: York Basil Blackwell, 1989 and Perkin, J. *Women and Marriage in Nineteenth Century England* Chicago: Lyceum, 1989.

32. Jeffreys, S. *The Spinster and Her Enemies: Feminism and Sexuality 1880–1930* Spinifex 1995; Israel, B. *Bachelor Girl: 100 Years of Breaking the Rules—A Social History of Living Single* New York: HarperCollins, 2003; Vicinus, M. *Independent Women: Work and Community for Single Women, 1850–1920,* London: Virago Press, 1985.

33. See Anderson, M. 'The Social Implications of Demographic Change' in Chapter 1. Thompson F. M. L. (ed.) *The Cambridge Social History of Britain 1750–1950,* Vol.2, Cambridge: Cambridge University Press, 2008.

34. This Act allowed women to petition for custody of children up to the age of seven and for access to children over that age. The age was increased to 16 with the Custody of Infants Act 1873.

35. Married Women's Property Acts 1870 and 1882.

36. Gleadle, 2001, P. 82, op cit.

37. Lewis, J. *Women in England 1870–1950: Sexual Divisions and Social Change,* Wheatsheaf, 1984; Rose. S. O. *Limited Livelihoods: Gender and Class in Nineteenth Century England,* London: Routledge, 1992; John, A. V. (ed.) *Unequal Opportunities: Women's Employment in England and Wales 1850–1918,* Oxford: Basil Blackwell, 1986.

38. Information supplied by Judith Hodson, Work Experience Administrative Assistant and School Archivist Varndean School.

39. Judith Hodson, Varndean archivist.

40. This was a time of great educational reform as reported by Delamont, S. 'The Contradictions in Ladies' Education'

in Delamont, S. and Duffin, L. (eds.), *Nineteenth Century Woman: Her Cultural and Physical World*, London: Croom Helm, 1978.

41. Dyhouse, C. *Girls Growing Up in Late Victorian and Edwardian England*, London: Routledge 1981, Chapter 2.

42. Vlaeminke, M. *The English Higher Grade School, A Lost Opportunity*, London: Routledge, 2000.

43. Judith Hodson, Varndean archivist.

44. See Holcombe, L. *Victorian Ladies at Work: Middle-class Working Women in England and Wales 1850–1914*, Hamden, CT, 1973.

45. See Cannadine, D. Keating, J. Op cit, p.42 and also pp.18 and 64; and Sheldon, N. *The Right Kind of History: Teaching the Past in Twentieth-Century England*, London: Palgrave Macmillan, 2011; and, Sutherland, G. 'Education' in Thompson, F. M. L. (eds.) *The Cambridge Social History of Britain 1750–1950*, Cambridge: Cambridge University Press, 1990, p.119. The 1880 Act was called the Elementary Education Act.

46. Pupil teachers are discussed in Berry, M. Teacher *Training Institutions in England and Wales: A Bibliographical Guide to Their History,* London: Society for Research into Higher Education, 1973; Dent, H. C. *The Training of Teachers in England and Wales, 1800–1975*, London: Hodder and Stoughton, 1977; Widowson, F, '"Educating Teacher": Women and Elementary Teaching in London, 1900–1914', in Leonore Davidoff and Belinda Westover, *Our Work, Our Lives, Our Words: Women's History and Women's Work,* Basingstoke: Macmillan Education, 1986.

47. Helena's CV: WL: 7HLN/A/01.

48. There is some discrepancy in her dates at Brighton and Liverpool on her CV in 7HLN/A/01. On careful examination it would appear that she was a student at Edge Hill in 1903 and left there in 1905 (as confirmed in Montgomery, F. and Flinn, M. *A Vision of Learning: Edge Hill University 1885–2010*, Third Millennium Publishing Limited, 2010) and her letters of recommendation from Sarah Hale (Principal of Edge Hill). This is contrary to the information on Helena's CVs. This appears to be an

innocent error, but surprising given Helena's attention to detail.

49. 1900–1905 she held the Soames Educational Trust Scholarship (one granted annually), the Hack Scholarship (because first on list of students) and a Science and Art Scholarship (again first on the list of students) according to her archive. See WL: 7HLN/A/01. Again there is no corroborative evidence of this.

50. Sutherland, 1990, op cit, p.119.

51. Ibid.

52. Widdowson, F. 'Educating Teacher: Women Elementary Teaching in London, 1900–1914' in Davidoff, L. (ed.), *Our Works, Our Lives, Our Words: Women's History and Women's Work,* Basingstoke: Macmillan, pp.95–123.

53. Fry, G. K. 'Sir Robert Laurie Morant (1863–1920)', *Oxford Dictionary of National Biography* 2004.

54. Morant became Permanent Secretary in 1903 and was recognised as being responsible for the Education Act 1902.

55. Code of Regulations for Public Elementary Schools in Great Britain, HM Stationary Office, 1900, pp.4, 54 and 60; Edwards, E. *Women in Teacher Training Colleges 1900–1960,* Routledge, 2004, p.9; and Cannadine, 2011, op cit pp.42–43, 63.

56. WL: 7HLN/A/01.

57. This would appear to be a scholarship programme: see Cannadine, 2011, op cit p.22. It was abolished in 1907, Wardle, D. *English Popular Education 1780–1975,* Cambridge: Cambridge University Press, 1975, p.74.

58. WL: 7HLN/A/01.

59. 'The York Place Varndean Story' by Joan Miller, published privately in 1988 to celebrate the centenary of the school, refers to the King's Prize in 1902: 'In the Advanced Physiology examination the fifteen girls entered gained the outstanding result of seven first-class and eight second-class passes; Elsa Kirby, who obtained the highest marks in the country was awarded the coveted King's Prize.' Judith Hodson, archivist at Varndean School could provide records of school awards from 1911 onwards only. There is no mention of a King's Scholarship or prize. The reference to it

comes from Helena's CV.

60. Such a scholarship would entitle them to a scholarship for further teacher training, Cannadine, 2011, op cit and Wardle, 1975, op cit.

61. Later Mrs North.

62. General reference dated February 1905. Letter from Miss Syson, WL: 7HLN/A/01.

63. General reference Mr W. Done BA, Principal of the Education Committee for the County Borough of Brighton, Pupil Teacher Centre, Pelham Street, Brighton 13 February 1905 WL: 7HLN/A/01.

64. Cannon, undated, op cit.

65. *Varndean Chronicle*, Special Edn. July 1947. WL: 7HLN/A/29, the school became 'Varndean' in 1932.

66. Ibid.

67. Montgomery, 2010, op cit, p.1.

68. Ibid.

69. Ibid, p.12.

70. Ibid, p.18.

71. It is possible that there was a family connection with Liverpool, as her Aunt Eliza died there in 1906 according to the England and Wales National Probate Calendar 1858–1966.

72. Montgomery, 2010, op cit, p.19.

73. Ibid, 80 per cent of students studying at Edge Hill came from the counties of Lancashire, Yorkshire, Cheshire and Cumberland.

74. Montgomery, 2010, op cit, p.12.

75. Ibid.

76. Ibid.

77. Ibid, p.13.

78. Ibid.

79. Ibid.

80. WL: 7HLN/A/01. Her CV was presumably for employment but it is difficult to know exactly for which job applications.

81. Montgomery 2010, op cit, p.34.

82. Ibid.

83. Ibid.

84. Ibid, p.13.

85. Ibid, p.17.

86. Ibid.

87. Ibid.

88. Ibid.

89. Ibid, p.34.

90. Ibid, p.35.

91. Ibid.

92. Ibid.

93. Ibid.

94. Ibid, p.36.

95. Ibid, p.37.

96. WL: 7HLN/A/01. February 1918.

97. Montgomery, 2010, op cit, p.38.

98. Ibid.

99. *Edge Hill Magazine* 1908, Montgomery, 2010, op cit, p.38.

100. W: 7HLN/A/01. She notes on her CV that every pupil passed successfully.

101. Cannon, undated, op cit.

102. Ibid.

103. WL: 7HLN/A/01.

104. Cannon, undated, op cit.

105. WL: 7HLN/A/02.

106. Ibid.

107. WL: 7HLN/A/01.

108. Ibid.

109. WL: HLN/A/01.

110. Ibid.

111. She would retake (and pass) this exam in 1930 as an external student WL: 7HLN/A/37.

112. WL: 7HLN/A/01.

113. This developed from the David Stow's Glasgow Normal Seminary, the first institution in Britain established specifically for the training of teachers. It received a government grant to take over all other teacher training colleges in Scotland. Harrison, M. M. and Marker, W. B. (eds.) *Teaching the Teacher — The History of Jordanhill College of Education 1823–1993*, John Donald, 1996.

114. Letter from the Director of Studies to Helena Normanton, 8 April 1914. WL: 7HLN/A/01.

115. She uses the word 'tutor' on her CV rather than governess. Governess had a possibly demeaning and negative connotation, see Hughes, K. *Victorian Governess*, London: Hambledon Press, 1993 and Hollis, P. (ed.), *Women in Public 1850–1900: Documents of the Victorian Women's Movement* London: George Allen and Unwin, 1979.

116. WL: 7HLN/A/01.

117. Southport in 1910. *The Times* obituary, 8 October 1968.

118. *The Times*, 'North West Ham', 27 June 1911.

119. Maroula, J. and Purvis, J. *The Women's Suffrage Movement, New Feminist Perspectives*, Manchester University

Press, 1998, p.52.

120. Ibid p.54.

121. Burton, A. *Burdens of History: British Feminists, Indian Women and Imperial Culture 1865–1915,* University of North Carolina Press, 1994, p.53.

122. WL: 7HLN/D/07. This file demonstrates Helena's membership of this group until 1954.

123. May 1915 'The English Woman.'

124. Burton, 1994, op cit, p.54.

125. Normanton, H. *Sex Differentiation in Salary*, National Federation of Women Teachers, 1915.

126. Letter from the University of London addressed to Helena at 273 Willesden Lane informing her that she had been added to the list of University extension lecturers, WL: 7HLN/A/01.

127. Extension lectures were a means by which women could access university teaching at a time when some universities were closed to them, or if they were unable to attend university for any reason. It was begun in 1867 by Professor James Stuart, a Cambridge don, and the movement later became known as the London Society for Extension of University Teaching. The lectures were offered in major cities in England. Dyhouse, C. *No Distinction of Sex? Women in British Universities 1870–1939*, London: University College London, 1995.

128. Letter from the registrar of the University Extension Board, University of London to Helena, 24 February 1916, WL: 7HLN/A/01.

129. WL: 7HLN/A/01.

130. Ibid. Reference by W. Done BA, 7 March 1913.

131. Ibid. Reference by Ernest Rayns 17 January 1913.

132. Ibid. Reference by M. E. Tassell 28 February 1907.

133. Ibid.

134. Taylor, A. *Annie Besant: A Biography*, Oxford: Oxford University Press, 1991.

135. See Lloyd, T. O. *The British Empire, 1558–1995,* Oxford: Oxford University Press, 1996; Levine, P. *The British Empire: Sunrise to Sunset*, Harlow: Longman, 2007.

136. As explained in the introduction of Normanton, H. *India in England,*

Ganesan Publishers, 1921. This was a reprint of many of the leading articles in the weekly *India.*

137. Chandrika Kaul, 'Montagu, Edwin Samuel (1879–1924)', *Oxford Dictionary of National Biography*, Oxford: Oxford University Press, 2004.

138. Robert Stevens, 'Hewart, Gordon, First Viscount Hewart (1870–1943)', *Oxford Dictionary of National Biography*, Oxord: Oxford University Press, 2004.

139. Richard A. Cosgrove, 'Pollock, Sir Frederick, Third Baronet (1845–1937)', *Oxford Dictionary of National Biography*, Oxford: Oxford University Press, 2004.

Notes to Chapter 2

1. Speech by Helena to members of the Suffragette Fellowship, 6 February 1950. WL: 7HLN/4.

2. Barbara Taylor, 'Wollstonecraft, Mary (1759–1797)'; Pat Rogers, 'Burnley, Fanny (1752–1840'; Isobel Grundy, 'Montgu, Lady Mary Wortley (bap.1689, d.1662)'. All *Oxford Dictionary of National Biography* Oxford: Oxford University Press, 2004.

3. See Clark, A. *Working Life of Women in the Seventeenth Century*, London: Frank Cass, 1919.

4. Drake, B. *Women and Trade Unions*, London: Virago, 1920, p.3.

5. Frow, R and Frow, E. (eds.) *Political Women 1800–1850* London: Pluto Press 1989, Chapter 3.

6. Morgan, S. 'Domestic Economy and Political Agitation: Women and the Anti-Corn Law League 1839–1846', in Gleadle, K. and Richardson S (eds.), *Women in British Politics*, Basingstoke: Macmillan, 2000.

7. Midgley, C. *Women Against Slavery*, London: Routledge 1992, pp.87–9, 39–40, 142–5.

8. For a comprehensive study, see Holcombe, L. *Wives and Property: Reform of the Married Women's Property Law in Nineteenth Century England,* Toronto and Buffalo: University of Toronto Press, 1983.

9. Midgley, C. 1992, op cit.

10. See Walkowitz, J. R. *Prostitution and Victorian Society* Cambridge: Cambridge

University Press, 1980.

11. See Hutchins, B. *Women in Modern Industry,* London: G. Bell, 1915, p.110.

12. Janet Howarth, 'Fawcett, Dame Millicent Garrett (1847–1929)', *Oxford Dictionary of National Biography*, Oxford: University Press, 2004.

13. Joannou, M. And Purvis, J. (eds.) *The Women's Suffrage Movement: New Feminist Perspectives,* Manchester: Manchester University Press, 1998, pp.2 and 43; such as the Pankhursts, see Pankhurst, S. *The Suffragette Movement,* London: Longmans Green and Co., 1931.

14. Caird, M. *The Morality of Marriage and Other Essays on the Status and Destiny of Women,* London: G. Redway, 1897, pp.131–156.

15. Grand, S. *The Heavenly Twins,* republished University of Michigan Press, 1993. There was a real concern about venereal disease.

16. Caine, B. *English Feminism 1780–1980,* Oxford: Oxford University Press, 1997, p.137.

17. This would cause conflicts, see Caine, B. 'Generational Conflict and the Question of Ageing in Nineteenth and Twentieth Century Feminism', *Australian Cultural History,* 14 (1995) 92–108.

18. Bodichon, B. *Reasons for and Against the Enfranchisement of Women,* National Society for Women's Suffrage. London: McCorquodale & Co, 1872.

19. Bland, L. *Banishing the Beast, Sexuality and the Early Feminists,* New York: New York Press, 1995.

20. Tickner, L. 'The Political Imagery of the British Women's Suffrage Movement' in Beckett, J. and Cherry, D. (eds.), *The Edwardian Era,* London: Phaidon, 1987, pp.100–116.

21. Abel, R. *The Making of the English Legal Profession 1800–1988,* Washington: Beard Books, 1988, p.74.

22. For a full explanation, see Liddington, J. and Norris, J. *One Hand Tied Behind Us: The Rise of the Women's Suffrage Movement,* London: Virago, 1978.

23. See Mappen, E. F. 'Strategists for Change: Socialist Feminist Approaches to the Problems of Women's Work', in John, A. V. (ed.), *Unequal Opportunities: Women's Employment in England,*

1800–1918, Oxford: Oxford University Press, 1986.

24. This is explored in Lewis, J. *The Politics of Motherhood,* London: Croom Helm, 1980.

25. Kersley, G. *Darling Madame: Sarah Grand and Devoted Friend,* London: Virago Press, 1983.

26. This was the pseudonym of Ben and Elizabeth Wolstenholme Elmy. Sandra Stanley Holton, 'Elmy, Elizabeth Clarke Wolstenholme (1833–1918)', *Oxford Dictionary of National Biography*, Oxford: Oxford University Press, 2004.

27. Ethelmer, E, 'Feminist', *Westminster Review,* 149 (1898), 60–5.

28. John Davis, 'Webb (Martha) Beatrice (1858–1943)', *Oxford Dictionary of National Biography,* Oxford: Oxford University Press, 2004.

29. Webb, B, 'The Awakening of Women', *New Statesmen,* suppl. 'On the Awakening of Women', 2 Nov. 1911.

30. WL: 5SPG.

31. Showalter, E. *Inventing Herself: Claiming a Feminist Intellectual Heritage* 2001, Scribner Books, p.172.

32. Schreiner, O. *Woman and Labour,* London: Virago, 1911.

33. As reported in *The Vote,* 20 Feb 1920.

34. For example Elizabeth Blackwell.

35. For example, in an interview with *The Evening News* 28 December 1919.

36. Menkel-Meadows, C. 'Portia in a Different Voice; Speculating on a Woman's Lawyering Process', 1 *Berkeley Women's Law Journal,* 39, 1985, pp.39–63.

37. Ibid p.40.

38. Ibid p.55.

39. Ibid p.56.

40. Ibid p.57.

41. Ibid p.63.

42. McGlynn, C. *The Woman Lawyer: Making the Difference,* Oxford: Oxford University Press, 2005.

43. Bacik, I. Costello, C. Drew, E. *Gender in Justice: Feminising the Legal Profession,* Trinity College Law School, 2003.

44. Gilligan, C *In a Different Voice,* Harvard University Press, 1982.

45. Bacik, 2003, op cit, p.34 and Rhode, D. 'Gender and the Professions' in Schultz, U and Shaw, G (eds.) *Women in the World's Legal Profession,* Oxford: Hart,

2003, p.7.

46. There is no corroborative material in her WL papers but she was at their victory dinner after the passing of the Sex Disqualification (Removal) Act and we can surmise that she was a member.

47. Ray Strachey was the chairperson: *Evening News,* 9 March 1920 and *Evening Mail*, 9 March 1920. Barbara Caine, 'Strachey, Rachel Pearsall Conn [Ray] (1887–1940)', *Oxford Dictionary of National Biography*, Oxford: Oxford University Press, 2004.

48. Purvis, J. *Emmeline Pankhurst: A Biography,* London: Routledge, 2002, p.68; Pugh, Martin *The Pankhursts,* London: Vintage, 2008, p.116; and Crawford, E. *The Women's Suffrage Movement: A Reference Guide 1866–1928,* London: University College London, 1999.

49. Pugh, M. 2008 op cit. Although Pugh refers to it as 'The Committee to Secure the Admission of Women to the Legal Profession,' it must be the same group given Pankhurst's involvement, p.116. Mitchell, D. *Queen Christabel,* Macdonald and James, 1977, pp.55–6.

50. It is mentioned in Pugh ibid; Auchmuty, R. *Whatever Happened to Miss Bebb,* Legal Studies, Vol. 31, No. 2, pp.209 and 212; Lang, E, *British Women in the Twentieth Century,* T. Werner Laurie 1929, and Crawford, 1999, op cit, and some contemporary newspaper reports.

51. Auchmuty, 2011 p.212. 'Entry to the legal profession had been one of the objects of the feminist societies for many years, and a special committee, with Mr Samuel Garrett as its chairman, had existed for the purpose of securing this reform': Strachey, R. *The Cause,* Virago, 1928, p.235.

52. Rosser described Chrystal MacMillan as one the 'older' generation, active suffragettes, joining the Bar in vindication of their efforts for women's rights. Rosser dismisses MacMillan as making 'no headway'—see WL: LOCKET.

53. One of the litigants in *Bebb v The Law Society* [1914] 1 Ch. 286. There is little evidence about this committee except the reports of its celebration dinner.

54. For example, *The Daily News,* 24 December 1903.

55. WL: 7HLN/D/08. 1918 The National Women Citizens Association (1917–1975) was founded in 1917. It centred on how women could be active citizens. From 1913, autonomous local WCAs were formed throughout the UK with an objective to stimulate women's interest in social and political issues in order to prepare them for active citizenship. In 1917 it became clear that women would get the vote. The National Union of Women Workers called a meeting of British women's organizations to discuss the implications. The NUWW established the Provisional Central Committee on the Citizenship of Women, with members drawn from interested societies. Later that year, 42 affiliated societies were accepted by the executive committee. Helena was the first secretary. By 1918 the first branches appeared.

56. WL: 5SPG.

57. Deirdre Beddoe, 'Thomas, Margaret Haig, suo jure Viscountess Rhondda (1883–1958)', *Oxford Dictionary of National Biography*, Oxford: Oxford University Press, 2004; Online edn, Sept 2012.

58. Initially set up to change the law on six points: satisfactory legislative provision on child assault, widowed mothers, the unmarried mother and her child, and equal rights for guardianship for married couples, equal pay for teachers and equal opportunities for both sexes in the civil service.

59. Her contact with French lawyers is recorded in a folder in her archives: WL: 7HLN/A/27.

60. This was an organization founded in 1908 in the USA (Chicago-Kent College) in 1924 (until 1969) to promote high professional standards amongst women law students and lawyers (http://www.lib.utexas.edu/taro/utlaw/00003/law-00003.html).

61. WL: 7HLN/A/28.

62. WL: 7HLN/D/11. 1936–1938.

63. WL: 7HLN/B/02. 1929–1937.

64. WL: 7HLN/A/28.

65. WL: LOCKET.

66. WL: 7HLN/B/03. 1932–1947.

67. WL: 7HLN/B/03.

68. This has been examined in many

works, including: Spender, D. *There's Always Been a Women's Movement This Century,* London: Pandora,1984; Alberti, J. *Beyond Suffrage: Feminists in War and Peace, 1914–1928,* London: Macmillan 1989; Harrison, B. *Prudent Revolutionaries: Portraits of British Feminists Between the Wars,* Oxford: Oxford University Press, 1987; Dyhouse, C. *Feminism and the Family in England, 1880–1930,* Oxford: Oxford University Press, 1989; Pugh, M. *Women and the Women's Movement in Britain, 1914– 1959,* London: Macmillan, 1992; Kent, S. K. *Making Peace: The Reconstruction of Gender in Interwar Britain,* Princeton University Press, 1993.

69. Thane, P, 'What Difference Did the Vote Make?' in Vickery, A. (ed.) *Women, Privilege and Power,* Stanford University Press. 2001, pp.253–254.

70. They separated in about 1884.

71. This was introduced by the Guardianship of Infants Act 1925 which gave equal rights to both parents on divorce and emphasised that the interests of the child was the 'paramount consideration' for the courts when deciding custody.

72. The case of *R v Greenhill* (1863) 4 A & E 624 is a good example of that double standard and follows *R v De Manneville* [1804] 5 East 221.

73. The mother's adultery was seen as an absolute bar to custody. In *Seddon v Seddon and Doyle* (1862) 2 SW & Tr 640 the mother had had an adulterous relationship (the court recognised that her husband's behaviour had driven her to this) but she was denied custody. The judge considered that 'it will probably have a salutary effect on the interest of public morality, that it should be known that a woman, if found guilty of adultery, will forfeit as far as the court is concerned, all rights to the custody of or access to her children', see p.641.

74. *Re Besant* [1879] 11 Ch. 508 CA. Anne Taylor, 'Besant, Annie (1847–1933)', *Oxford Dictionary of National Biography,* Oxford University Press 2004, Online edn. 2008.

75. In 1877 Besant and Charles Bradlaugh were prosecuted for publishing Charles Knowlton's pamphlet 'Fruits on Philosophy'. They were acquitted by the Court of Appeal, see: Browne, J. *Charles Darwin: The Power of Place,* Princeton University Press, 2002; Marvell, R. *The Trial of Annie Besant and Charles Bradlaugh,* London: Elek/Pemberton, 1976.

76. Shanley, M. L. *Feminism, Marriage and the Law in Victorian England 1850–1895,* Tauris, 1989; Sachs, A. and Wilson, J. H. *Sexism and the Law: A Study of Male Beliefs and Legal Bias in Britain and the United States,* Oxford: Martin Robertson, 1978; O'Donovan, K. *Sexual Divisions in Law,* London: Weidenfeld & Nicolson, 1985.

77. http://www.guardian.co.uk/news/ datablog/2013/jan/30/university- applications-subjects-age-gender- country

78. For a comprehensive history of women and universities see Dyhouse, op cit, 1995.

79. University of London: www.london. ac.uk/history; and Zimmern, A. *The Renaissance of Girls' Education in England: A Record of Fifty Years' Progress,* London: A. D. Innes & Company, 1898.

80. Leslie Howsam, 'Orme, Eliza (1848– 1937)', *Oxford Dictionary of National Biography,* Oxford: Oxford University Press, 2004.

81. Howsam, L. 'Sound-Minded Women: Eliza Orme and the Study and Practice of Law in Late-Victorian England' (1989), 15 *Atlantis* 44. Mossman, M. J. *The First Women Lawyers: A Comparative Study of Gender, Law and the Legal Professions,* Oxford: Hart, 2006, page 128.

82. Dean Burgon from Oxford declared in 1847 that the statute admitting women to examinations was a reversal of the law of nature, which was also the law of God and that women were inferior to men and would be inferior until the end of time, Green, V. H. H. *A History of Oxford University,* Batsford, 1974 p.186. G. Martin Murphy, 'Burgon, John William (1813–1888)' *Oxford Dictionary of National Biography,* Oxford: Oxford University Press, 2004.

83. A. H. Miller 'Neaves, Charles, Lord Neaves (1800–1876)', Rev. Shiels, *Oxford Dictionary of National Biography,*

Oxford: Oxford University Press, 2004 (this entry professes that Lord Neaves was well-disposed towards the teaching of women at universities).

84. *Jex-Blake v Senatus of Edinburgh. University* (1873) 11 M 784.

85. Between 1875 and 1914 the number of women becoming teachers rose by 862.1 per cent, Holcombe, L. *Victorian Ladies at Work: Middle-Class Working Women in England and Wales 1850–1914*, 1973, Newton-Abbot: David and Charles, p.34.

86. WL: HLN/07.

87. Montgomery, F. and Flinn, M. *A Vision of Learning. Edge Hill University 1885–2010*, Third Millennium Publishing Limited, 2010, p.17.

88. Daniel Duman, *The English and Colonial Bars in the 19th Century*, London: Routledge, 1983.

89. Holton, S. S. *Feminism and Democracy. Women's Suffrage and Reform Politics in Britain, 1900–1918*, Cambridge: Cambridge University Press 1986; Holton, S. S. *Suffrage Days: Stories From the Women's Suffrage Movement*, London: Routledge, 1996; Purvis, J. and Holton, S. S. (eds.) *Votes for Women*, London: Routledge, 2000; Liddington, J. *The Life and Times of a Respectable Rebel: Selina Cooper (1864–1946)*, London: Virago, 1984.

90. J. A. Hamilton 'Bovill, Sir William (1814–1873)', Rev Mary Heimann, *Oxford Dictionary of National Biography*, Oxford: Oxford University Press, 2004 where it is noted that Bovill was known for not being impartial.

91. Jane Howarth 'Fawcett, Dame Millicent Garrett (1847–1929)', *Oxford Dictionary of National Biography*, Oxford: Oxford University Press, 2004.

92. 1897.

93. 1903.

94. Jane Purvis, 'Pankhurst, Dame Christabel Harriette (1880–1958)', *Oxford Dictionary of National Biography*, Oxford: Oxford University Press, 2004.

95. Her membership card is preserved with her archives WL: 7HLN/A/07.

96. Holton, S. 1986, op cit, Chapter 6, pp.116–133.

97. Clarke, P. *Hope and Glory, Britain 1900–1990*, Penguin Books, 1997, p.94.

98. Alberti, 1989, op cit.

99. For further discussion see: Braybon, G. Women *Workers in the First World War*, London: Taylor and Francis Ltd, 1990; Martin D. Pugh, 'Politicians and the Woman's Vote 1914–1918', *History*, October 1974, Vol. 59 Issue 197, pp.358–374; Grayzel, S *Women and the First World War*, Pearson, 2002; Thom, D. *Nice Girls and Rude Girls: Women Workers in World War I (Social and Cultural History Today)*, I. B. Tauris & Co. Ltd, 1998; Holloway, G. *Women and Work in Britain Since 1840 (Women's and Gender History)*, Routledge, 2005; Wall, R. and Winter, J. (eds.) *The Upheaval of War: Family, Work and Welfare in Europe 1914–18*, Cambridge: Cambridge University Press, 1998; Law, C. *Suffrage and Power: Women's Movement 1918–1928 (Social and Cultural History Today)*, I. B. Tauris Publishers, 2000.

100. See *Chapter 1*.

101. In 1918, quoted in Clarke, 1997, op cit p.98.

102. Representation of the People Act 1918, section 4.

103. They had to occupy premises worth at least £10 per annum.

104. They were excluded for five years after the war.

105. Parliament (Qualification of Women) Act 1918, section 1.

106. *Beckenham Advertiser*, December 16 1948, 'Obituary'.

107. Ewen, A. Cameron, 'Clark, Gavin Brown (1846–1930)', *Oxford Dictionary of National Biography*, Oxford: Oxford University Press, 2004.

108. Ibid.

109. She expresses this sentiment in letters to Marie Stopes WL: 7HLN/A/18.

110. Legal writer and judge, Wilfred Prest, 'Blackstone, Sir William (1723–1780)', *Oxford Dictionary of National Biography*, Oxford: University Press, 2004.

111. Blackstone, W. *Commentaries on the Laws of England* (1765) as reprinted Morrison, W. (ed.), Cavendish Publishers, 2001.

112. Ibid Vol.1, p.430.

113. For more detail on coverture and property see Holcombe, L. *Wives and Property: Reform of the Married Women's Property Law in Nineteenth*

Century England, Toronto and London: University of Toronto Press, 1983.

114. This was often a strong theme and illustrated in Victorian novels: see Wynne, D. *Women and Personal Property in the Victorian Novel,* Ashgate, 2010.

115. As per Lord Denning in *Williams and Glyn's Bank v Boland* [1979], Ch 312 at p.432.

116. See Vicinus, M. 'Distance and Desire: English Boarding School Friendships, 1870–1920', in Duberman et al (eds.) *Hidden From History: Reclaiming the Gay and Lesbian Past,* New York/ Harmondsworth: Penguin, 1991.

117. Allen, G. *The Woman Who Did,* London: John Lane Publishers, 1895.

118. Equity is a system of law that is separate from the common law. Since 1873 with the passing of the Judicature Acts, equity and common law can be considered in the same court.

119. Masson, J, Bailey-Harris, R. and Probert, R. *Cretney's Principles of Family Law* (8th edn.), Thomson Sweet and Maxwell 2008 at 3–002 and 3–006. Cornish, W. and Clark, G. de N. *Law and Society in England 1750–1950,* London: Sweet & Maxwell, 1989, pp.398–403. For a thorough examination, see Holcombe, 1973, op cit.

120. Section 1 Married Women's Property Act 1870.

121. Holcombe, 1973, op cit.

122. Married Women's Property Act 1882.

123. Masson, 2008, op cit, p.153 at 006.

124. Workman, J. 'Wading Through the Mire: An Historiographical Study of the British Women's Movement Between the Wars', *University of Sussex Journal of Contemporary History,* 2, 2001.

Notes to Chapter 3

1. Cowper, F. *A Prospect of Gray's Inn* London: Stevens, 1951, p.117.

2. WL: 7HLN/A/01.

3. 'Foundations of Freedom', Helena Normanton, *The Vote* (The Organ of the Women's Freedom League), March 3, 1916 , Vol. XIII, p.945.

4. This started in 1917 and emerged from the National Union of Women's Workers. Its purpose was to prepare women for citizenship when they gained the vote and the right to participate fully in the public sphere. It also aimed to stimulate women's interest in social and political issues. WL: GB 106 5/NWC.

5. WL: 7HLN/C/23. She was editor from 1919–1922.

6. WL: 7HLN/A/08 and 03. She intended to rent out rooms and draw an income from this, but the rooms were seldom let and the house itself was in need of expensive decoration.

7. For a more detailed study see Mossman, M. J. *The First Woman Lawyers: A Comparative Study of Gender Law and the Legal Professions,* Oxford: Hart, 2006.

8. Ivy Williams, as quoted in *Law Journal,* 34, 1904, 1–2.

9. *Gloucestershire Echo,* 'The Miscellany', 16 January 1904.

10. Sex Disqualification (Removal) Act 1919.

11. Auchmuty, R. 'Whatever Happened to Miss Bebb? *Bebb v. The Law Society* and Women's Legal History', *Legal Studies,* Vol. 31, No. 2, June 2011, pp.199–230, p.222.

12. This is something she long campaigned for. See Logan, A. 'Professionalism and the Impact of England's First Women Justices 1920–1950', pp.833–850 in *Historical Journal,* 49(3) (2006); Logan, A. *Making Women Magistrates: Feminism, Citizenship and Justice in England and Wales 1918–1950,* London: PhD University of Greenwich, 2002, p.150; and Logan *Feminism and Criminal Justice: A Historical Perspective,* Palgrave, 2008.

13. Woolf, V. *A Room of One's Own; Three Guineas,* London: Penguin,1938, p.120.

14. WL: LOCKET.

15. Pugh, M. *Women and the Women's Movement in Britain, 1914–1999,* Basingstoke: Macmillan, 2000, p.90.

16. Zimmeck, M. 'Strategies and Stratagems for the Employment of Women in the British Civil Service, 1919–1939', pp.901–924, *Historical Journal,* 27(4), 1984, p.909.

17. Logan, 2002, op cit.

18. *The Vote,* 6 May 1921 (front page).

19. See Caine, B. *English Feminism 1780–1980,* Oxford: Oxford University Press, 1997, p.173.

20. Introduced by Lord Buckmaster, HL

Deb, 26 February 1919, Vol 33, c339.

21. Introduced by Benjamin Spoor on 21 March 1919. HC Bill 38 (1919).

22. This had its second reading on 22 July 1919 (Lord Chancellor) HL Deb, 22 July 1919, Vol 35, cc.891–911.

23. Maitland, F. W. and Horne, A. *The Mirror of Justices*, reprinted by Nabu Press, 2013.

24. Mossman, M. J. op cit, pp 113–121.

25. Philippa Levine, 'Grey, Maria Georgina (1816–1906)', *Oxford Dictionary of National Biography*, Oxford: Oxford University Press, 2004.

26. The CLE was established in 1852 by the Inns. Its function was to supervise education of Bar students there. It employed professors to lecture the students. CLE archive, Institute of Advanced Legal Studies Library, University of London.

27. Lady Lowry QC (Vice President of the Association of Women Barristers) in the *Association of Women Barristers Magazine*, Winter/Spring, 2004.

28. Kamm, J *Indicative Past: A Hundred Years of the Girls' Public School Trust,* Allen & Unwin, 1971, p.16.

29. Mossman, 2006, op cit, p.116.

30. The minutes and memoranda of the governing Council of Benchers.

31. This meant 'proper and practical.'

32. 'The year "That Awa"' [this means 'the year that away'] (December 1875), 6 *Englishwoman's Review*, p.533 (the article describes Orme and Richardson's work and office); 'Women as Lawyers' (November 1875), 6 *Englishwoman's Review*, p.510.

33. Mary Richardson a fellow law student of Orme's at UCL, Mossman, 2006, op cit, p.124.

34. Abel-Smith, B and Stevens, R. (with Rosalind Brooke) *Lawyers and the Courts: A Sociological Study of the English Legal System 1750–1965*, London: Heinemann, 1967, pp.192–3.

35. Mossman, 2006, op cit, p.132.

36. 'Women at the Bar', *Law Journal*, 12 December 1903, p.620.

37. Kirk, H. *Portrait of a Profession: A History of the Solicitor's Profession, 1100 to the Present Day*, London: Oyez Publishing, 1976, p.132.

38. Mossman, 2006, op cit.

39. A occupation now gone, but at the turn of the 20th-century it was a male occupation which involved drafting pleadings. Special pleaders did not have to be barristers (but could be). They did not appear in court but had to hold a licence to practise. Often a job before call to the Bar. See Kershaw, M. 'From Beeching to Woolf', *Liverpool Law Review*, 19(1), 47–51, 1997.

40. Lady Lowry QC (Vice President of the Association of Women Barristers) in the *Association of Women Barristers Magazine,* Winter/Spring, 2004.

41. See *Englishwomen's Review* 151 (1878) 60. In 1878 a small group for the Promotion of Legal Education for Women was set up in London.

42. In 1892 Cornelia Sorabji passed a Bachelor of Civil Law from Oxford University, see Suparna Gooptu, 'Sorabji, Cornelia (1866–1954)', *Oxford Dictionary of National Biography*, Oxford: Oxford University Press, 2004; and also Howsam, 1989 at pp.46 and 49.

43. Middle Temple records MT. 1/MPA/22. See also Lang, 1929, p.146 and January 1904, *Lady Law Students' Englishwoman's Review,* 49.

44. MT3/MEM.

45. 13 March 1903.

46. 24 April 1903.

47. *Jex Blake case*; *Hall v Society of Law Agents, Scottish Law Reporter*, Vol. 38, p.776 and *Beresford Hope v Lady Sandhurst* 23 QBD 70. p.90.

48. Lord Chancellor Halsbury. (G. R. Rubin, 'Giffard, Hardinge Stanley, First Earl of Halsbury (1823–1921)', *Oxford Dictionary of National Biography*, Oxford: Oxford University Press, 2004). Lord Chief Justice Alvestone. Mr Justice Kekewich (J. B. Atlay, 'Kekewich, Sir Arthur (1832–1907', rev. Hugh Mooney, *Oxford Dictionary of National Biography*, Oxford: Oxford University Press, 2004), Mr Justice Wright, Mr Justice Farwell; Mr Justice Walton and Mr Justice Joyce.

49. MT3/MEM.

50. Auchmuty, R, 'Whatever Happened to Miss Bebb? *Bebb v. The Law Society* and Women's Legal History', *Legal Studies*, Vol. 31, No. 2, June 2011, pp.199–230 points out that the four litigants in the *Bebb case* were presented by the media

as acceptable 'would-be' members of the
legal profession, unlike Pankhurst whose
behaviour was considered ;disgraceful',
see p.214.

51. Lang, 1929, op cit.

52. *Bebb v Law Society* [1914] 1 Ch.
286, included the following litigants:
Gwyneth Bebb, Karen Costello (both
first-class Oxford graduates), Maud
Ingram (a Cambridge History and Law
graduate and solicitor's office employee)
and Lucy Nettlefold (a Newnham law
student).

53. Maitland, F. W. and Horne, A. *The
Mirror of Justices,* op cit. A manuscript
kept in the Parker Library, Corpus
Christi College, Cambridge. The
author is unknown but believed to
be Andrew Horn, a lawyer and legal
scholar (1275–1328). It was relied on by
William Blackstone and was the basis
for his argument regarding the doctrine
of coverture.

54. Christian, E. B. V. *A Short History
of Solicitors*, London: Reeves, 1896.
The author states that it is difficult to
suppose a reason for this statement
except ignorance. He also states that
women were further excluded from
becoming judges alongside 'open lepers,
idiots, lunatics and deaf mutes.'

55. *Bebb v Law Society*, p.294.

56. An example of this is Lord Neaves
judgment in *Jex-Blake* which explained
women's absence from Scottish universities by quoting Don Pedro d'Ayala
(Spanish ambassador at the Scottish
Court of James IV) who commented
that Scottish women '... are the absolute
mistresses of their houses, and even of
their husbands in all things concerning
the administration of their property,
income or expenditure ...' From this
Neaves J concluded that women were
aware that 'their proper place was at
home, learning to rule their husbands,
and bring up their children ...'

57. Sachs. A. and Wilson J. H. *Myth of
Males Protectiveness,* Oxford: Oxford
University Press, 1978.

58. The Mines Act 1842 prohibited women
working underground. Fredman, S.
Women and Law 1997, Oxford: Oxford
University Press, p.72.

59. The Factory Act 1844 introduced a 48
hour week for women.

60. John, A. (ed.) *Unequal Opportunities.
Women's Employment in England
1800–1918*, Blackwell, 1986.

61. Hutchins, B. L. and Harrison, A, *A
History of Factory Legislation*, P. S. King
& Son Ltd, 1911.

62. Abel, R. L. *The Making of the Legal
Profession 1800–1988*, Beard Publishers,
1998 p.17.

63. The Supreme Court (formerly House
of Lords) still only sits in London, as
does the Court of Appeal. Barristers
were often members of a 'circuit'. This
was essential for practising outside
London. In the past the King would
have travelled over the country hearing
appeals from the manorial courts. Later
he would appoint judges to act on his
behalf and they would travel the country
on designated circuits hearing cases. This
was intended to enable the equitable
distribution of justice. These routes later
became known as 'circuits'.

64. Middle Temple, Inner Temple, Gray's
Inn and Lincoln's Inn. The Bar Council
and Inns of Court are still based in
London. The Inns were established
by serjeants-in-law: elite barristers, a
role established around 1300. Their
apprentices were known as 'barristers'.
No new serjeants were created after
the Judicature Act 1873 as they were
deemed unnecessary. Abel, R, 1998, p.35.

65. Senate Annual Statement 1983–4.

66. Being 'called' licenses a barrister to
practise law.

67. Abel, 1998, op cit p.35.

68. WL: 7HLN/A/01, letter from Henry
Pensford, under treasurer of Middle
Temple acknowledging her application
to be admitted as a student there.

69. Abel, 1998, op cit, p.48: during this
period the Inns operated as a kind of
'finishing school'.

70. Ibid, p.49.

71. Ibid, p.50.

72. Ibid.

73. Ibid, p.41.

74. Ibid, p.38.

75. Ibid.

76. The dinners had to be eaten in the Hall
of the Inn where the student was a
member.

77. WL: LOCKET.

78. Abel, 1998, op cit, p.37.
79. A bencher is a senior barrister who is a governor of an Inn and a member of its council. It is the highest type of membership of an Inn.
80. Abel, 1998, op cit, p.38.
81. Ibid.
82. Polden, Patrick, 'Portia's Progress: Women at the Bar in England 1919–1939', *International Journal of the Legal Profession*, Vol. 12, No.3, Nov 2005, p.294.
83. George Wilfred Holford Knight 1877–1936, barrister and Labour MP for Nottingham South 1931–1935, see David Howell, 'National Labour (*act.* 1931–1945)', *Oxford Dictionary of National Biography*, Oxford: Oxford University Press, 2013.
84. He would later be her sponsor at Middle Temple and join her for her first dinner, see *Chapter 4*.
85. Polden, 2005, op cit, p.317; and *Law Times*, 1912–13, p.317.
86. January 1917. As reported in the *Pall Mall Gazette*, 17 January 1917.
87. *The Observer*, 'Women and the Bar', 10 February 1919.
88. Lincoln's Inn Black Books, 2001, p.7.
89. Auchmuty, 2011, op cit. It was not just the franchise that had been a success, women's campaigns had others for example with regard to property: the Married Women's Property Acts 1870, 1874, and 1882; limited success with divorce (with the Matrimonial Causes Act 1878); the repeal of the Contagious Diseases Acts in 1883.
90. 'Women and the Bar', *The Observer*, 10 February 1919.
91. *Daily Graphic,* 16 February 1918.
92. Ibid.
93. WL: LOCKET.
94. These are all contained within WL: 7HLN/A/01.
95. A parliament is the Inn's sovereign body and its ultimate authority. It is made up of benchers and sits at various times during the year.
96. WL: 7HLN/A/01.
97. February 22 1918 'Women as Barristers', *The Vote*, p.155.
98. WL: 7HLN/A/01.
99. Ibid.
100. Undated and unheaded. It is worth noting that Helena was under no illusions that because the vote had been won all other reforms would come automatically. This view was held by other feminists in respect of further social and economic changes, hence Viscountess Rhondda's comment that the vote was 'a far cry from the end of the road': see Caine, 1997, op cit, p.283.
101. WL: 7/HLN/A/01.
102. This was a reference to Bertha Cave.
103. Auchmuty, 2006, op cit p.230.
104. A discourse on the law.
105. *The Contemporary Review* May 1913 No. 569. WL: 7HLN/A/03 loose items, Scrapbook 2 of 2.
106. 1851–1919, see David Davies, 'Eady, Charles Swinfen, First Baron Swinfen (1851–1919)', rev. Hugh Mooney, *Oxford Dictionary of National Biography*, Oxford: Oxford University Press, 2004. He had opposed Miss Bebb.
107. 1913–1918.
108. 1918–1919, National Archives: T1/12155. The Master of the Rolls was and is the second most senior judge in England. The most senior is the Lord Chief Justice.
109. *Evening Standard,* 2 March 1918.
110. 8 March 1918.
111. A law society named after Lord Hardwicke (a past Lord Chancellor, see Peter, D. G. Thomas, 'Yorke, Phillip, First Earl of Hardwicke, 1690–1764', *Oxford Dictionary of National Biography,* Oxford: Oxford University Press, 2004).
112. Scrapbook WL: 7HLN/A/01. The motion was moved by Mr F. Van Den Berg.
113. 1884–1920, judge, and MP for Newbury (1906), *The Times*, Obituary, December 28 1920. A handwritten note in her papers states that Mr Justice Mackarness was the first bencher of the Middle Temple to express his regrets to Miss Normanton on her rejection.
114. 12 May 1919.
115. 30 February 1918, WL: 7HLN/A/01.
116. 5 March 1918, WL: 7HLN/A/01.
117. WL: 7HLN/A/01.
118. Albert Napier, 'Schuster, Claud, Baron Schuster (1869–1956)', *Oxford Dictionary of National Biography*, Oxford University Press, 2004. Hall, J. G. And Martin, D. F. *Yes Lord Chancellor:*

A Biography of Lord Schuster, 2003, Chichester: Barry Rose Law Publishers.

119. He was sympathetic to the women's movement, ibid Hall, op cit, p.134.

120. John Campbell, 'Smith, Frederick Edwin, First Earl of Birkenhead (1872–1930)', *Oxford Dictionary of National Biography*, Oxford: Oxford University Press, 2004.

121. There is no mention of Helena in his biography, Napier, A. ibid. Her future father-in-law father was an MP and may have had some influence, but there is no evidence to support this assertion.

122. WL: 7HLN/A/05

123. The Lord Chancellor, the President of the Probate Divorce and Admiralty Division, the Master of the Rolls, and the judges of the King's Bench, Chancery, and Probate Divorce and Admiralty Divisions, each of the judges to whom the appeal was directed, and the benchers of the Inn from whose decision the appeal arose. He said that it should be addressed to the House of Lords.

124. WL: 7HLN/A/05.

125. Ibid.

126. *Daily Telegraph*, 11 June 1919.

127. Lang, E. *British Women in the Twentieth Century* 1929, T. Werner Laurie, pp.163–4.

128. WL: 7HLN/A/29. This was at the YMCA, Victoria Hall, Derby, 18 March 1918.

129. WL: 7HLN/A/29.

130. This is a reoccurring title given to her: Polden, 2005, op cit p.308, described her as a 'pioneer'; flyers at debates described her as this. In *Chapter 4* we see that this was a label often used by the newspapers when referring to Helena.

131. WL: 7HLN/A/29. Clifton Villa, Glenthorne Road, 9 June 1918.

132. This was a London University Student Union (1893–1933), University College London Students Bodies' Records.

133. WL: 7HLN/A/03. 9 April 1919.

134. WL: 7HLN/A/03.

135. Annual Ladies' Night Debate on 9 April 1919 at the Union Society of London, WL: 7HLN/A/03.

136. *The Evening Standard*, 10 April 1919.

137. WL: 7HLN/A/03, flyer for Monday 5 May 1919 Public Meeting in Central Hall, Westminster.

138. WL: 7HLN/A/03, flyer for 22 May 1919 Public Protest Meeting, St. Peters Hall, Bournemouth.

139. Helena was possibly empowered due to exercising her right to vote for the first time in the general election the month before (*Gloucestershire Echo*, 14 December 1918).

140. WL: 7HLN/A/03.

141. WL: 7HLN/A/03. 17 January 1919.

142. WL: 7HLN/A/03. The appeal was heard by a committee composed of: Master Muir Mackenzie (a civil servant: Robert Stevens, 'Mackenzie, Kenneth Augustus Muir, Baron Muir Mackenzie (1845–1930)', *Oxford Dictionary of National Biography*, Oxford: Oxford University Press, 2004), Master Macmorrans, Master Honoratius Lloyd and Master de Colyar.

143. The Barristers' and Solicitors' (Qualification of Women) Bill.

144. Lord Buckmaster, as quoted in Lincoln's Inn Black Books, 2001, p.7.

145. WL: HLN/A/03.

146. 28 October 1952, letter from Helena to Ian Jacob Jackson, Director General of the BBC, WL: 7HLN/08.

147. *Dyson v Attorney General* (1911), 1 KB 410.

148. Barristers and Solicitors (Qualification of Women) Bill, February 1919.

149. William Goodhart, 'Buckmaster, Stanley Owen, First Viscount Buckmaster (1861–1934)', *Oxford Dictionary of National Biography*, Oxford: Oxford University Press, 2004.

150. HL Deb11 March 1919 vol 33 c591, Lord Buckmaster (Liberal). Lord Chancellor from 1915–16.

151. 8 March 1919.

152. *Bebb v Law Society* [1914]. As this applied to solicitors only.

153. WL: 7HLN/A/03, AGM held on 24 June 1919 at De Montford Hall, Leicester. Motion proposed by Mrs Tanner for the Women's Freedom League; seconded by Mrs Oliver Strachey.

154. Auchmuty, 2011, op cit, p.218.

155. Copy of letter in WL: 7HLN/A/01.

156. T. L. Stevenson, 12 December 1918, WL: 7HLN/A/03.

157. WL: 7HLN/A/03, letter dated

December 5 1918.

158. Chris Wrigley, 'Henderson, Arthur (1863–1935)', *Oxford Dictionary of National Biography*, Oxford: Oxford University Press, 2004; Leventhal, F. M. *Arthur Henderson*, 1989, Manchester Manchester. University Press.

159. WL: 7HLN/A/03.

160. WL: 7HLN/A/03. 27 September 1918.

161. HC Bill 38 (1919).

162. WL: 7/HLN/A/01.

163. The second reading is when the principles of a Bill are considered.

164. There were no debates on the second reading of the Sex Disqualification (Removal) Bill.

165. *Daily Mail,* 'Women's Inn of Court', 18 March 1919.

166. 21 March 1919, one of the three clauses was to remove the disqualification of women from holding civil or judicial appointments.

167. Smith, H. L. 'Sex Versus Class: British Feminists and the Labour Party Movement 1919–1929', *The Historian,* 47, 1984, p.19.

168. Takayanagi, 2012, op cit, p.70.

169. Takayangi, 2012, op cit, p.40.

170. HC Deb, 4 Apr 1919, Vol 114, c1625–1628.

171. Strachey, 1928, op cit, p.375.

172. Skordaki, E 'Glass Slippers and Glass Ceilings: Women in the Legal Profession', 3 *International Journal of the Legal Profession*, 10, 1996.

173. Middle Temple Scrapbook.

174. HC Deb, 4 Jul 1919, Vol 117, c1307, Lt-Col Sir Samuel Hoare (Conservative).

175. Ibid cc1336–8 Robert Cecil.

176. HC Deb 4 July 1919, Vol. 117, cc1283–1285, Major Waldorf Astor (Conservative). See Takayangi, 2012, p.54.

177. HL Deb 24 Jul 1919, Vol. 35, c.1047.

178. WL: 7HLN/A/08.

179. It had its second reading on 22 July 1919.

180. HL Deb 22 Jul 1919, Vol. 35, c. 892, Lord Chancellor.

181. War Cabinet Committee of Home Affairs 16 and 28 May 1919. TNA, CAB 26/1. HAC 28 16/5/19 item 6 & HAC 30 28/5/19 item 4.

182. Takayangi, 2012, op cit, p.54.

183. Strachey, 1935, op cit, felt the Bill only opened up the legal profession to women, see p.375.

184. Takayanagi, op cit, p.56.

185. Strachey, op cit, p.375.

186. Takayanagi, op cit, p,70.

187. Thane, 2001, op cit.

188. Takayanagi, 2012, op cit, p.71.

189. Strachey, 1928, op cit, p.375.

190. As recorded in the annual report of the National Union of Societies for Equal Citizenship in 1919 (of which Helena had been the first general secretary in 1917).

191. Smith, H. L. (ed.) *British Feminism in the Twentieth Century,* University of Massachusetts Press, 1990, p.52.

192. 1872–1968, feminist activist and sister-in-law to Ray Strachey. Barbara Caine, 'Strachey, Philippa (1872–1968)', *Oxford Dictionary of National Biography*, Oxford: Oxford University Press, 2004.

193. The LSWS changed its name to the London Society for Women's Service in 1919. In 1926 it would become the London and National Society for Women's Service: Crawford, ibid, Chapter 2, p.356.

194. Takayanagi, 2012, p.59.

195. Ibid, p.60.

196. Ibid.

197. Ibid.

198. Ibid.

199. WL: 7HLN/A/05.

200. For example, *Bulletin,* 15 December 1918, 'Admission to Middle Temple before Christmas'. There was also speculation in the *Daily Express,* 16 December 1919, 'Britain's First Portia: Miss Normanton expecting the Call' and the *Globe,* 16 December 1919, 'Women Lawyers Advent: Applicant's View'.

201. WL: 7HLN/A/05.

202. Strachey, 1928, op cit, p.375.

203. Ibid.

204. Lang, 1929, op cit, p.164.

205. WL: 7HLN/A/01.

206. Polden, 2005, op cit. The other Inns also accepted women, after Helena: Theodora Llewellyn Davies at Inner Temple, 9 January 1920, Marjorie Powell at Lincoln's Inn 16 January 1920 and Mary Selina Share Jones at Gray's Inn on 27 January 1920.

Notes to Chapter 4

1. The Woolsack was the seat of the Lord Chancellor (a lawyer) who was, in 1919, the Speaker in the House of Lords. This changed with the Constitutional Reform Act 2005, when the first person to be elected to the new role of Lord Speaker was a woman, Baroness Hayman.

2. *The Gentlewoman*, 27 December 1919, p.1029.

3. *Evening News*, 28 December 1919.

4. This is perhaps a misquote as her book, *Every Day Law For Women*, says that she was 12, see Chapter 1, or possibly the interview was a fabrication, as Helena must have been aware of the etiquette of the Bar and its rules on self-advertising.

5. Olga Balachowsky-Petit became the first woman to practise, see Clark, L. *Women and Achievement in Nineteenth-Century Europe*, Cambridge: Cambridge University Press, 2008, p.227.

6. In reality women barrister's careers were often restricted to crime or family work. They did not manage to move into more lucrative fields for some time, see Polden, P. 'Portia's Progress: Women at the Bar in England 1919–1939', *International Journal of the Legal Profession*, 293–335, p.320.

7. *Evening News*, 30 December 1919.

8. They do not forget the women who tried and 'failed' before Helena and indeed list them: Bertha Cave (1903 application to Gray's Inn), Miss Victoria Poulton, Miss Jane Cormack, and Mrs Weldon.

9. 30 December 1919.

10. The former Miss Bebb of *Bebb v Law Society* [1914], see *Chapter 3*.

11. Tuesday 30 December 1919.

12. *Evening News,* 30 December 1919.

13. M. A. Elston, 'Lind-af-Hageby, (Emilie Augusta) Louise (1878–1963)', *Oxford Dictionary of National Biography*, Oxford: Oxford University Press, 2004. The trial to which they refer was in 1913 when she brought an unsuccessful action against Dr C. W. Saleeby (1878–1940), a prominent eugenicist and temperance campaigner who, she alleged, had accused her of being 'a systematic liar' in her campaign against vivisection. The *Nation and Athenaeum*, Vol. 13, 1913, p.127 described her advocacy as 'brilliant.'

14. Words said against her in her anti-vivisection work.

15. *Daily Chronicle*, 30 December 1919.

16. *The Observer*, 4 January 1920.

17. Given the rules on self-advertising the wisdom of such actions was questionable.

18. 30 December 1919, WL: 7HLN/02.

19. *The Woman Teacher*, 9 January 1920.

20. WL: 7HLN/A/0.

21. Ibid.

22. Ibid.

23. On the same night Mrs Thomson (Ms Bebb) also had her first dinner at Lincoln's Inn. She too was treated well, see Auchmuty, R. 'Whatever Happened to Miss Bebb? *Bebb v The Law Society* and Women's Legal History,' Legal Studies, Vol. 31 No. 2, June 2011, pp.199–230, p.224.

24. Hubert Sweeney was a barrister at 1 Plowden Buildings. He had been a teacher in a London Board School before joining Middle Temple. In 1906 he was chosen to contest (unsuccessfully) Wigan for the Lancashire and Cheshire Women Textile and Other Worker's Representative Committee: Crawford, Elizabeth *The Women's Suffrage Movement in Britain and Ireland: A Regional Survey,* Routledge, 2006; and Liddington, J. and Morris, J. *One Hand Tied Behind Us: The Rise of the Women's Suffrage Movement*, London: Virago, 1978.

25. WL: 7HLN/A/03. Loose items from Scrapbook 2 of 2. Also reproduced *Daily Mirror* 12 January 1920, 'Verse in her Honour'.

26. *Daily Express,* 12 January 1920.

27. Letter dated 19 January 1920, WL: 7HLN/A/17. Cobb would go on become the first woman to hold a brief, Lang, E. *British Women in the Twentieth Century,* T Werner Laurie, 1929, p.166.

28. Polden, P. 2005, op cit, p.322.

29. Ibid, p.322.

30. *Manchester Guardian*, 31 January 1920.

31. Polden, 2005, op cit, p.295.

32. Ibid.

33. Ibid.

34. Ireland called its first woman to the Bar in November 1921, Frances Kyle, and later that day Averill Deverell was

also called and went on to become the first woman to practise at the Bar. Bar Council of Ireland: http://www.lawlibrary.ie/viewdoc.asp?fn=/documents/aboutus/history/default.htm&m=2#chap21. Margaret Kidd would become the first member of the Scottish Bar in 1923. Isobel Anne Poole, 'Kidd, Dame Margaret Henderson (1900–1989)', *Oxford Dictionary of National Biography*, Oxford: Oxford University Press, 2004, 1882.

35. *The Daily News,* 3 March 1919.

36. March 1919, see Lady Lowry QC, *A Brief History of Women at the Bar*, Association of Women Barristers, Winter/Spring, 2004.

37. 13 February 1920, *The Christian Science Monitor*, Boston, USA, 'Views of English Woman Barrister'. We cannot be certain that this report is reliable.

38. This was the publication of an international Christian news organization.

39. This was a residential club founded in 1920 by the WFL. Prior to this, the WFL had run a café at its headquarters in Holborn, which provided lunches and lectures. The lease was purchased by Dr Elizabeth Knight and maintained by her until her death in 1933. Membership was open to both men and women who had sympathy with progressive thought. It was to become the rallying point for the extension of the franchise movement, therefore it attracted suffrage sympathisers. It also provided vegetarian food which maintained a link between vegetarianism and the movement. The club closed in 1962. For a more detailed account, see Crawford, 2006, p.125.

40. *The Vote*, 20 February 1920.

41. WL: 8SUF/B/042, 8SUF/B/041 and 8SUF/B/153. Alice Schofield-Coates (1881–1875) was a prominent suffragette and Women's Freedom League volunteer. She had been force fed and forcibly removed from the railings of the House of Commons for failing to leave. She was an activist who had addressed suffragette meetings with Mrs Pankhurst. Later she ran a vegetarian restaurant and became a councillor working for teachers' rights.

42. The only reference to Mrs Mustard can be found at the Special Collection at the WL: 7AMP/0/074. This consists of a photograph of a 'committee' in which she can be seen with others at Caxton Hall (a central location for the WSPU). She was presumably a suffragette and women's rights worker.

43. George Wilfred Holford Knight 1877–1936, barrister and Labour MP for Nottingham South 1931–1935. Author of *Oxford Dictionary of National Biography*, Oxford University Press, 2013.

44. Possibly Helena's pupil master.

45. Janet Gibson is listed on the 'Roll of Honour of Suffragette Prisoners 1905–1914', WL: 7LAC/2.

46. WL: 7HLN/A/01 Scrapbook. Letter dated 14 January 1921.

47. Reported 9 March 1920 in both the *Evening News* & *Evening Mail*.

48. Although it is referred to as a banquet in Auchmuty, 2006, op cit, p.224.

49. WL: 7HLN/A/02.

50. He was lawyer, Conservative Unionist MP and loyal friend of women's organizations. E. H. H. Green, 'Hills, John Waller (1867–1938)', *Oxford Dictionary of National Biography*, Oxford: Oxford University Press, 2004. Hills had played an important role in the passing of the Sex Disqualification (Removal) Act 1919, see Takayanagi, Mari Catherine, *Parliament and Women, c.1900–1945*, University of London, Kings College, PhD, 2012, p.61 (he was responsible for a clause that allowed universities to admit women to membership and degrees), p.62 (he wanted to remove the marriage bar) and p.64 (wanted full equality for women).

51. Frederic Wrottesley, 'Pollock, Ernest Murray, First Viscount Hanworth (1861–1936)', rev. Alec Samuels, *Oxford Dictionary of National Biography*, Oxford: Oxford University Press, 2004.

52. Robert Stevens, 'Hewart, Gordon, First Viscount Hewart (1870–1943)', *Oxford Dictionary of National Biography*, Oxford: Oxford University Press, 2004.

53. H. C. G. Matthew, 'Haldane, Richard Burdon, Viscount Haldane (1856–1928)', *Oxford Dictionary of National Biography*, Oxford: Oxford University Press, 2004.

54. Deirdre Beddoe, 'Thomas, Sybil

Margaret, Viscountess Rhondda (1857–1941)', *Oxford Dictionary of National Biography*, Oxford: Oxford University Press, 2004.

55. Janet Howarth, 'Fawcett, Dame Millicent Garrett (1847–1929)', *Oxford Dictionary of National Biography*, Oxford: Oxford University Press, 2004.

56. Lang, 1929, p.165. Chrystal MacMillan was an executive member of the National Union of Women's Suffrage Societies and one of the first female barristers.

57. Sankey, 'Duke, Henry Edward, First Baron Merrivale (1855–1939)', rev. H. C. G. Matthew, *Oxford Dictionary of National Biography*, Oxford: Oxford University Press, 2004.

58. Chapman was a supporter of women's suffrage from his student days (Cecil Chapman, *The Poor Man's Court of Justice: Twenty-five Years as a Metropolitan Magistrate*, London: Hodder and Stoughton, 1925, p.58). He was chairman of the Men's League for Women's Suffrage, although he eventually gave up this position in order to remain a magistrate following Home Office intervention (John, A. V, 'Between the Cause and the Courts: The Curious Case of Cecil Chapman' in C Eustance, J Ryan and L Ugolini (eds.) *A Suffrage Reader: Charting Directions in British Suffrage History*, Leicester: Leicester University Press, 2000, pp.145–161).

59. Hall, L. *Sex, Gender and Social Change*, Palgrave MacMillan, 2012, p.102. Indeed, throughout his career as a magistrate he sought to forward women's interests including through public speaking and publications on women and law. His other political role was serving as a Conservative councillor for Chelsea on London City Council between 1896 and 1898 (*Who Was Who, 1929–1940* (2nd. edn.), London: Adam & Charles Black, 1967, p 239).

60. Auchmuty, 2006, op cit.

61. Ibid.

62. Lord Chief Justice until 1921 and he had led the prosecution in *R v Seddon* 1912 (fly paper poisoning murder case).

63. Lang, 1929, op cit.

64. *Manchester Guardian*, 9 March 1920.

65. Lang, 1929, op cit.

66. Reported 9 March 1920 in both the *Evening News* and the *Evening Mail.*

67. *Evening Mail,* 9 March 1920.

68. Abel, R. L. *The Making of the Legal Profession 1800–1988*, Beard Books, 1998, p.50.

69. Gower, L. C. B. 'English Legal Training: A Critical Survey', 13 *Modern Law Review*, pp.137–140, 2009.

70. Information kindly supplied by Theresa Thom, Gray's Inn and Guy Holborn, Lincoln's Inn.

71. Ibid and Abel, 1998, op cit, p.41.

72. Abel, 1998, op cit.

73. Ibid.

74. Ibid.

75. Although now missing (private information), there is an extract in *Graya*, No. 89, pp.39–41.

76. Ibid.

77. Ibid.

78. Polden, 2005, op cit.

79. *Graya*, op cit.

80. Noted on her CV. WL: 7HLN/A/01.

81. Ibid.

82. Hazel Fox, 'Williams, Ivy (1877–1966)', *Oxford Dictionary of National Biography*, Oxford: Oxford University Press, 2004.

83. *Law Journal*, 1921, Vol 56, p.215.

84. Ibid.

85. Bacik, I, Costello, C and Drew E, 'Gender Injustice: Towards the Feminisation of the Legal Professions?', Law School, Trinity College Dublin, Dublin, 2003, p.431.

86. *Evening Standard*, 13 January 1921.

87. WL: 7HLN/A/07.

88. The re-occurring issue of self-advertising has not been dealt with as a theme because it is essential to the chronology of Helena's story. It has an effect on her subsequent behaviour. It is difficult to know if other women were subjected to these constant accusations or indeed if male barristers suffered in this way too. On the face of things it may be misogyny.

89. WL: 7HLN/A/07.

90. S. V. FitzGerald, 'Edge, Sir John (1841–1926)', rev. Roger T. Stearn, *Oxford Dictionary of National Biography*, Oxford: Oxford University Press, 2004. He was a man of Irish descent, who was called to both the Irish and the English

Bars. He took silk in 1886 and was made a High Court judge in India. He retired in 1908 and became treasurer at Middle Temple in 1919.

91. WL: 7HLN/A/07.
92. She must have felt that this was encouraging press intrusion.
93. WL: 7HLN/A/07.
94. WL: 7HLN/A/07.
95. Boulton, W. W. 1953, Butterworths, see Evans, K. *The Language of Advocacy,* 1998, Oxford: Oxford University Press, p.31.
96. Polden, 2005, op cit, p.327.
97. Polden, 2005, op cit, p.327.
98. Purcell, C. G. *Cases and Other Authorities on Legal Ethics 1870–1934,* London Foundation Press, 1946.
99. For a discussion of press behaviour see Bingham, A. *Gender Modernity and the Popular Press in Inter-War Britain,* Oxford University Press Monograph, 2004 and Bingham, A. *Family Newspapers. Private Lives and the British Popular Press 1918–1978,* Oxford: Oxford University Press, 2009.
100. WL: 7HLN/A/06. 31 May 1920.
101. *Daily Express*, 14 January 1921.
102. *Daily Chronicle,* 14 January 1921.
103. *Daily Sketch,* 14 January 1921.
104. *Daily Telegraph,* 'Women Bar Students', 14 January 1921.
105. *Daily Express,* 'The Feminine Rake', 26 January 1921.
106. MT. 3/MEM.
107. *The Vote* January 21 1921.
108. Polden 2005, op cit, p.295.
109. Ibid.
110. Abel, 1998, op cit, p.75.
111. Polden, 2005, op cit, p.298.
112. Ibid.
113. Ibid.
114. Ibid.
115. Ibid, p.301.
116. Ibid, p.300.
117. Ibid, p.301: it was not until after the Second World War that entrants with a law degree were in the majority and that the figure would probably be the same for women.
118. MT.3/MEM.
119. WL: 7HLN/A/01.
120. Williams went on to be the first woman called to the Bar of England and Wales and therefore the first woman barrister,

see Hazel Fox, op cit, 2004.
121. Achieved in 1930, WL: 7HLN/A/37.
122. Polden, 1996, op cit, p.322.
123. Ibid.
124. Lincoln's Inn Black Books, 2001, pp.555–560.
125. British Phone Books 1880–1984. p.862.
126. Statement re *The Times* November 1921, November 22 1922, WL: HLN/A/07. The British Phone Books (1880–1984) register her as being at this business address in 1924, p.734. She remained here until 1929, p.937, when she moved to 3 Dr Johnson's Buildings.
127. Polden. 2005, op cit. Only individual addresses were printed and given that the Inns have accommodation in them it is not a clear guide.
128. Abel,1998, op cit, p.53.
129. Ibid.
130. Ibid.
131. WL: LOCKET.
132. Miss A. W. Hastings was awarded a Middle Temple 'prize' in 1922, letter from Middle Temple to Helena 27 October 1925, WL: 7HLN/A/01.
133. Polden, P. 2005, op cit.
134. WL: 7HLN/A/17.
135. Polden, 2005, op cit.
136. WL: LOCKET.
137. Polden, 2005, op cit, p.295.
138. Polden, 2005, op cit, p.306.
139. Notes by Elsie Cannon, Helena's niece. WL: 7HLN/C/09.
140. *The Evening Standard,* 26 October 1921.
141. *New York Times,* 'Woman Barrister of England Here', 7 January 1925.
142. Ibid.
143. *Washington DC Star*, 12 April 1925.
144. WL: 7HLN/A/17.
145. Letter from Helena to Mater Scott KC, treasurer of Middle Temple, 11 November 1922.
146. Document on opinion paper in response to *Evening Standard* report of 18 November 1922, 'Barristers Hidden Tresses', WL: 7HLN/A/07.
147. Ibid.
148. Kramer, D. *Heywood Broun. A Biographical Portrait*, New York: Current Books, 1949.
149. She was to an extent unsuccessful as they offered a passport in the name 'Ruth Hale, also known as Mrs Heywood Broun.' She refused to accept

this.

150. Helena gave them a guided tour of the Temple, this was recorded and commented on in the *Daily Star* of 24 July 1924.

151. *Evening Standard*, 'Women Barristers Hidden Tresses', 18 November 1922.

152. *Oxford Times*, 'What's In a Name', 2 January 1925.

153. Statement by Helena re *The Times*, 22 November 1922.

154. WL: 7HLN/A/07.

155. 18 January 1935. Letter from Hutchinson and Co, WL: 7HLN/A/07.

156. *Evening Standard*, 18 November 1922.

157. Ibid.

158. Abel, 1998, op cit, p.330.

159. Rosser describes Davy '…bit of a practice at the divorce Bar, mainly through legal aid, "plodded on" until 1929. Decided to become a solicitor for the "good of the cause." She felt too few solicitors willing to brief women. She felt women barristers "future prospects were hard and dim." She linked up with another solicitor and opened an office in the East End called "Berthen and Davy." Did a lot of poor persons work and had support from Sir George Fowler'—see WL: LOCKET. Evidence that Davy sent Rosser briefs, mostly police court matrimonial troubles, which Rosser explained, 'I was more than pleased to have them.'

160. Theodora Llewellyn Davies was the adopted child of J. M. Barrie and a pupil of Theobald Mathew, 4 Paper Buildings, Temple. She would go on to run the Howard League for Penal Reform. Mathew was an Irish Catholic and a common law junior who never took silk; significantly he was one of first juniors to take a female pupil.

161. The Inn is led by the treasurer, who is elected to serve for a one-year term.

162. *Evening Standard*, 18 November 1922.

163. Abel, 1998, op cit, p.49.

164. Polden, 2005, op cit, p.302.

165. Ibid.

166. Ibid.

Notes to Chapter 5

1. WL: 7HLN/A/18. 28 November 1933. Letter from Helena to the LNSWS.

2. Abel, R. *The Making of the English Legal Profession 1800–1988*, Washington: Beard Books, 1988, Table 1.12, p.330.

3. *Northern Daily Telegraph*, 9 July 1935.

4. Polden, P. 'Portia's Progress: Women at the Bar in England 1919–1939', *International Journal of the Legal Profession*, Vol.12, No.3, Nov 2005, p.297.

5. Abel, 1998, op cit, p.311 Table 1.1.

6. Ibid, Table 1.12 p.330.

7. *Northern Evening Dispatch*, 'What Women Barristers are Doing', 17 February 1925.

8. *Liverpool Courier*, 'Women Who Make Good at The Bar', 25 May 25 1926.

9. Strachey, R. *Careers and Openings for Women* London: Faber and Faber, 1935.

10. Hughes, D. W. *Careers for Our Daughters*, London: Black Publishers, 1936.

11. Polden, 2005, op cit, p.314.

12. As noted earlier, Helena's father and mother were a piano manufacturer (or tuner) and 'publican.'

13. WL: LOCKET.

14. *Evening Standard*, 'Portia in Court', 20 November 1922.

15. Ibid.

16. Abel, 1998, op cit, p.60.

17. Polden, 2005, op cit, p.315.

18. Ibid. Polden gives two examples of this career route: Beatrice Honor Davy (called 1922 at Inner Temple) and Marion Billson (called 1924, so not a direct contemporary of Helena).

19. Ibid. Polden lists Beroe Bicknell, Doris Belcher, Esther Dangerfield, Irene Davies and Denise Chorlton as following this path. Bicknell also wrote books.

20. WL: LOCKET.

21. Ibid.

22. Ibid.

23. Flood, J. *Barristers Clerks, The Law's Middlemen*, Manchester: Manchester University Press, 1983.

24. WL: LOCKET.

25. Cretney, S. *Family Law in the Twentieth Century, A History*, Oxford: Oxford University Press, 2011, pp.306–7, mentions legislation dating back to 1495 to assist the poor with fees, but with the Rules of the Supreme Court (Poor Persons) 1913 came the Poor Persons'

Procedure. This allowed the Poor Persons' Department of the High Court to refer a person with assets of less that £50 to a 'reporting solicitor.' Following their report the court could admit the applicant as a 'poor person,' i.e. enable them to be exempt from court fees and they would be assigned a solicitor or counsel from a list of volunteers who would run the case but could not take a fee.

26. WL: LOCKET.

27. Polden, 2005, op cit; Auchmuty, R. 'Whatever Happened to Miss Bebb? *Bebb v. The Law Society* and Women's Legal History', *Legal Studies*, Vol. 31 No. 2, pp.199–230.

28. Lang, E. L. *British Women in the Twentieth Century*, T Werner Laurie, 1929 and Gates, G. E. *The Women's Year Book,* Women's Publishers, 1923, p.43.

29. Held in the High Court of Justice, Probate Divorce and Admiralty Division (Divorce).

30. Many of her cases were divorce cases, for example, 3 March 1930 *Evening Standard* & *Evening News*, *Nottingham Evening News*, *Northern Despatch* (and *Daily Mirror* 4 March 1930): 'Judge Bans Secrecy Over Divorce Names.' 16 February 1931 letter from Dehn & Lauderdale, solicitors thanking her for her work on a divorce case, WL: 7HLN/A/17.

31. David Davies, 'Horridge, Sir Thomas Gardner (1857–1938)', rev. Hugh Mooney, *Oxford Dictionary of National Biography*, Oxford: Oxford University Press, 2004; a solicitor who converted to the Bar and became a KC and Liberal MP for Manchester East, where he campaigned for the release of Chinese slaves in African gold mines. He stood down from politics and returned to the Bar as a High Court judge, hearing mainly divorce cases although he was involved in the *Casement* treason trial.

32. WL: 7HLN/A/09. 2 January 1923, letter from C. Damer Snell, official shorthand writer at the Royal Courts of Justice.

33. This is no record of how she came to be briefed by these solicitors, possibly they already briefed someone senior in her chambers.

34. Forty per cent of divorce petitions were from women between 1858–1900, see Stone, L. *Road to Divorce, England 1530–1987,* Oxford: Oxford University Press, 1990.

35. This is a legal term that means the defendant has been served with the papers and is a set procedure which has to be followed that shows the jurisdiction of the court and details of the legal action. This gives the defendant an opportunity to reply and appear.

36. Cretney, 2011, op cit, p.194.

37. An equitable doctrine that means that no one would be granted relief if they were guilty in some way. A good example of this is *Clarke v Clarke and Clarke* (1865) 34 LJ (PA&M) 94, where the husband's one off act of adultery with a prostitute was enough to debar him from divorcing his wife who was having an incestuous affair with her brother.

38. In *Gipps v Gipps and Hume* (1864) 11 HLC 1 the husband drove the wife to prostitution and then lived off her earnings. He was denied a divorce on the grounds of connivance.

39. Sections 29 and 30.

40. WL: 7HLN/A/07.

41. *Chicago Tribune* (Paris edition), 22 December 1922.

42. WL: 7HLN/A/29. 2 January 1923.

43. WL: 7HLN/A/07.

44. WL: 7HLN/A/07.

45. WL: 7HLN/A/07.

46. Case book No. 2 1930–1940, WL: 7HLN/A/13.

47. Ibid.

48. Abel, 1998, op cit, p.97.

49. Western Circuit Minute Book No. 2.

50. Odgers was a prolific writer of law texts, e.g. *The Principles of Pleadings and Practice in Civil Actions in the High Court of Justice*, London: Stevens & Sons, 1912; *Odgers on the Common Law in England*, London: Sweet & Maxwell, 1927; *Principles of Practice and Evidence,* Butterworths, 1911.

51. Western Circuit Minute Book No.2

52. WL: 7HLN/A/07. April 1923 (No day recorded).

53. Helena's friend and supporter Holford Knight wrote under a pen name of 'Eldon Junior' and this matter relates to an article he wrote in which he depicted

a female bar student despairing about the jealousy that surrounded her at the Bar. Helena noted in her scrapbook that she 'wondered the authorities did not do something about this kind of thing.' This suggests that she and Holford Knight may have fallen out.

54. WL: 7HLN/A/07. Undated.
55. Heilbron, H. *Rose Heilbron,* Oxford: Hart Publishing, 2012, pp.135–139.
56. Ibid, p.185.
57. Ibid, p.186.
58. Ibid, p.189.
59. Ibid, p.208.
60. Ibid, pp.138–9.
61. Polden, 2005, op cit, p.318.
62. Ibid, p.324.
63. Ibid, p.318.
64. Ibid, p.314.
65. The great Victorian barrister. C. Biron, 'Hall, Sir Edward Marshall (1858–1927)', rev. Mike Clarke, *Oxford Dictionary of National Biography*, Oxford: Oxford University Press, 2004.
66. WL: 7HLN/A/17, letter from Helena to Venetia Stephenson, 3 March 1927.
67. Case book No. 2 1930–1940 is in her archives, see WL: 7HLN/A/13.
68. WL: 7HLN/A/14.
69. Abel, 1998, op cit, p.120.
70. Ibid, p.22
71. Ibid.
72. Heilbron, 2012, op cit, p.18.
73. Ibid p.22.
74. Ibid, p.23.
75. Ibid, pp.27–28.
76. Abel, 1998, op cit, Table 1.36, p.368.
77. http://www.measuringworth.com/ ukcompare/relativevalue.php
78. Abel, 1998, op cit, p.60.
79. Ibid, p.61.
80. *Daily Express*, 'Woman Counsel and the Jury', 7 February 1924.
81. *Evening News*, 'A Brief From the Dock', 17 September 1932.
82. WL: LOCKET.
83. *Daily Express*, 'First Woman in the Old Bailey: Women Counsel and the Jury', 7 February 1924; the story was repeated two years later in *Evening News* .March 1926.
84. *Daily Express* 7, February 1924. It has often been suggested that Elsie Bowerman was the first woman to appear in the Old Bailey, but she was

not called until November 1924.
85. Various examples appear in later endnotes.
86. *Daily Express,* 8 February 1924.
87. WL: LOCKET.
88. Ibid.
89. 1851–1929, barrister, MP and Old Bailey judge from 1920. His photo-graphic portrait hangs in the National Portrait Gallery. He gained a reputation for being sympathetic to homosexual offences, see Houlbrook, M. *Queer London: Perils and Pleasures in the Sexual Metropolis 1918–1957,* Chicago: University of Chicago Press, 2006.
90. This behaviour was probably not uncommon as Rosser describes a similar experience in her account of her career (WL: LOCKET) when, on her first court appearance she was left alone to examine the witness. She called the witness, and told the judge she would start with 'page 205 of the depositions'. Sir Henry Dickens, 'fixed a fierce look on me and said "I have never trusted a woman in my life and I am not going to start now. You are quite wrong; it is page 204." He then sat back, threw off his wig and roared with laughter at his own joke. So did the court. He was technically right for there was one word "and" left on page 204.' Rosser seems to have been unfazed by this experience commenting, 'We proceeded merrily for the rest of the afternoon.'
91. *Wolverhampton Express,* 'Woman Barrister. Gallant Sergeant Offers to Help Her Out', 7 February 1924.
92. *Daily Express*, 'Woman Counsel and the Jury', 7 February 1924.
93. *Daily Express* (Lighting up time), 'Win For A Woman Barrister.', 8 February 1924.
94. Prison had three divisions. The third division was for habitual and common criminals, they were kept in their cells and given productive work. First and second division convicts were inside for more trivial offences and kept separate from the third division prisoners for fear of contamination. See Lytton, C. *Prisons and Prisoners,* Peterborough: Broadview Press Ltd, 2008, p.20.
95. *Daily Express* (Lighting up time), 'Win For A Woman Barrister', 8 February

1924.

96. *Manchester Evening News*, 8 February 1924.

97. Henry Snell MP 1865–1944 Labour, Woolwich east, David Howell, 'Snell, Henry, Baron Snell (1865–1944)', *Oxford Dictionary of National Biography*, Oxford: Oxford University Press, 2004.

98. Receipt from the RCJ dated 16 December 1927. WL: 7HLN/A/17.

Notes to Chapter 6

1. Delafield, E. M. *The Provincial Lady in America* (1934), London: Virago Press,1984, p.286.

2. Boros, C.L *Justice Henry Fielding's Influence on Law and Literature* New Jersey: Xlibris Corp 2010, Chapter 6; Oakland, J. *British Civilisation* Routledge, 2010, p.166; Rackley, E. *Women, Judging and the Judiciary: From Difference to Diversity*, Routledge, 2012, p.52.

3. This is discussed further in Chapters *7* and *8.*

4. Rosser was the daughter of a Welsh businessman and Liberal councillor. This job was arranged for her by Lloyd George in 1920 after she moved from St. Hugh's, Oxford, to the London School of Economics to study for a thesis, see WL: LOCKET.

5. *Daily Star,* 24 July 1924, 'American Lady Lawyers Visited the UK.'

6. Moran, J. *Star Authors: Literary Celebrity in America,* Pluto Press, 1999, p.17.

7. WL: 7HLN/A/10. Copy of letter dated 17 June 1924.

8. WL: 7HLN/A/10. September 1924 letter from Helena to Major Pond.

9. WL: 7HLN/A/10. 5 September 1924 letter from Pond to Helena.

10. The *New York Times*, 7 January 1925, 'Woman Barrister of England Here'.

11. Ibid.

12. *Washington Herald*, 'Fight for Maiden Name Wins Aid', 24 November 1924.

13. The Comptroller General was appointed by President Harding and was the Director of the General Accounting Office. This had legislative powers and was set up to ensure the fiscal and managerial accountability of the Federal Government.

14. WL: 7HLN/A/10. Letter dated 16 December 1924.

15. Delafield, 1934, op cit.

16. Ibid, p.263.

17. Ibid, p.285.

18. Ibid, p.289.

19. Ibid.

20. *New York Times,* 'Woman Barrister of England Here', 7 January 1925.

21. *Westminster Gazette*, 'Woman's Passport: First to be granted in maiden name', 29 December 1924.'

22. Also reported in the *Sunday Express*, 28 December 1924. Ruth Hale was married to the journalist, Heywood Broun, and challenged the US State Department in 1921 over the right to be issued with a passport in her maiden name. They refused this but issued one as 'Ruth Hale, also known as Mrs Broun', a compromise of sorts. She was a founding member of the Lucy Stone League, whose motto read 'My name is a symbol for my identity and must not be lost.' See Kramer, D. *Heywood Broun: A Biographical Portrait* New York: Current Books, 1949.

23. *Overseas Daily Mail*, 3 January 1925.

24. *Empire News*, 'Passport Report', 4 January 1925.

25. WL: 7 HLN/A/10.

26. WL: 7HLN/A/10.

27. WL: 7HLN/A/10.

28. WL: 7HLN/A/10.

29. As reported in the *New York Times*, 'Woman Barrister of England Here', 7 January 1925. The *Adriatic* left Liverpool on 27 December 1924: UK Incoming Passenger Lists 1878–1960.

30. 21 January 1925. WL: 7HLN/A/10.

31. WL: 7HLN/A/10.

32. WL: 7HLN/A/10.

33. WL: 7HLN/A/10. 28 February 1925.

34. For example Lang E. M. *British Women in the Twentieth Century* London, T Werner Laurie, 1929 p.166.

35. *Law Journal*, 21 November 1925, 941.

36. Ibid. Ruby Black, 1896–1957, journalist and biographer of Eleanor Roosevelt, born in Texas, member of National Women's Party, Birth Control League, Woman's National Press Club and editor of *Equal Right's Magazine*; Stannard, U. *Mrs Man* Germain Books, 1977,

pp.206–207 and Howes, D. *American Women,* Vols 1–3, Richard Blank Publishing Co. 1935, p.51.

37. Page 36 of Helena's Scrapbook. WL: 7HLN/A/01.
38. *Law Journal,* 21 Nov 1925, 941.
39. WL: 7HLN/A/10. 7 March 1925.
40. 13 March 1925, as reported in the *Philadelphia Bulletin.* WL: 7HLN/A/10.
41. WL: 7HLN/A/10.
42. 4 April 1925 Letter to Helena c/o a hotel in Quebec. WL: 7HLN/A/10.
43. June 1925, The Canadian White Ribbon Tidings, Quebec province. Helena scribbled on this report of her speech, 'In England there is a respect for law,' in which she is described as 'the first woman barrister.' In red ink she wrote, 'I shall never get this error out of the Press.'
44. Canadian Pacific Line, passenger No. 208: Details from UK incoming passenger lists 1878–1960.
45. WL: 7HLN/A/10. 22 May 1925.
46. 26 May 1925. Letter from Stella Wolfe Murray journalist at *Women's News and Views.* WL: 7HLN/A/17.
47. WL: 7HLN/A/17.
48. *Chicago Illinois Tribune,* 1 March 1925.
49. 4 April 1925 letter to Helena c/o hotel in Quebec from National Woman's Party, Washington. WL: 7/HLN/A/10.
50. WL: 7HLN/A/11.

Notes to Chapter 7

1. Thane, P. 'What Difference Did the Vote Make?' in Vickery, A. (ed.) *Women, Privilege and Power,* Stanford University Press, 2001, pp.253–4.
2. For example, 19 November 1926 when she was 'blackballed by the United Law Society. Letter from Mr. Guedalla, solicitor, to Helena to say both he and his son had proposed to join it and that she was blackballed. He was very upset. WL: 7HLN/A/17. No records for the society exist.
3. 6 July 1925. Letter from Cartwright Sharp of 3 Elm Court to Helena. WL: 7HLN/A/26.
4. WL: 7HLN/A/04.
5. WL: 7HLN/A/01.
6. 15 October 1926. Letter from John Lewenstein Solicitors, Hull concerning

the case of *Moody v Lee and Beaulah.* WL: 7HLN/A/26.
7. Ibid.
8. *Yorkshire Post,* 'Lady Barrister and Cooking. Retried Hull Case. Keen Prosecution of Plaintiff', 30 November 1926.
9. Ibid.
10. Ibid.
11. Much has been written on this situating of women and women's work, see O'Donovan, K. *Sexual Divisions in Law,* London: Weidenfeld and Nicolson, 1985; and Eisensteien, Z. R. *The Radical Future of Liberal Feminism,* London: Longman, 1981.
12. See Helena's reply 25 January 1927 WL: 7HLN/A/17.
13. 12 January 1928. Letter to Joan Firmin, Women's Union College, WC1, WL: 7HLN/A/17. She apologised for not replying sooner but had sprained her ankle.
14. MT.3/DIS/67.
15. WL: 7HLN/A/17. Letter dated 5 March 1927. From Helena to Miss Venetia Stephenson (at 1 Garden Court, Temple).
16. In a letter Helena warned Stephenson that someone was spreading rumours and gossip about her (Stephenson) and that Helena had done all she could to 'refute them.' Stephenson's 'crime' was to get 'a little too much work.' WL: 7HLN/A/17. Stephenson was 30 when she entered Gray's Inn in 1922 and was called in 1924. She often waited with Helena for dock briefs but never secured a tenancy. She worked as a law reporter (she was removed from the divorce courts for reporting the more salacious aspects) and died in poverty, see Polden, P. 'Women at the Bar in England, 1919–1939,' *International Journal of the Legal Profession,* Vol. 12, No.3, Nov 2005, pp.308–309. She was the first woman to defend a prisoner in a murder trial (he was hanged) see Franz, N. A. *English Women Enter the Profession,* Cincinnati Publishers, 1965. WL: 7HLN/F/03.
17. Stephenson was described by her contemporary, Enid Rosser as 'an arid woman, who "hung around the Old Bailey and London Session" but she was not an asset to the cause largely because

she was lacking in charm and manners.' See WL: LOCKET.

18. These papers are carbon copies of letters from Helena to a woman journalist. They concerned an unnamed woman barrister: 'I will not give the woman barrister's name yet' and seem to concern a plagiarism case involving an undated article in Nash's magazine. Helena stated that she had taken the advice of Sir Duncan Kurley KC. Nash's magazine brought a case for infringement of copyright against the *Sunday Express*. 'They' (Nash's Magazine?) 'are holding their hand until they see the outcome of the libel action against me [Helena], a highly speculative piece of litigation. I have a watertight defence of privilege and justification. Mr Cartwright Sharp is acting for me.' This is confusing and unclear.

19. *Daily Sketch*, '"Cat" for Human Satyr, Crook Who Terrorised Women, Court Censure, Sentence of Three Years' Penal Servitude', 20 November 1927; also reported in the *Daily Mirror, Islington Post*, 18 November 1927 and *Paisley Daily Express,* 17 November 1927.

20. Before Sir Ernest Wild, recorder.

21. 26 November 1928. Letter HN to MT informing them there would be a letter in the *Daily Chronicle* apologising for an article in which they attacked her.

22. WL: 7HLN/A/17. 14 May 1928. Letter from Helena to Albert Crewe of 3 Plowden Buildings, Temple (She would join these chambers in 1932).

23. 25 Aldersmead Road.

24. British Phone Books 1880–1984, p.1023. She would only remain there for a year, as in 1931 she is recorded as being in chambers at 3 Plowden Buildings, Middle Temple and until 1939.

25. WL: 7HLN/A/13.

26. WL: 7HLN/A/01.

27. WL: 7HLN/A/07. 30 October 1934.

28. Mr H. C. Mossop.

29. The papers went back to 1898.

30. WL: 7HLN/A/21.

31. *Lancashire Post*, 'Woman Barristers Defence of Young Husband', 3 March 1930.

32. *Edinburgh Evening News*, 1 March 1930.

33. This appears to be Sir Travers Christmas Humphreys, see F. H. Cowper, 'Humphreys, Sir (Richard Somers) Travers Christmas (1867–1956)', rev. Alec Samuels, *Oxford Dictionary of National Biography*, Oxford: Oxford University Press, 2004. He was a respected judge who had been a junior barrister in the criminal libel action against Lord Alfred Douglas's father. He was also the junior barrister in the *Crippen case* and the similar fact evidence precedent of *R v Smith*.

34. He was a KC whose mother was Ethel Gordon Fenwick, 1857–1947, a nursing pioneer and campaigner for a nationally accepted nursing certificate, see http://www.kingscollections.org/nurses/d-f/fenwick-ethel-gordon

35. *Edinburgh Evening News*, 1 March 1930.

36. Ibid.

37. WL: 7HLN/A/04. Handwritten note in her papers.

38. Cretney, S. *Family Law in the Twentieth Century,* Oxford: Oxford University Press, 2011, p.176.

39. British Phone Books. p.1245.

40. WL: 7HLN/A/22.

41. A barrister who practises mainly in crime, not the most lucrative of employments.

42. *The Northern Echo*, 5 August 1931.

43. Dunn ran a holiday club for fellow employees at the Messrs Rowntrees of York.

44. *News of the World*, 25 October 1931.

45. Binding over is not a sentence but a disposal which requires that the convicted defendant refrain from committing another crime (or specified behaviour) within a fixed period set by the court or faces being returned to court when a recognizance, a promise to pay money, somewhat like a bond, can be forfeited. It is an ancient process traceable to the Justices of the Peace Act 1361.

46. *Liverpool Post*, 'Women Counsel Popular', 16 September 1932.

47. 21 September 1932, as reported in *Sketch Weekly*.

48. Ibid.

49. Next to the report of 17 September 1932, *Evening News*, 'A Brief From the Dock.' 7HLN/A/01.

50. WL: 7HLN/A/01. 9 April 1933.

51. *News of The World*, 22 January 1933.
52. Page 29. WL: 7HLN/A/04.
53. *Daily Express*, 16 September 1933; *Jersey Morning News*, 'Attacked Maid Prevents a Robbery, Screams Frighten Intruders at Dancer's Home', 16 September 1933; *The Star*, 15 September 1933; *Marylebone Mercury*, 23 September 1933.
54. Frank Povey (aged 26) and his brother Reginald Povey (aged 21).
55. *Daily Express*, 16 September 1933.
56. This must have been Cecil Whiteley who was a KC and judge. He had a distinguished career, also acting for the prosecution with Travers Humphreys in the 'Brides in the Bath' case and the defence in the Thompson and Bywaters murder trial in 1922: a clear example of social attitudes towards women's sexual desires. Bywaters had attacked and killed his lover's husband. She was hanged (probably pregnant) despite the fact that there was no evidence she physically participated in the murder and scarcely any that she planned the attack other than cryptic love letters. She was styled a wicked women, who indulged in extra-marital and illicit sex with her lodger.
57. WL: 7HLN/A/04.
58. *The Queen*, 'Women in the News, Women as Barristers', 29 November 1933.
59. WL: 7HLN/A/07. 10 March 1933.
60. WL: 7HLN/A/07. 13 March 1933.
61. 4 April 1933.
62. WL: 7HLN/A/07. 24 August 1933.
63. See *Chapter 9*.
64. WL: 5CMW/A.
65. Unreported. But see *The Times*, 'Convict & Custody of Child', 11 December 1933.
66. This must be Sir Rigby Philip Watson Swift, who was from the North of England and although he lived in Sussex made a point of going on circuit every two years. He had been a successful barrister, KC and then judge who presided over many infamous cases of the day. He was a strong supporter of marriage but recognised that the divorce law was harsh and could produce diffi-cult results, see J. E. Singleton, 'Swift, Sir Rigby Philip Watson (1874–1937)', rev. Alec Samuels, *Oxford Dictionary of National Biography*, Oxford: Oxford

University Press, 2004.
67. *Sunday Times*, 10 December 1933.
68. P. 26. WL: 7HLN/A/04.
69. *Daily Herald*, 'Prisons Within Prisons, 11 January 1934.
70. WL: 7HLN/A/04.
71. *The Spectator*, 'A Victim of the Law', 11 November 1922, p.33.
72. *Daily Express*, 'Feminists give a big hand to woman barrister Helena Normanton', 24 January 1936. Also in *Wood Green Sentinel*, 30 January 1936; *Grimsby Evening Telegraph*, 23 January 1936; *Daily Mirror*, 24 January 1936; and *News of the World*, 26 January 1936.
73. Cohabitation was not unusual at this time because of the difficulties with divorce and there was legislation that recognised these unions, see Thane, P. *Happy Families? History and Family Policy*, 2010. Report for the British Academy, p.28.
74. *News Review*, 30 January 1936.
75. 7 May 1936.
76. Lady Emma Clark Beilby (1858–1936) was a campaigner for women's entry to the engineering profession, see Law, C. *Women, A Modern Political Dictionary*, I. B. Tauris Publishers, 2000, p.24. She was married to a Scottish Industrial Chemist (C. H. Desch, 'Beilby, Sir George Thomas (1850–1924)', rev. John Bosnell, *Oxford Dictionary of National Biography*, Oxford: Oxford University Press, 2004) and it is unclear why she withdrew her gift.
77. *Worthing Herald*, 'Woman with "Curious Psychic Powers", Users of "Subtle Craft" Fined at Worthing Court', 14 September 1936.
78. WL: 7HLN/A/04.
79. Kollar, R. *Searching for Raymond: Anglicanism, Spiritualism and Bereavement Between Two World Wars*, Lexington Books, 2000, p.140.
80. Walker-Smith, D. *Lord Reading and His Cases: The Study of a Great Career*, New York: Taylor Francis, Macmillan, 1934, p.21.
81. Ibid.
82. *Daily Sketch*, 6 February 1934. Also, *Daily Sketch*, 'Canada is the first to appoint a female KC', 11 November 1934. They reported that there were two eligible women in England. The most

senior was Helena who had not been given silk nor applied for it.

83. Abel, R. *The Making of the English Legal Profession,* Beard Publishing, 1988, p.98. Silks were appointed by the Lord Chancellor and until 1945 this was virtually automatic for anyone who applied. Until 1961 an applicant had to notify all the juniors on his or her circuit with greater seniority so that they could apply before him or her if they so wished.

84. See Bar Council website for the application form and criteria.

85. Abel op cit.

86. WL: 7HLN/A/22.

87. 5 July 1934.

88. Polden, 2005, op cit, p.322. Cross was born in 1908, whose maternal family were lawyers. She left St. Hilda's at 20 with a BA, joining Lincoln's Inn in 1928 and was called in 1931. She built up a strong practice with the aid of a solicitor who began at the same time as she did. She found Lincoln's Inn chilly and discovered her clerk never sought work for her. During the Second World War she took employment in Civil Defence and continued in this role after the war.

89. 'Women in Council', *Journal of the National Council of Women of Great Britain,* September 1946.

90. WL: 7HLN/A/06, for example on 19 September 1946 letters of congratulation would be received from St. Joan's Social and Political Alliance re her election to the General Council of the Bar.

91. WL: 7HLN/A/01. 12 July 1933.

92. WL: 7HLN/A/07. 18 July 1933.

93. WL: 7HLN/A/07. 28 July 1933.

94. WL: 7HLN/A/07. 2 August 1933.

95. WL: 7HLN/A/07. 3 August 1933.

96. This contains the civil rules of practice.

97. WL: 7HLN/A/01. 26 September 1934.

98. WL: 7HLN/A/07.

99. WL: 7HLN/A/07. 27 September 1934.

100. *Daily Sketch,* 'Shall We Ever See a Woman Judge? Why Portia is not a great success', 5 October 1934.

101. Charles Garfield Lott Du Cann was not only a barrister but also a prolific author on the legal profession and other topics such as *Adventures in Antiques,* Muller Publishers, 1965; *Teach Yourself to Live*, Hodder & Stoughton, 1955; and *The Loves of George Bernard Shaw*, Funk & Wagnalls Co., 1963.

102. WL: 7HLN/A/07. 19 December 1934.

103. WL: 7HLN/A/07. 9 January 1935.

104. Rosser described Colwill as an '"odd creature"…daughter of a clerk in the Temple. Found a place in chambers with Martin O'Connor, a highly suspect and crafty old Irishman whose reputation was not of the highest quality to put it mildly and with kindness…She was quite busy running around court…She wasn't a bad sort once you accepted her background and her chambers and she herself was quite honest and behaved with due professional propriety,' see WL: LOCKET.

105. There is large historiography concerning this case, but in summary, this was a successful defence by Marshall Hall for Madame (or Princess) Marguerite Fahmy in 1923 for the shooting dead of her husband, Egyptian Prince Fahmy Bey at London's Savoy Hotel. The death of the prince is frequently on lists of victims of the so-called Curse of the Pharaohs. Marshall Hall brought out Prince Fahmy's race and sexual habits, painting the victim as an evil-minded foreigner who threatened a 'white woman' for sexual reasons, whereupon she defended herself. The jury accepted it. The Egyptian ambassador wrote several angry letters to the newspapers criticising Marshall Hall's blackening of the victim and Egyptians in general. In any case Madame Fahmy was acquitted. Majoribanks, E. *Famous Trials of Marshall Hall,* London, 1950.

106. WL: 7HLN/A/17. 30 November 1937.

107. WL: 7HLN/A/17. 1 December 1937.

108. WL: 7HLN/A/17. 1 December 1937. Letter from Whitehall to Helena.

109. WL: 7HLN/A/17. 2 December 1937.

110. *Daily Mail,* 'Helena Normanton, Senior Woman Barrister, demands—Women Judges NOW', 2 December 1937.

111. Polden, P. 'The Lady of the Tower Bridge: Sybil Campbell, England's First Woman Judge' *Women's History Review,* Vol. 8, No. 3, 1999. The then Home Secretary was James Chuter Ede.

112. Ibid, p.507.

113. Ibid.

114. MT3/DIS/67 1938.

115. *Daily Telegraph*, 'Women JP's "Not Worth Anything"', 12 April 1938.
116. . *The People*, 'Women as Judges, Our Portias Now want to be Solomon's', 22 May 1938.
117. Page 44 of her Scrapbook. WL: 7HLN/A/04.
118. *Daily Mail*, 29 June 1938, WL: 7HLN/A/23.
119. Article by 'Hervey Middleton.'
120. 1 July 1938.
121. WL: 7HLN/A/23.
122. WL: 7HLN/A/23. Also reported in *Daily Mail*, 'Two Men Among 800 Women', 11 July 1938.
123. *Daily Mail*, 11 July 1938.
124. WL: 7HLN/A/23.
125. WL: 7HLN/A/23. 20 July 1938.
126. WL: 7HLN/A/23. 11 August 1938. Letter from Elise Cannon to her Aunt Helena, on *Good Housekeeping* notepaper (her workplace).
127. WL: 7HLN/A/23. 21 September 1938.
128. 4 May 1939 as reported in the *Sussex Daily News*.
129. WL: 7HLN/A/17. 8 September 1938.
130. WL: 7HLN/A/17. 13 September 1938.
131. Ibid, p.76.
132. Ibid.
133. WL: 7HLN/A/17. 17 September 1938.
134. WL: 7HLN/A/17. 19 September 1938.
135. WL: 7HLN/A/25. Letter from HN to prisoner G. Cheshunt. From 20 December 1938–10 January 1939.

Notes to Chapter 8

1. As quoted in the *Evening Standard*, 27 December 1944.
2. MT3DIS/68.
3. *Girl's Own Paper*, February 1939, p.257.
4. Osgoode Society for Canadian Legal History: Margaret Paton Hyndman, Transcript, p.127. Material provided by Professor Mary Jane Mossman.
5. Ibid.
6. MT3/DIS/69 June 1940.
7. Earengey was secretary to the Cheltenham WSPU and a barrister: see Crawford, E. *The Women's Suffrage Movement: A Guide 1866–1928*, Routledge 2000, pp.107, 182. Rosser describes her as 'wife of a county court judge, grandmother and old suffragette, made appearances before the county court and was much liked. Made a magistrate for the County of London and sat as a mag and did prison visiting at Holloway. She was an "asset"to the cause.' She was kind and encouraging to Enid, see: WL: LOCKET.
8. WL: 7HLN/A/03.
9. *News of the World*, 1 May 1943.
10. *Marylebone Mercury*, 5 June 1943.
11. *News of the World*, 1 April 1945.
12. Hyndman transcript, op cit.
13. WL: 7HLN/A/17. 26 December 1947. The Old Bailey Mess was described by Rosser (WL: LOCKET) as very friendly and barristers would lunch together there daily. It was open to all members of the Central Criminal Court Bar Mess, those barristers who were appearing in cases but were not members of the mess could use it by invitation. She said 'We would lunch there without any formality or order of precedence or seniority and it was a cheerful gossipy place.'
14. As later reported in the *Daily Mail*, 1 June 1948.
15. MT3/DIS/77.
16. As later reported in the *Daily Mail*, 1 June 1948.
17. *Daily Mail*, 1 June 1948.
18. *Daily Telegraph*, 11 December 1948.
19. Ibid.
20. *Beckenham Advertiser*, 16 December 1948.
21. *Evening Standard*, 18 May 1949.
22. Indeed, the *Midland Daily Tribune* of 24 March 1949 reported that she had applied once before, but had been passed over.
23. Abel, R. *The Making of the English Legal System*, Beard Books, 1998, p.98.
24. Ibid, p.99.
25. Heilbron, H, *Rose Heilbron*, Oxford: Hart, 2012, p.67–72.
26. WL: 7HLN/F/04.
27. WL: 7HLN/A/06: For example from the Foreign Office, the town clerk of Beckenham, girls' grammar schools and her past schools.
28. WL: 7HLN/A/06. 23 May 1949.
29. WL: 7HLN/A/07.
30. *News Review*, 5 May 1949. They were described as 'Silks Without Breeches.'
31. *Daily Telegraph*, 27 April 1949.
32. Heilbron, 2012, op cit, p.70.

33. *Daily Mail,* 26 May 1949.
34. 8 May 1951.
35. Ribs do have ligaments, but she probably meant bruising.
36. *The Times,* 30 July 1951.
37. *The Beckenham Advertiser,* 26 July 1951.
38. *Daily Graphic,* 'Women Talking', 24 July 1951.
39. *Overseas Weekly Mail,* 30 July 1951.
40. *Sussex Daily News,* 21 July 1951, *News Chronicle,* July 21 1951, *Colne News,* July 27 1951, *Yorkshire Post,* 23 July 1951, *London Daily Mail,* July 21 1951 and others, see WL: 7HLN/F/01.
41. WL: 7HLN/A/07. 2 May 1951.
42. *Evening Standard,* 10 February 1951.
43. MT3/DIS/77.
44. Letter in Middle Temple file: MT3/DIS/77.
45. 23 May 1951.
46. MT3/DIS/78.
47. *Britannia and Eve,* 'Modern Portia's', September 1952.
48. MT3/DIS/80.
49. Rosser practised from 1927–1933.
50. WL: LOCKET.
51. Abel, 1998, op cit, p.8.
52. For example Millicent Blewell Stone. WL: 7HLN/A/03.
53. Normanton, H. *Everyday Law for Women,* Ivor, Nicholson and Watson, 1932. 1st edn.
54. WL: 7HLN/C/15.
55. WL: 7HLN/C/16.
56. Normanton, H. (ed.), *The Trial of Alfred Arthur Rouse,* Edinburgh and London: William Hodge and Company, 1931.
57. Normanton, H. *The Trial of Norman Thorne, The Crowborough Chicken Farm Murderer,* Geoffrey Bles Publishers, 1929.
58. Browne, C. *Oliver Quendon's First Case,* Hutchinson Publishers, 1927.
59. WL: 7HLN/C/07. 11 October 1934.
60. WL: 7HLN/C/05.
61. WL: 7HLN/C/17.
62. WL: 7HLN/C/06.
63. *Woman,* November 1924 p.113.
64. *Woman,* December 1924 p.196.
65. *Woman,* October 1925 p.29.
66. *Woman,* April 1925 p.33.
67. WL: 7HLN/C/03. 11 October 1934.
68. Between 1924–1939, WL: 7HLN/C/03.
69. WL: 7HLN/C/03.
70. WL: 7HLN/C/03. 14 July 1925.
71. WL: 7HLN/C/03. 30 December 1925.
72. August 1922.
73. WL: 7HLN/C/22.
74. For an explanation of her mindset, see Burton, A. *Burdens of History: British Feminism, Indian Women and Imperial Culture 1865–1915,* University of North Carolina Press, 1994.
75. *The Englishwoman,* 'The Privy Council and Women', No. 91, July 1916.
76. *The Coming Day,* 'The Jury System and Women', November 1917, p.91.
77. *Teachers World,* 'Mock Trials and How to Arrange Them', 27 February 1929.
78. *The Nation USA,* 'Whitewashing British Rule in India', 19 June 1920 p.831.
79. *The Nation,* 'The Non-Cooperation Movement', 21 December 1921, p.721 (she argued abandonment was improbable).
80. *Advertising World*, August 1926 p.329.
81. *Coming Fashions Magazine,* 'Your Worldly Goods', April 1936, p.70.
82. 1936, numerous articles on the legal profession as a job for women — she was quite encouraging, but recommended that it is not for someone without a 'substantial economic background' as it takes time to get established.
83. *Daily Review,* 'My Child's Future', December 1938.
84. WL: 7HLN/C/07.
85. WL: 7HLN/C/11.
86. WL: 7HLN/C/11.
87. WL: 7HLN/C/11, 28 April 1937 Letter from Curtis Brown to Helena.
88. 'Mrs Warfield Denies Rumors on Gems, Trousseau, Aid to Nazis' by Helena Normanton, *New York Times,* 31 May 1937.
89. WL: 7HLN/C/11, letter from Helena to Simpson, 31 May 1937.
90. *The Star,* 4 and 5 June 1937.
91. WL: 7HLN/A/29.
92. For three guineas. She had to remind the Liverpool Women Citizens' Association Council that they owed her £1. 17s.0d for an address she gave in 1933.
93. WL: 7HLN/A/07.
94. WL: 7HLN/C Lovat Dickson Publishers, 6 August 1937.
95. WL: 7HLN/C Jarrolds Publishers, 8 August 1957.
96. *New York Times ,* 'Woman Barrister of England Here', 7 January 1925.

97. WL: 7HLN/A/18. 12 July 1939.
98. WL: 7HLN/A/17. 11 January 1957. Letter from Salisbury, Privy Council Office to Helena.
99. *Daily Express*, 'Lone Criminal Thanks Woman From Dock', 27 May 1937.
100. Also known as Sylvan de Hirsch-Davies.
101. WL: 7HLN/A/25. 27 May 1937. Letter from prisoner G Cheshunt (3668) to Helena.
102. WL: 7HLN/A/25. 29 May 1937.
103. WL: 7HLN/A/25. 31 May 1937. Letter from prisoner G Cheshunt (3668) to Helena.
104. WL: 7HLN/A/25. 2 June 1937, Letter from Helena's clerk to G Cheshunt.
105. 7HLN/A/25. 20 December 1937.
106. WL: 7HLN/A/25. 31 December 1937.
107. WL: 7HLN/A/25. 9 December 1938.
108. WL: 7HLN/A/25. 13 December 1938.
109. WL: 7HLN/A/25. 15 December 1938.
110. WL: 7HLN/A/25. 25 December 1938. He wrote thanking her for the books and saying that he had enjoyed them. He especially loved her cards—he loved beautiful things.
111. WL: 7HLN/A/25. 20 February 1939.
112. WL: 7HLN/A/25. 22 February 1939.
113. *Daily Express*, 'Women Win Another Chance for Convict', 13 October 1937.
114. Aged 52 and a carpenter.
115. WL: 7HLN/A/25. 14 February 1939.
116. WL: 7HLN/A/25. 20 February 1939.
117. Auctioneer, estate agent, junior bank clerk, advertising, male nurse, Irish tour guide, courier, strong, willing, and would do anything with his hands.
118. WL: 7HLN/A/25. 27 February 1939.
119. WL: 7HLN/A/25. 4 April 1939.
120. WL: 7HLN/A/25. 11 April 1939.
121. WL: 7HLN/A/04. 17 September 1939.
122. WL: 7HLN/A/25. 24 September 1939.
123. WL: 7HLN/A/25. 29 September 1939.
124. His wife was now an invalid. With the evacuation of the Brompton she was unable to have her lung removed. Without the operation there was no hope recovery.
125. WL: 7HLN/A/04. 30 October 1939.
126. WL: HLN/A/25. For example others include Wallace (Brixton 1484) who wrote her poems, he was extremely depressed and was only allowed to write about his health and the weather; Montagu Cohen (Wandsworth 2293)
thanking her for her help and fearful of leaving prison, he had seen the chaplain as she advised.
127. Cairns, J. A. R. *Careers for Girls*, London: Hutchinson, 1928, p.53.
128. Holtby, W, *Women and a Changing Civilisation*, London: Bodley Head, 1934, p.280.
129. Oliver, J. *What Shall I be? A Book of Careers*, London: Collins, 1938, pp.66–67.
130. Heal, J. *Book of Careers for Girls*, Bodley Head, 1955, p153.
131. WL: 7HLN/A/18. Letter to *Strand Magazine*, 1932.
132. WL: LOCKET.

Notes to Chapter 9

1. *Yorkshire Post*, 20 March 1954.
2. Cannon affectionately recalled how their marriage was one in which 'sparks could fly': WL: 7HLN/C/09.
3. WL: 7HLN/A/03.
4. WL: 7HLN/B/03.
5. WL: 7HLN/B/02.
6. This is the same piece of legislation that her own mother would have had to use if her husband had not died (and she had wished to divorce him).
7. Cretney, S. *Family Law in the Twentieth Century* Oxford: Oxford University Press, 2005, p.161
8. Ibid.
9. Ibid.
10. Ibid.
11. Ibid, p.162.
12. Forty per cent of divorce petitions were from women between 1858–1900, see Stone, L. *Road to Divorce, England 1530–1987*, Oxford: Oxford University Press, 1990.
13. Cohabitation was not new and often a direct result of the unsatisfactory divorce laws: see Thane, P. *Happy Families: History and Family Policy*, London: British Academy Policy Centre, 2011.
14. He was a Scottish Professor of Roman Law, see Eliza Orme, 'Hunter, William Alexander (1844–1898)', rev. C. A. Creffield, *Oxford Dictionary of National Biography*, Oxford: Oxford University Press, 2004.
15. Cretney, S. 2011, op cit, p.203.
16. Ibid, p.205.

17. This National Union of Women's Suffrage became the NUSEC in March 1919 with Eleanor Rathbone succeeding Millicent Fawcett. In 1932 it would separate its campaign and education functions to the National Council for Equal Citizenship. WL: NA1041.
18. Which amended the Matrimonial Causes Act 1857, section 27.
19. Masson, 2008, op cit and Thane, 2011, op cit, p.9.
20. Thane 2011, op cit.
21. Cretney, S. 2011, op cit, p.227.
22. WL: 7HLN/B/01.
23. Cretney, 2011, op cit, p.229.
24. Ibid.
25. WL: 7HLN/B/02. National Council for Equal Citizenship Annual Report 1932 p.5. This was the campaigning and education arm of the NUSEC.
26. WL: 7HLN/B/02.
27. *Daily Herald,* 'Prisons within prisons', 11 January 1934.
28. *Benson v Benson* 1933. Unreported. But see *The Times* 'Convict and Custody of Child', 11 December 1933.
29. WL: 7HLN/A/04 p.28.
30. Herbert, A. P. *Holy Deadlock*, London: Penguin, 1935.
31. Pound, R. *A P Herbert: A Biography* Michael Joseph, 1976; Reginald Pound, 'Herbert, Sir Alan Patrick (1890–1971)', rev. Katherine Mullin, *Oxford Dictionary of National Biography*, Oxford: Oxford University Press, 2004.
32. WL: 7HLN/B/03. 3 October 1934. Her observations on the draft Bill.
33. WL: 7HLN/B/0318 July 1934. Letter from Marjorie Green secretary for the NCEC.
34. WL: 7HLN/B/01.
35. WL: 7HLN/A/07.
36. WL: 7HLN/A/07. 27 September 1934.
37. WL: 7HLN/B/03.
38. WL: 7HLN/B/01.
39. WL: 7HLN/B/03.
40. 5 October 1934. Helena to Mrs Hubbock, WL: 7HLN/B/01.
41. WL: 7HLN/B/03. Letter from Mrs Hubbock to Helena 11 October 1934.
42. WL: 7HLN/B/03. 12 October 1934.
43. WL: 7HLN/B/03. 18 October 1934.
44. WL: 7HLN/B/03. 26 October 1934.
45. WL: 7HLN/B/03. 18 October 1934.
46. WL: 7HLN/B/03. 19 November 1935

at 4.30 pm at the Millicent Fawcett Hall.
47. WL: 7HLN/B/03. 24 October 1934.
48. WL: 7HLN/A/29. Letters from Mrs Barton, chairperson of Portsmouth Women Citizens' Association to HN on 11 January 1935, 17 January 1935, and 24 January 1935.
49. WL: 7HLN/B/03.
50. WL: 7HLN/B/02. 6 February 1936. Helena's observations document on the Marriage Bill 1936.
51. Ibid p.11 of the Scrapbook.
52. WL: 7HLN/B/03. 6 February 1936.
53. WL: 7HLN/03. Letter to Mrs Gray, 15 April 1935.
54. HLN/B/01.
55. Letter from Helena to Miss Wingate, Secretary NCEC, 26 January 1937. WL: 7HLN/B/02.
56. Cretney, 2011, op cit, p.247.
57. Letter asking her for 10s/6d, November 1938 WL: 7HLN/B/01.
58. This became a limited company in 1914 and was committed to divorce reform. At the beginning it demanded a Royal Commission to consider this and was responsible for the Gorell Report. It was 'highly influential', see Cretney, 2011 op cit, pp.214–216.
59. WL: 7HLN/A/18. 31 January 1939.
60. WL: 7HLN/A/18. 2 February 1939.
61. Masson, J, 2008, op cit.
62. Morgan, R. I. 'The Introduction of Civil Legal Aid in England and Wales 1914–1949' in *Twentieth Century British History*, 1994, 5(1): 38–76.
63. Cretney, 2011, op cit, p.281.
64. WL: 5WMA.
65. WL: 5SPG. This group was founded by Lady Rhondda in 1921 to promote changes in legislation that would help and promote women.
66. Ibid.
67. Cmd. 9678.
68. WL: 7HLN/B/03. She addressed the National Council for Legal Citizenship and NCW.
69. WL: 7HLN/B/01.
70. WL: 5MWA.
71. WL: 7HLN/A/18. Letter from Helena to Marie Stopes.
72. It was submitted on 20 February 1952, WL: 7HLN/B/05.
73. WL: 7HLN/B/01.

74. WL: 5CMW/A.
75. Ibid.
76. WL: 7HLN/B.
77. With the introduction of the Divorce Reform Act 1969.
78. WL: 7HLN/C/03.
79. WL: 7HLN/B/02.
80. WL: 7HLN/A/07.
81. *Who was Who* online edition 2014 and Law, C *Women, A Modern Political Dictionary*, p.115. This was an American society for liberal arts and sciences.
82. *Who was Who* 2014 also records her as being the ex-vice president.
83. *Who was Who* online edition 2014.
84. This is a Paris University friends society that upholds French culture and language.
85. Joanne Workman, 'Normanton, Helena Florence (1882–1957)', *Oxford Dictionary of National Biography*, Oxford: Oxford University Press, 2004
86. Ibid.
87. Ibid.

Notes to Chapter 10

1. 24 November 1957 from Herbert Marshall Advision Films, Bombay. Marshall was an actor.
2. WL: 7HLN/C/09.
3. *The Times,* Obituary, 16 October 1957; *Kentish Times,* 18 October 1957 and numerous others. See WL: 7HLN/F/05.
4. *The Times,* 10 January 1958.
5. *Brighton and Hove Herald,* 23 November 1957.
6. *Brighton Herald,* 19 October 1957.
7. For her fuller thoughts, on retirement, see *Chapter 8* of this work.

Selected Bibliography

Primary Sources

Middle Temple archives

Women's Library (WL)

WL: 5SPG

WL: 7HLN

WL: 5CMW

WL: 2WFL

WL: 2NSE

WL: 7AMP

WL: LOCKET

WL: Nettlefield 10/07

WL: 2LSW

WL: 3AMS/A & B

WL: 9/02/213 & 239

WL: 6JCS/A/1

WL: 7MGE/02/118

Contemporary Sources

'Women at the Bar' (12 December 1903) *Law Journal,* 620.

'The year "That Awa"' (December 1875) *Englishwoman's Review* 6, 533.

'Women as Lawyers' (November 1875) *Englishwoman's Review* 6, 510.

'Lady Law Students' (1904, January) *Englishwoman's Review,* p.49.

Allen, G. (1895) *The Woman Who Did,* London: John Lane Publishers.

Asquith, H. (1928) *Memories and Reflections,* London: Cassell.

Asquith, M. (1920) *Autobiography,* Bodley Head.

Bacik, I., Costello, C. and Drew, E. (2003) *Gender Injustice: Towards the Feminisation of the Legal Professions?* , Trinity College, Dublin Law School.

Birkett, Lord. (1961) *Six Great Advocates,* Hardmondsworh, Penguin Books.

Bodichon, B. (1872) *Reasons For and Against the Enfranchisement of Women,* The National Society for Women's Suffrage. London: McCorquodale & Co.

Booth, C. (1918) *A Memoir, by his Wife,* London: MacMillan.

Fawcett, M. G. (2002) *Josephine Butler: Her Work and Principles,* Portrayer Publishers.

Foster, J. (1885) *Men at the Bar,* London: Reever & Turner.

Gates, G. E. (1923) *The Women's Year Book,* London: Women's Publishers.

Heal, J. (1955) *Book of Careers for Girls,* London: Bodley Head.

Herbert, A. P. (1935) *Holy Deadlock,* London: Penguin.

Holtby, W. (1934) *Women and a Changing Civilisation,* London: Bodley Head.

Howes, D. (1935) *American Women Vols 1–3,* Richard Blank Publishing Co.

Hutchins, B. (1911) *A History of Factory Legislation,* P. S. King & Son Ltd.

Kramer, D. (1949) *Heywood Broun: A Biographical Portrait,* New York: Current Books.

Lang, E. M. (1929) *British Women in the Twentieth Century,* London: T Werner Laurie.

MacGill, E. (1955) *My Mother the Judge,* Toronto: Ryerson Press.

Majoribanks, E. (1950) *Famous Trials of Marshall Hall,* London: Penguin.

Marsden, D. (1911, Nov 23) 'Notes of the Week', *The Freewoman.*

Montgomery Hyde, H. (1955) *United in Crime,* London: Heinemann.

Normanton, H. (1916, March 3) 'Foundations of Freedoms', *Vote: The Organ of the Women's Freedom League,* Vol. XIII, p.945.

(1931) *The Trial of Alfred Arthur Rouse,* Edinburgh and London: William Hodge and Company.

(1932) *Everyday Law for Women,* London: Richard Clayton & Sons.

(1921) *India in England,* Ganesan Publishers.

(1915) *Sex Differentiation in Salary 1915,* National Federation of Women Teachers.

(1929) *The Trial of Norman Thorne, The Crowborough Chicken Farm Murderer,* London: Geoffrey Bles Publishers.

Odgers, B. (1927) *Odgers on the Common Law in England,* London: Sweet & Maxwell.

(1911) *Principles of Practice and Evidence,* London: Butterworths.

(1912) *The Principles of Pleadings and Practice in Civil Actions in the High Court of Justice,* London: Stevens & Sons.

Oliver, J. (1938) *What Shall I Be? A Book of Careers,* London: Collins.

Pankhurst, S. (1932) *The Home Front,* London: Gay and Hancock.

Purcell, C. G. (1946) *Cases and Other Authorities on Legal Ethics 1870–1934,* London: Foundation Press.

Schreiner, O. (1911) *Woman and Labour,* London: Virago.

(1878) *60 Englishwomen's Review*, 151.

Strahan, J. (1919) *The Bench and Bar of England*, London: Blackwood.

Strachey, R. (1928) *The Cause: A Short History of the Women's Movement in Great Britain*, London: Virago.

(1935) *Careers and Openings for Women*, London: Faber & Faber.

Strahan, J. (1919) *The Bench and Bar of England*, London: Blackwood.

Walker-Smith, D. (1934) *Lord Reading and His Cases: the Study of a Great Career*, New York: MacMillan.

Webb, B. (1911, Nov 2) 'The Awakening of Women', *New Statesmen* (supplement 'On the Awakening of Women').

Whiteley, C. (1942) *Cecil Whiteley, Brief Life*, MacMillan.

Zimmern, A. (1898) *The Renaissance of Girls' Education in England: A Record of Fifty Years' Progress*, London: A. D. Innes & Company.

Secondary Sources

Journal articles

Auchmuty, R. 'Whatever Happened to Miss Bebb? *Bebb v The Law Society* and Women's Legal History', *Legal Studies*, Vol. 31, No. 2, 199–230.

Logan, A. (2006) 'Professionalism and the Impact of England's First Women Justices 1920–1950', *Historical Journal* 49(3), 833–850.

Mossman, M. J. (1988) 'Portia's Progress: Women as Lawyers — Reflections on Past and Future', *Windsor Yearbook of Access to Justice*, 252.

Polden, P. (Nov 2005) 'Portia's Progress: Women at the Bar in England, 1919–1939', *International Journal of the Legal Profession*, 293–335.

(1999) 'The Lady of the Tower Bridge: Sybil Campbell, England's First Woman Judge', *Women's History Review*, Vol. 8, 505–526.

Workman, J. (2001) 'Wading Through the Mire: An Historiographical Study of the British Women's Movement Between the Wars', *University of Sussex Journal of Contemporary History*, 2.

Books

Abel, R. (1998) *The Making of the English Legal Profession 1800–1988*, Washington: Beard Books.

Kennedy, H. (1978) 'Women at the Bar' in R. Hazell, *The Bar on Trial,* London: Quartet Books, 148–62.

Law, C. (1997) *Suffrage and Power: The Women's Movement 1918–1928,* London: I. B. Tauris & Co.

(2001) *Women, A Modern Political Dictionary,* London: I. B. Tauris & Co.

Sorabji, R. (2010) *Opening Doors: The Untold Story of Cornelia Sorabji,* London: I. B. Tauris & Co.

Takayanagi, M. C. (2012) *Parliament and Women, c.1900–1945,* University of London: King's College PhD.

Thane, P. (2001) 'What Difference Did the Vote Make?' in Vickery, A. *Women, Privilege and Power,* pp.253–288, Stanford: Stanford University Press, 253–88.

(2012) *Sinners? Scroungers? Saints?: Unmarried Motherhood in Twentieth Century England,* Oxford: Oxford University Press.

(2011) *Happy Families?: History and Family Policy,* London: British Academy Policy Centre.

A fuller list of Secondary Sources is available at www.WatersidePress. co.uk/HN

Index

Mothering Justice: Working with Mothers in Criminal and Social Justice Settings

Edited by Lucy Baldwin

With a Foreword by Vicky Pryce

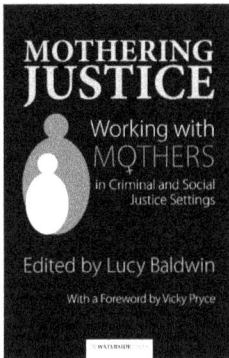

Written by experts with first-hand experience, *Mothering Justice* is the first whole book to take motherhood as a focus for criminal and social justice interventions.

'A valuable addition for those working with women in criminal justice, and other statutory/voluntary agencies … A focus on vulnerable mothers … is long overdue'— *Probation Journal*

'This book … will add to and develop understanding in relation to working with mothers in criminal justice'— *Vicky Pryce (from the Foreword)*

Paperback & eBook

ISBN 978-1-909976-23-8 | 2015 | 320 pages

Sir William Garrow: His Life, Times and Fight for Justice

by John Hostettler and Richard Braby

With a Foreword by Geoffrey Robertson QC

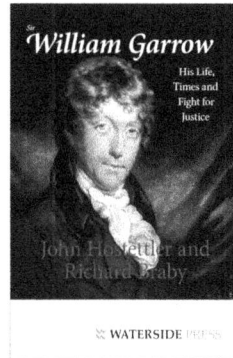

A comprehensive account of lawyer William Garrow's life, career, family and connections as depicted in the award-winning BBC series *Garrow's Law*.

'A law book yes, but boring no, a delight to read'— *Internet Law Book Reviews*

'A blockbuster of a book'— *Phillip Taylor MBE of Richmond Green Chambers*

'Informative, entertaining and a really good read … rescues Garrow from undeserved obscurity'— *Littlehampton Gazette*

Paperback & eBook

ISBN 978-1-904380-69-6 | 2011 | 352 pages

www.WatersidePress.co.uk